Essential Text Book

Of

Research Methodology and Biostatistics

By

Dr. Mahboob Ali (Author)

Dr Izharul Hasan (Co-Author)

Self Academia Publishing, Seattle, Washington, United State

Book Details

Paperback:

Publisher: Self academia publishing; 1st Ed 2021

Language: English

ISBN- 9798523246609

Imprint: Independently published

Product Dimensions: 6 x 9 inches

@2021 by publishing platform and author

Corresponding email: mahboobnium786@gmail.com

PREFACE TO THE FIRST EDITION

The Unani System of Medicine is one of the ancient medicines ever practiced in the world. The documentary evidences of Unani medicine dated back to 460 B.C. The great Hippocrates was the first formal physician of Unani medicine and known as **Father of Medicine**. Hippocrates was the man who liberalized the medicine from the domain of Demon, evil spirit and myth of primitive society. For the first time he emphasized the role of various exogenous and endogenous factors in disease causation. Hippocrates postulated the theory of Humours, Tabiyat – an inherent quality responsible for initiation and maintenance of the attributed functions of any compound including human body and of human genesis. Because of this pioneer work in the field of medicine in primitive days of imagination he is rightly the **father of medicine**. *Further* **Galen,** a great physician promoted the concept, theory and treatment of *Unani* medicine. After Galen the Unani Medicine was accepted by Arab physician like **Abu Bakr Razi and Ibne Sina** who gave more strength to this system and exposed or proved scientifically to it. After Arabs, the Unani system of medicine entered in India. In India, **Hakeem Ajmal Khan** tried his best in the progress of the progress of *Unani* medicine. He gave a new approach towards the scientific or research study. He is the only person who started research work in *Unani* medicine i.e., he deputed Hakeem Saleemuzzaman to coduct a research study as to see the efficacy of 'Asrol' in Hypertension. Because of his great contributions, *Unani* System of Medicine exists till date. Now it is our duty to promote our system so that the best means of 'art of healing' may exist and get progress in future.

There is a need of time to evaluate the efficacy of Unani Drugs, formulation and unani therapy as well as to elaborate the concept of diagnosis and mode of treatment of Unani system of medicine. And this cannot be achieved without knowing the method of research or research study. For the development of *Unani* system of medicine and to expose the importance and efficacy of the uncovered *Unani* drugs or *Unani* formulations, a good research study should be conducted. For conducting a good research, a researcher must have deep knowledge about the research process and research study. Keeping it in mind, I tried my best to write **this book on Research methodology and Biostatistics**. I have attempted to give information and principles which the researchers are expected to know during research. This book deals with core knowledge of Biostatistics and research study with the key concepts and key points of research. *This book has been written as per syllabus of Post Graduate course of Unani Medicine designed by CCIM.* This book consists of all important points which are mandatory to be understood for the research study such as essential criteria for clinical trial, research report, ICMR Guidelines and method of writing a research paper etc.

I hope this book will be considered as an informative source, students-oriented and best source for references for researcher and postgraduate's students. There may be any mistake in writing the book. If anybody found any mistake, please advise me about that. I will be really happy by healthy suggestions and constructive criticism from thoughtful readers.

Dr Mahboob Ali

Dr Izharul Hasan

INDEX

Chapter 1: INTRODUCTION

Research, Research Methods and Research Methodology

RESEARCH: It can be defined as "Research is a systematized effort to gain a new knowledge."

Research is a logical and systematic search for new and useful information on a particular topic. In the well-known nursery rhyme Twinkle Twinkle Little Star How I Wonder What You Are the use of the words how and what essentially summarizes what research is. It is an investigation of finding solutions to scientific and social problems through objective and systematic analysis. It is a search for knowledge, that is, a discovery of hidden truths. Here knowledge means information about matters. The information might be collected from different sources like experience, human beings, books, journals, nature, etc. A research can lead to new contributions to the existing knowledge. Only through research is it possible to make progress in a field. Research is indeed civilization and determines the economic, social and political development of a nation. There are vast areas of research in other disciplines such as languages, literature, history and sociology. Whatever might be the subject, research has to be an active, diligent and systematic process of inquiry in order to discover, interpret or revise facts, events, behaviours and theories. Applying the outcome of research for the refinement of knowledge in other subjects, or in enhancing the quality of human life also becomes a kind of research and development.

Research is done with the help of study, experiment, observation, analysis, comparison and reasoning. Research is in fact ubiquitous. For example, we know that cigarette smoking is injurious to health; heroine is addictive; cow dung is a useful source of biogas; malaria is due to the virus protozoan plasmodium; AIDS (Acquired Immuno Deficiency Syndrome) is due to the virus HIV (Human Immuno Deficiency Virus). How did we know all these? We became aware of all these information only through research. More precisely, it seeks predictions of events, explanations, relationships and theories for them.

OBJECTIVES OF RESEARCH: The prime objectives of research include as:

(1) to discover new facts (2) to verify and test important facts (3) to analyse an event or process or phenomenon to identify the cause and effect relationship 2 (4) to develop new scientific tools, concepts and theories to solve and understand scientific and nonscientific problems (5) to find solutions to scientific, nonscientific and social problems and (6) to overcome or solve the problems occurring in our everyday life.

RESEARCH METHODS: It can be defined as "Methods to convert a research problem into an operational one to get conclusion".

Research Methods are the various procedures, schemes and algorithms used in research. All the methods used by a researcher during a research study are termed as research methods. They are essentially planned, scientific and value-neutral. They include theoretical procedures, experimental studies, numerical schemes, statistical approaches, etc. Research methods help us collect samples, data and find a solution to a problem. Particularly, scientific research methods call for explanations based on collected facts, measurements and observations and not on reasoning alone. They accept only those explanations which can be verified by experiments.

RESEARCH METHODOLOGY: is a systematic way to solve a problem. It is a science of studying how research is to be carried out. Essentially, the procedures by which researchers go about their work of describing, explaining and predicting phenomena are called research methodology. It is also defined as the study of methods by which knowledge is gained. Its aim is to give the work plan of research. It is necessary for a researcher to design a **methodology** for the problem chosen.

IMPORTANCE OF RESEARCH METHODOLOGY:

In Research Study It is necessary for a researcher to design a methodology for the problem chosen. One should note that even if the method considered in two problems is same the methodology may be different. It is important for the researcher to know not only the research methods necessary for the research under taken but also the methodology. For example, a researcher not only needs to know how to calculate mean, variance and distribution function for a set of data, how to find a solution of a physical system described by mathematical model, how to determine the roots of algebraic equations and how to apply a particular method but also need to know

    a. Which is a suitable method for the chosen problem?
    b. What is the order of accuracy of the result of a method?
    c. What is the efficiency of the method? And so on.

More precisely, research methods help us to get a solution of a problem. On the other hand, research methodology is concerned with the explanation of the following:

    a. Why is a particular research study undertaken?
    b. How did one formulate a research problem?
    c. What types of data were collected?
    d. What particular method has been used?
    e. Why was a particular technique of analysis of data used?

The study of research methodology provides us the necessary training in choosing methods, materials, scientific tools and training in techniques relevant for the problem chosen.

Chapter 2: FUNDAMENTALS OF BASIC RESEARCH

Basic Research is an investigation on basic principles and reasons for occurrence of a particular event or process or phenomenon. It is also called theoretical research. Study or investigation of some natural phenomenon or relating to pure science is termed as basic research. Basic researches sometimes may not lead to immediate use or application. It provides a systematic and deep insight into a problem and facilitates extraction of scientific and logical explanation and conclusion on it. It helps build new frontiers of knowledge. The outcomes of basic research form the basis for many applied research. Researchers working on applied research have to make use of the outcomes of basic research and explore the utility of them. Research on improving a theory or a method is also referred as fundamental research. For example, suppose a theory is applicable to a system provided the system satisfies certain specific conditions. Modifying the theory to apply it to a general situation is a basic research. Attempts to find answers to the following questions actually form basic research as:

    a. Why are materials like that?
    b. What are they?
    c. How does a crystal melt?
    d. Why is sound produced when water is heated?
    e. Why do we feel difficult when walking on seashore?
    f. Why are birds arrange them in '>' shape when flying in a group?

Fundamental research leads to a new theory or a new property of matter or even the existence of a new matter, the knowledge of which has not been known or reported earlier.

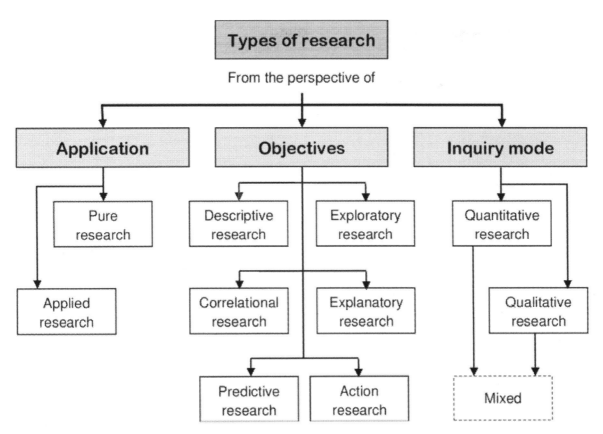

Figure: Types of Research

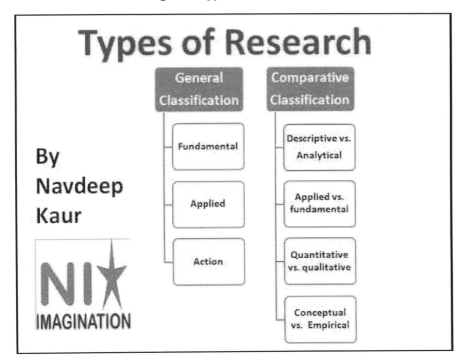

Figure: Types of Research by Navdeep Kaur

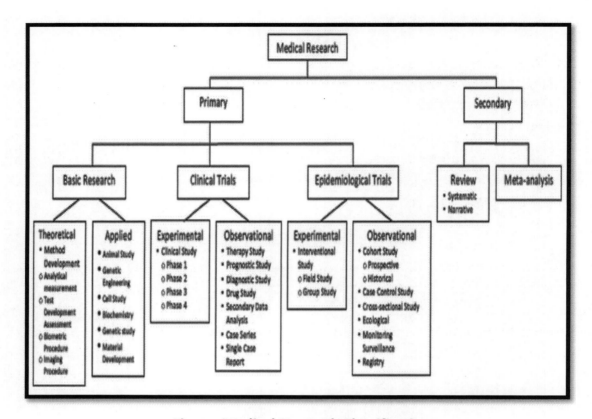

Figure: Medical Research Classification

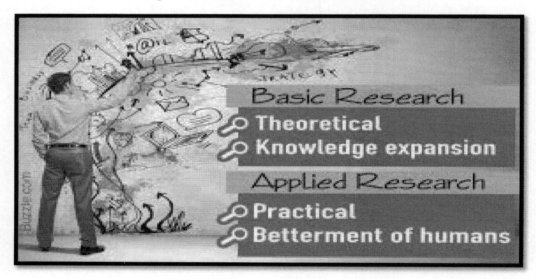

Figure: Basic and Applied Research

APPLIED RESEARCH

Applied research is a methodology used to solve a specific, practical problem of an individual or group. The study and research is used in medicine, business, and education in order to find solutions that may cure diseases, solve scientific problems or develop technology.

In an applied research one solves certain problems employing well known and accepted theories and principles. Most of the experimental research, case studies and inter-disciplinary research are essentially applied research. Applied research is concerned with actual life research such as research on increasing efficiency of a machine, increasing gain factor of production of a material, pollution control, preparing vaccination for a disease, etc. Obviously, they have immediate potential applications. Some of the differences between basic and applied research are summarized in table I. Thus, the central aim of applied research is to find a solution for a practical problem which warrants solution for immediate use, whereas basic research is directed towards finding information that has broad base of applications and thus add new information to the already existing scientific knowledge. The basic and applied researches can be quantitative or qualitative or even both. Quantitative research is based on the measurement of quantity or amount.

HISTORICAL RESEARCH

One type of qualitative **research** is **historical research**, which involves examining past events to draw conclusions and make predictions about the future. The steps in **historical research** are: formulate an idea, formulate a plan, gather data, analyze data, and analyze the sources of data.

In Historical Research, historical aspect of USM from its origin to the present time, biographer of *unani* physicians and some other contribution to the USM is studied.

CONCEPTUAL RESEARCH

Conceptual research is defined as a methodology wherein **research** is conducted by observing and analyzing already present information on a given topic. **Conceptual research** doesn't involve conducting any practical experiments. It is related to abstract concepts or ideas.

In conceptual research concept of USM are discussed, their origin and development is studied. Effect of different branches of knowledge on the concept and their authenticity is taken under consideration.

EMPIRICAL RESEARCH

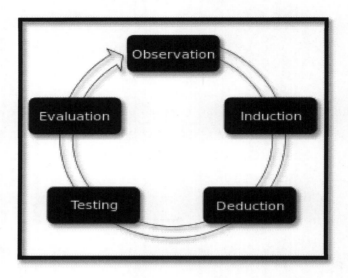

Empirical research is research using empirical evidence. It is a way of gaining knowledge by means of direct and indirect observation or experience. Empiricism values such research more than other kinds. Empirical evidence (the record of one's direct observations or experiences) can be analyze quantitatively or qualitatively. Quantifying the evidence or making sense of it in qualitative form, a researcher can answer empirical questions, which should be clearly defined and answerable with the evidence collected (usually called data). Research design varies by field and by the question being investigated. Many researchers combine qualitative and quantitative forms of analysis to better answer questions which cannot be studied in laboratory settings, particularly in the social sciences and in education.

Empirical research is based upon observation and it is a data base research like experimental research. Empirical research is appropriate when proof is sought that certain variable affects other variable.

Applied research aims at finding a solution of an immediate problem facing a society while fundamental research is mainly concerned with generalization and with the formulation of a theory.

QUALITATIVE RESEARCH
Steps of Qualitative Research

- All qualitative studies have a distinct starting and ending point
- The step are as follows (in some cases)

- Identification of the phenomenon to be sdudied
- Identification of the participants in the study (purposive sample collecting)
- Generation of hyphtheses
- Data collection (continual observance)
- Data analysis

Interpretation/Conclusions

Qualitative research is concerned with qualitative phenomena i.e. phenomena involving quality or kind e.g. Estimation of reasons of human behavior.

Qualitative research is defined as a market research method that focuses on obtaining data through open-ended and conversational communication.

This method is not only about "what" people think but also "why" they think so. For example, consider a convenience store looking to improve its patronage. A systematic observation concludes that the number of men visiting this store are more. One good method to determine why women were not visiting the store is to conduct an in-depth interview of potential customers in the category.

On successfully interviewing female customers, visiting the nearby stores and malls, and selecting them through random sampling, it was known that the store doesn't have enough items for women and so there were fewer women visiting the store, which was understood only by personally interacting with them and understanding why they didn't visit the store, because there were more male products than female ones.

Therefore, the qualitative research methods allow for in-depth and further probing and questioning of respondents based on their responses, where the interviewer/researcher also tries to understand their motivation and feelings.

QUANTITATIVE RESEARCH

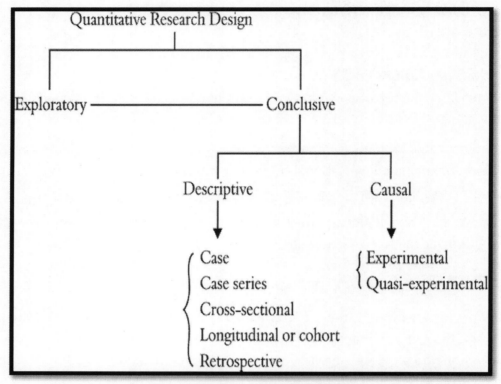

Figure: Quantitative Research

In natural sciences and social sciences, quantitative research is the systematic empirical investigation of observable phenomena via statistical, mathematical, or computational techniques.[1] The objective of quantitative research is to develop and employ mathematical models, theories, and hypotheses pertaining to phenomena. The process of measurement is central to quantitative research because it provides the fundamental connection between empirical observation and mathematical expression of quantitative relationships.

Quantitative data is any data that is in numerical form such as statistics, percentages, etc. The researcher analyses the data with the help of statistics and hopes the numbers will yield an unbiased result that can be generalized to some larger population.

Quantitative research is based up on the measurement of quantity or amount. It is applicable to phenomena which can be expressed in terms of quantity.

LITERARY RESEARCH

Literary Research is the backbone of various **research** branches. **Literary Research** includes - To find out all possible information about a particular text or **literature** in published or unpublished matter in various forms such as, manuscript, book etc. In literary research, the material or literature of USM, especially Manuscripts are worked out and their translation, preservation, editing and compilation are also done.

Branches of Literary research:

- Documentation and publication.
- Collection and study of medical information from archeological and other sources.
- Collection of unpublished work, manuscripts, palm etc.
- Maintenance and development of museum and libraries.

Methodology in literary Research:

Research methodology revolves around the:
- Critical study of available literature.
- Methodology collection
- Proper clarification
- Printing and communication
- Collecting the unpublished manuscripts from various sources.
- Participation in seminar.

Quality of literary Research:

- Honesty
- Straight forwardness
- Accuracy
- Cautious approach
- Conviction to reject in consistent theories.
- Analysis of all aspect of evidence.
- Old literature not to be destroyed.

CLINICAL RESEARCH

Clinical research is a branch of healthcare science that determines the safety and effectiveness (efficacy) of a medicine, diagnostic products and treatment regimens intended for human use. These may be used for prevention, treatment, diagnosis or for relieving symptoms of a disease. Clinical research is different from clinical practice. In clinical practice established treatments are used, while in clinical research evidence is collected to establish a treatment.

OBJECTIVES OF CLINICAL RESEARCH OR TRIAL:

1. To evaluate the safety and efficacy of drug (like *Unani* drugs those are already claimed by *unani* Hakim).
2. To develop new herbal *Unani* drug.
3. To develop an effective, cheap, economical easily available and safe *Unani* drug.
4. To develop new indications of drugs or to change dose, formation or route of administration

TYPES OF CLINICAL RESEARCH:

Treatment Research generally involves an intervention such as medication, psychotherapy, new devices, or new approaches to surgery or radiation therapy.

Prevention Research looks for better ways to prevent disorders from developing or returning. Different kinds of prevention research may study medicines, vitamins, vaccines, minerals, or lifestyle changes.

Diagnostic Research refers to the practice of looking for better ways to identify a particular disorder or condition.

Screening Research aims to find the best ways to detect certain disorders or health conditions.

Quality of Life Research explores ways to improve comfort and the quality of life for individuals with a chronic illness.

Genetic studies aim to improve the prediction of disorders by identifying and understanding how genes and illnesses may be related. Research in this area may explore ways in which a person's genes make him or her more or less likely to develop a disorder. This may lead to development of tailor-made treatments based on a patient's genetic make-up.

Epidemiological studies seek to identify the patterns, causes, and control of disorders in groups of people.

An important note: some clinical research is "outpatient," meaning that participants do not stay overnight at the hospital. Some is "inpatient," meaning that participants will need to stay for at least one night in the hospital or research center. Be sure to ask the researchers what their study requires.

OTHER TYPES OF CLINICAL RESEARCH:

1. Disease oriented research
2. Drug Oriented Research
3. Clinical pharmacological research

1. Disease Oriented Research :

- To study the etiology- regarding temperament, akhlat etc.
- To study the theory of pathogenesis
- To study the clinical methods
- To study the principal and method of treatment
- To study the prognosis of disease
- To study the complication of disease

2. Drug Oriented Research:

- To study the safety and efficacy of *Unani* drugs.
- Clinical studies and therapeutic trials of single and compound drugs in different diseases.

3. Clinico-Pharmacological research:

- Scientific validation of regimental therapy i.e. dalak, riyazat, fasd, hijamat, irsale ilq.
- Scientific validation of fundamentals and practical demonstration of applied aspects of original concepts and theories of *Unani* System of Medicine.
- To develop parameters for assessment of *Mizaj* in healthy as well as diseased individuals and its scientific validation.
- To study different physiological, pathological, and biochemical's parameters in subjects having different *Mizaj*.s
- To study the susceptibility to different diseases in subjects having different *Mizaj*.

CLINICAL TRIALS AND VARIOUS BRANCHES OF UNANI MEDICINE:

In *Unani* Medicine, Clinical trial may be concerned with the following:

- Evaluation of unani drug (most common)
- Surgical procedures like fasd (venisection) etc.
- Radio therapy
- Medical advice as diet and exercise policy.
- Regimental therapy as Hijamat, dalak (massage) etc.
- Alternative approach to patient management.

PHASES OF CLINICAL TRIALS

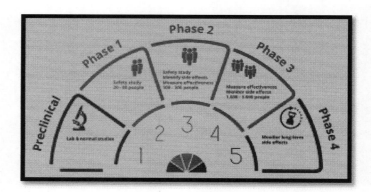

CLINICAL TRIALS: Clinical trials are a kind of clinical research designed to evaluate and test new interventions such as psychotherapy or medications. Clinical trials are often conducted in four phases. The trials at each phase have a different purpose and help scientists answer different questions.

DEVELOPMENT OF NEW UNANI DRUGS OR FORMULATION:

When a new formulation or a new route of administration is tested or when the process of manufacturing is being changed or medicine is going to be used for a new indication – then it is essential to do new preliminary studies beginning from animal pharmacology and toxicology experiment because in these cases the drug is thought to be new drug and it has to be passed through various phases of clinical trial.

PHASES OF A CLINICAL TRIAL:

Before the use of every new drug on a large scale, it has to be passed through the process of testing namely; Pre-clinical testing of the drug on animals and clinical testing of experimental drug (previously unproven in humans, therefore "experimental") in humans.

PRE-CLINICAL TESTING OF THE DRUG ON ANIMALS:

It is mandatory to carry out the pre-clinical testing of the experimental drug before permission is given by the authorities to start phase 1st human studies.

To prove that the drug works as it was hypothesized and does not produce any negative side effects, it is first thoroughly tested in animals. This stage of testing is commonly referred to as the "pre-clinical" stage. The purpose of these animal studies is to prove that the drug is not carcinogenic, mutagenic or terratogenic or harmful in any other way, and to understand how the drug is absorbed and excreted. Once the drug appears to be safe, and possibly effective in animals, the approval for testing the experimental drug in humans via an International New Drug application is requested.

Drug regulatory authorities have made if mandatory to generate principal data with newer compounds with a view to confirm efficacy and safety in animal species before it can be permitted for clinical trials in human subjects. Pre –clinical studies in animals provide basis for extrapolation from animals to main.

CLINICAL TESTING OF EXPERIMENTAL DRUG (PREVIOUSLY UNPROVEN IN HUMANS, THEREFORE "EXPERIMENTAL") IN HUMANS:

The main aim of clinical trial is to test or study of the experimental drugs through various phases. The clinical testing of experimental drugs in humans is normally done in three phases (Phase I, II, and III) with more and more people included in each subsequent. Before moving to the next phase of development, the data are fully analyzed to ensure the experimental drug is safe and well tolerated. After successful completion of all the three phases of testing, the result are submitted to the licensing authority to obtain a New Drug Approval (NDA). Additional (late phase III /or post-marketing / phase IV) testing is done to look at the long term safety.

I PHASE: To study the toxic pharmacological effect of drug

II PHASE: To study the efficacy and safety of the drug on limited number of patients and effective dose is established.

III PHASE: To study safety and efficacy in large population.

IV PHASE: Studies performed after marketing of the pharmaceutical product known as PMS – Post marketing surveillance.

CLINICAL TRIAL PHASE I:

Phase I trial look at how well a new drug is tolerated and are used to determine the highest dosage that can be safely given. Phase1st trial aim to determine the maximum tolerated dose in humans; pharmacodynamic effect, adverse reaction, if any, with their nature and intensity; and pharmacokinetic behavior of the drug as far as possible. These studies are often carried out in healthy adult volunteers which are 20-100 in number, usually in a hospital setting where they can be closely watched and treated should there be any side effects. Clinical, physiological and biochemical observation are carried out for monitoring. In certain cases like testing of anticancer drugs, carried out in patients suffering from the disease for which the medicine is intended by expert clinical pharmacologist.

The main purpose of a phase 1st trial is to see the tolerance dose and therefore to get an indication of the dose that might be used safely in subsequent studies. A low dose is given to a small group of people, and then a slightly larger dose to the next group, and so on, while the patients are closely monitored for side effects. At least two subjects should be assessed on each dose.

PHASE II CLINICAL TRIAL (EXPLORATORY TRIAL)

Once experimental drug has been proven to be safe and well tolerable in healthy volunteers, it must be tested in the patients to see its therapeutic effects and safety. This phase is of long duration and may take several months to years. These studies are usually limited to 3-4 centers and carried out by clinicians specialized on the concerned therapeutic areas and having adequate facilities to perform the necessary investigations for efficacy and safety. Such trials are preferably designed as randomized including, blinding controlled studies, using for control groups either an existing alternative treatment or a placebo. The dosage scheduled established in such studies are then used for a more extensive clinical study.

Additionally, Phase II studies are often designed to determine the correct dosage that is the dosage with the least number of side effects that is most effective. These are often referred to as dose-ranging studies.

Phase II clinical trial is further divided into two following phases:

PHASE II A: It is a preliminary trial whose purpose is to decide between two possibilities:

The treatment is not effective in at least 'x' percent of the patients.

The treatment is effective in at least 'x' percent of the patients.

These are Pilot clinical trials to evaluate efficacy and safety in selected populations of about 100-300 patients, who have the disease or condition to be diagnosed, prevented or treated. These often involve hospitalized patients who can be closely monitored. The purpose is to focus on dose response, type of patient, frequency of dosing or number of other issues involved in safety and efficacy.

PHASE II B: Following the treatment has been judged to be scientifically effective in a phase I or a Phase II A clinical trial, this phase starts. The primary objective is to obtain a precise estimate of the effectiveness of the treatment.

PHASE III (CONFIRMATORY   CLINICAL TRIAL):

In this phase, experimental drug is tested in several hundred to several thousand patients with the disease/condition of interest. The large-scale testing provide s a more thorough understanding of the drug's effectiveness, benefits/risks and range/severity of possible adverse side effect.

The purpose of these trial is to obtain sufficient evidence about the efficacy and safety of drug in a large number of patients, generally in comparison with standard drug and/ or placebo as appropriate. If the drug is already approved/marketed in other countries, Phase III data should generally be obtained on at least 100 patients distributed over 3-4 centres primarily to confirm the efficacy and safety of the drug.

Data on Adverse drug reactions (ADRs) is observed during clinical use of the drug should be reported along with a report on its efficacy in the prescribed format.

PHASE IV STUDIES AND POST MARKETING SURVEILLANCE (PMS):

These studies are performed after marketing of product. These are done on the basis of the product characteristics on which the marketing authorization was granted to assess the therapeutic value, treatment strategies used and safety profile. Phase IV studies should use the same scientific and ethical standard as applied in pre-marketing studies. After a product has been placed in the market, clinical trials designed to explore new indications, new methods of administration or new combinations, etc. are normally considered as trials for new pharmaceutical products.

The PMS can be broadly defined as the study of the drug use and drug effects after marketing.

A Phase IV study trial is interventional and is carried out using a licensed formulation within the terms of its product license. It is conducted either in general practice or   hospital, primarily to extend the efficacy data base, although collection of safety data will form an essential part of such a study.

A Phase IV trial differs from a PMS study which is observational and non-interventional and conducted primarily to monitor safety when a medicine (which is generally newly introduced) is prescribed in every day clinical practice. Simple measures of efficacy may be included in order that risk/benefit judgment to be made. Observation on a comparator drug may also be incorporated into the design of a post marketing surveillance study

EXPERIMENTAL RESEARCH

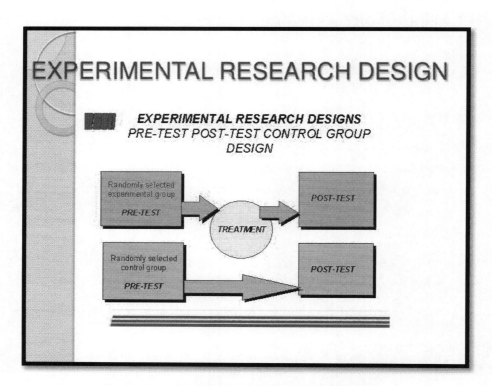

Figure: Experimental Research Design

Definition:

Experimental research is a study that strictly adheres to a scientific research design. It includes a hypothesis, a variable that can be manipulated by the researcher, and variables that can be measured, calculated and compared. Most importantly, experimental research is completed in a controlled environment. The researcher collects data and results will either support or reject the hypothesis. This method of research is referred to a hypothesis testing or a deductive research method. Purpose of Experimental Research seeks to determine a relationship between two variables—the dependent variable and the independent variable. After completing an experimental research study, a correlation between a specific aspect of an entity and the variable being studied is either supported or rejected.

The simplest example of an experimental research is conducting a laboratory test. As long as research is being conducted under scientifically acceptable conditions – it qualifies as an experimental research. A true experimental research is considered to be successful only when the researcher confirms that a change in the dependent variable is solely due to the manipulation of the independent variable.

It is important for an experimental research to establish cause and effect of a phenomenon, which means, it should be definite that effects observed from an experiment are due to the cause. As naturally, occurring event can be confusing for researchers to establish conclusions. For instance, if a cardiology student conducts research to understand the effect of food on cholesterol and derives that most heart patients are non-vegetarians or have diabetes. They are aspects (causes) which can result in a heart attack (effect).

Aims of Experimental Research

Experiments are conducted to be able to predict phenomenon. Typically, an experiment is constructed to be able to explain some kind of causation.

Experimental research is important to society because it helps us by improving our everyday life.

Types of experimental research design:

There are three basic types of experimental research designs as:

a. **Pre-experimental designs,**
b. **True experimental designs , and**
c. **Quasi-experimental designs.**

The different types of experimental research design are based on the how the researcher classifies the subjects according to various conditions and groups.

1. Pre-Experimental Research Design: This is the simplest form of experimental research design. A group, or various groups, are kept under observation after factors are considered for cause and effect. It is usually conducted to understand whether further investigation needs to be carried out on the target group/s, due to which it is considered to be cost-effective.

The pre-experimental research design is further bifurcated into three types:

• One-shot Case Study Research Design

- One-group Pretest-posttest Research Design
- Static-group Comparison

2. True Experimental Research Design: True experimental research is the most accurate form of experimental research design as it relies on statistical analysis to prove or disprove a hypothesis. It is the only type of Experimental Design that can establish a cause-effect relationship within a group/s. In a true experiment, there are three factors which need to be satisfied:

- Control Group (Group of participants for research that are familiar to the Experimental group but experimental research rules do not apply to them.) and Experimental Group (Research participants on whom experimental research rules do apply.)
- Variable which can be manipulated by the researcher
- Random distribution

This experimental research method is commonly implemented in physical sciences.

3. Quasi-Experimental Research Design: The word "Quasi" indicates resemblance. A quasi-experimental research design is similar to experimental research but is not exactly that. The difference between the two the assignment of a control group. In this research design, an independent variable is manipulated but the participants of a group are not randomly assigned as per conditions. The independent variable is manipulated before calculating the dependent variable and so, directionality problem is eliminated. Quasi-research is used in field settings where random assignment is either irrelevant or not required.

The degree to which the researcher assigns subjects to conditions and groups distinguishes the type of experimental design.

TYPES OF EXPERIMENT

A. Controlled Experiments

A controlled experiment often compares the results obtained from experimental samples against *control* samples, which are practically identical to the experimental sample except for the one aspect whose effect is being tested (the independent variable). A good example would be a drug trial. The sample or group receiving the drug would be the experimental group (treatment group); and the one receiving the placebo or regular treatment would be the control one. In many laboratory experiments it is good practice to have several replicate samples for the test being performed and have both a positive control and a negative_control. The results from replicate samples can often be averaged, or if one of the replicates is obviously inconsistent with the results from the other samples, it can be discarded as being the result of an experimental error (some step of the test procedure may have been mistakenly omitted for that sample). Most often, tests are done in duplicate or triplicate. A positive control is a procedure similar to the actual experimental test but is known from previous experience to give a positive result. A negative control is known to give a negative result. The positive control confirms that the basic conditions of the experiment were able to produce a positive result, even if none of the actual experimental samples produce a positive result. The negative control demonstrates the base-line result obtained when a test does not produce a measurable positive result. Most often the value of the negative control is treated as a "background" value to subtract from the test sample results. Sometimes the positive control takes the quadrant of a standard curve.

B. *Natural experiments*

The term "experiment" usually implies a controlled experiment, but sometimes controlled experiments are prohibitively difficult or impossible. In this case, researchers resort to *natural experiments* or quasi-experiments. Natural experiments rely solely on observations of the variables of the system under study, rather than manipulation of just one or a few variables as occurs in controlled experiments. To the degree possible, they attempt to collect data for the system in such a way that contribution from all variables can be determined, and where the effects of variation in certain variables remain approximately constant so that the effects of other variables can be discerned. The degree to which this is possible depends on the observed correlation between explanatory variables in the observed data. When these variables are not well correlated, natural experiments can approach the power of controlled experiments. Usually, however, there is some correlation between these variables, which reduces the reliability of natural experiments relative to what could be concluded if a controlled experiment were performed. Also, because natural experiments usually take place in uncontrolled environments, variables from undetected sources are neither measured nor held constant, and these may produce illusory correlations in variables under study.

OBSERVATIONAL STUDY

All epidemiological studies can be divided into observational and experimental or interventional studies. Observational studies are further subdivided in Descriptive and Analytical studies.

Observational studies observe and measure the effects on disease rates of exposures of interest (as they occur in the population) and draws inferences from a sample to a population where the independent variable is not under the control of the researcher because of ethical concerns or logistical constraints.

Like experiments, observational studies attempt to understand cause-and-effect relationships. However, unlike experiments, the researcher is not able to control (1) How subjects are assigned to groups and/or (2) Which treatment each group receives. Therefore, a sample survey is an example of an observational study.

The observational studies collect evidence/evidences based on the observations on routine records, reports and routine happenings. Under observational epidemiology, an epidemiologist measures the incidence and prevalence of disease, deaths, defect or disability or any other event in the community or population and does not intervene. John Snow's Studies on Cholera in London were observational studies. For an observational science to be valid, the experimenter must know and account for confounding factors. In these situations, observational studies have value because they often suggest hypotheses that can be tested with randomized experiments or by collecting fresh data. In addition, observational studies (e.g., in biological or social systems) often involve variables that are difficult to quantify or control. Observational studies are limited because they lack the statistical properties of randomized experiments.

TYPES OF OBSERVATIONAL STUDY:

> A. **Descriptive studies**
> B. **Analytical studies**

A. DESCRIPTIVE STUDIES

The four Ws of descriptive epidemiology or studies are:

> **What:** Health event/disease of concern
>
> **When:** Time
>
> **Where:** Place
>
> **Who:** Person

The descriptive studies in epidemiology simply describe the occurrence of disease in the community and it measures the incidence, prevalence, trends and distribution of disease or diseases in population. Descriptive studies use date of routine reports or records or data of special surveys. *Descriptive studies describe the health status of the community. It is based on parameters like under-five mortality, infant mortality, per capita income, life expectancy, total adult literacy, poverty rates, school enrolment, nutritional status, percentage of children immunized, percentage of population using improved drinking water sources and sanitation facilities, incidence of ARI and diarrhea, prevalence of HIV/AIDS, etc. The* descriptive studies are most commonly used to produce evidence-based data for appropriate action. Since time immemorial, the observations made on occurrence are the first step towards scientific investigations. In essence, the descriptive epidemiology describes the status of health, disease, nutrition and immunization in population.

The descriptive epidemiology follows the approach of count, divide and compare (CDC). CDC means identifying and counting cases, dividing number of cases by the size of population in which they occurred to arrive at rates and compare these rates over different time, place and different group of people. In essence descriptive epidemiology describes the health events in terms of time, place and person (TPP). This can be better understood in terms of 3 Ws, i.e. When (Time) did the disease occur—Date of onset of disease, Where (Place) did it occur and Who (Person) were affected most by the disease? Compiling, analyzing and interpreting data by time, place and person provides important clues to the causes or risk factors of disease and mode of transmission, and these clues can be helpful in generating hypotheses.

HEALTH EVENTS IN TERMS OF TIME, PLACE AND PERSON (TPP)

A. HEALTH EVENTS IN TERMS OF TIME DISTRIBUTION:

It consist of *Long-term or Secular Trends,* Seasonal Distribution, Short-term Variations and Cyclical Variations

1. Long-term (Secular Trends)

Long-term study of incidence of disease is called "secular trend" of disease. The time distribution of malaria from the year 1935 to 2010 indicates that over the years the reported incidence of malaria has declined from 100 million in the past to 1.49 million cases in 2010. In India, we reached a low level of incidence of malaria in 1965 when it was just 0.1 million and it escalated to 6.47million in the year 1976. This marked the resurgence of malaria in India. After 1976, the incidence of malaria stabilized at high incidence of over 2 million cases per year and since 2002 it has shown some decline to the level of 1.84 and 1.65 million in the year 2002 and 2003 respectively; it further declined to 1.49 million in the year 2010.

The decline to 0.1 million cases in 1965 speaks of success of interventions of malaria control programme. The rise of incidence to 6.47 in 1976 speaks of resurgence and failure of interventions/programme.

Table 1: Secular trend of malaria in India		
Years	Malaria cases in millions	P. falciparum cases
1976	6.47	0.75
1984	2.18	0.65
1986	1.79	0.64
1987	1.66	0.66
1988	1.85	0.68
1989	2.05	0.76
1990	2.02	0.75
1992	2.13	0.88
1993	2.21	0.85
1994	2.51	0.99
1995	2.93	1.14
1996	3.04	1.18
1997	2.66	1.01
1998	2.22	1.03
1999	2.28	1.14
2000	2.03	1.05
2001	2.09	1.01
2002	1.84	0.90
2003	1.87	0.86
2006	1.79	0.84
2007	1.51	0.74
2008	1.53	0.77
2009	1.56	0.84
2010	1.59	0.77

Impact of Observations

The epidemiological observations of high incidence of malaria in 1976 necessitated change in strategy of malaria eradication programme and modified plan of operation was evolved (MPO of malaria) in 1977.

A further long-term trend of falciparum malaria (which is killer malaria) indicates rising trend that over the years and now 50% of malaria is due to Plasmodium falciparum or Pf malaria. This observation is a cause of concern. Drug resistance in Pf malaria and insecticide resistance in mosquitoes has added more problems. Right now the epidemiological situation of Pf malaria is grim.

Application

By studying the disease like malaria over the years we can determine:

- The success or failure of national programme of malaria.
- It helps for re-planning and and re-thinking about the strategies.
- It helps us to know the changing pattern of disease as malaria incidence has increased significantly in India.

2. Seasonal Distribution

The incidence of malaria is not uniform all over the year. The incidence rises in the months of July to October because of favorable conditions for transmission of malaria. After rains, the mosquito breeding and density of vector increases and transmission becomes favorable, hence the incidence rises. This is known as seasonal variations in malaria occurrence. Rise of malaria in these months is a caution to get ready with the system to fight disease: mounting spray operation well before transmission period and adequate coverage with indoor residual insecticides, stepping up operations of surveillance in these months and raising the target of active case detection during transmission season. Thus, seasonal variations of malaria help us to gear up plans to fight against malaria.

3. Short-term Variations

Day of week and time of day: For occurrence of road traffic accidents, occupational diseases/exposures displaying data by day of the week or time of the day may be more informative. Pattern of these occurrences may suggest hypothesis and possible explanation.

Epidemic curve: Distribution of cases by date of onset or by hour of onset, the epidemiologist can draw an epidemic curve or histogram. In epidemic curve 'Y' axis shows number of cases and 'X' axis shows the date of onset. The shape and other features of an epidemic curve can suggest hypothesis about the time and source of exposure and the mode of transmission.

The short-term fluctuation in the occurrence or incidence of malaria indicated that the disease has attained and epidemic proportion or outbreaks in certain years. Malaria is an endemic disease in the country. When it occurs beyond the expected level (usually compared with past year or past year's occurrence) then we call this behavior as an epidemic proportion of occurrence, i.e. "when the malaria occurrence is clearly in excess of normal occurrence or expected occurrence then it is termed as epidemic of malaria".

In the years 1994, 1995 and 1996 (Table 2), there were fluctuation in occurrence of malaria, as incidence of malaria in these years increased beyond two million, hence these were the epidemic years for malaria in several places. The incidence of malaria suddenly increased as also the number of deaths reported (Table 2 and 3).

Table 2: Deaths due to malaria 1976-2010

Years	Deaths	Years	Deaths
1976	59	1993	354
1984	247	1994	1122
1985	213	1995	1151
1986	323	1996	1010
1987	188	1997	879
1988	209	1998	664
1989	268	2006	1707
1990	353	2008	935
1991	421	2009	1144
1992	422	2010	767

Table 3. Areas affected by malaria outbreaks 1994–2006

Years	States	No. of districts affected
1994	Rajasthan, Haryana, Manipur, Nagaland	13
1995	Maharashtra, WB and Assam	28
1996	Rajasthan, Haryana	8
1997	Gujarat, Goa and WB	4
1998	Goa, Maharashtra	2
1999	Andhra Pradesh, Assam, Bihar and WB	23
2000	Karnataka, UP and MP	5
2003	Rajasthan, Large epidemic—several districts	
2004	Assam, Goa, Haryana, Gujarat, Karnataka, Manipur and, Maharashtra	44
2005	Assam, Goa, Haryana Gujarat, Karnataka, Manipur, Maharashtra	48
2006	Karnataka and West Bengal	5

Reported incidence of deaths due to malaria in the country from 1976 to 2010 indicates that during the years 1994, 95 and 96 the deaths were far excess than the previous years, hence these deaths were clearly in excess of expected level. Therefore, these years (94, 95 and 96) were epidemic years for malaria as many deaths were reported in these years from the states of Orissa, Rajasthan, Haryana, Madhya Pradesh, Maharashtra, Gujarat, Karnataka and Assam (Table 3). Unit of determining the outbreak of malaria should be district or community development block or CHC/PHC or sub centre (Section).

4. Cyclical Variations

Malaria has cyclic pattern, in unstable malarial areas, outbreak/epidemic occur every 8–10 years under natural conditions. In effective and efficient control programme conditions cycle may appear after 15–20 years whereas under the partial implemented control programme situation the cycle may come after 5–7 years. Cyclical variations are observed as spikes or rise in incidence of disease at regular interval of one or two years in some diseases like measles and smallpox (which has now been eradicated). This is probably due to accumulation of susceptible individuals, i.e. young children who received no vaccination against measles. Measles outbreaks are generally due to accumulation of measles susceptibles children including both unvaccinated children and those who were vaccinated but failed to seroconvert. Approximately 15% of children vaccinated at 9-month are not protected after measles vaccination. Similarly, meningococcal meningitis shows cyclic trends after every 8–12 years.

B. HEALTH EVENTS IN TERMS OF PLACE DISTRIBUTION

Distribution of disease in a district, state or county, or a geographical area is significant determinant and provides clue for prevalence of special risk factors in that area.

Malaria as a disease is a public health problem in India; its distribution is not uniform all over India. Some states show high incidence while some states have low incidence of malaria.

During 2008, 1.53 million cases of malaria were reported from the country with 0.77 million being those of P. Falciparum. Ten states contributed 84% of total cases. Incidence of malaria was high in the state of Odisha, Jharkhand, MP, and Assam.

Two-fifth cases of Pf malaria in the country were reported from Odisha alone. Odisha and Jharkhand combined contributed 52% of cases of Pf malaria in India. Over half of the cases were from these two states.

These two states have high percentage of tribal people, health services are poorly developed, surveillance and treatment facilities not easily accessible because of lack of infrastructure facilities. Problem of drug resistance may be acute in tribal belts of these states. *On the basis of observational or descriptive epidemiology, this provides a ground for analytical epidemiology for testing of various hypotheses or speculations.*

Geographical mapping of malaria or geographical information system (GIS) of a disease provides useful information and helps classify the areas for different control strategies. Based on geographical distribution of malaria the problem areas were broadly classified as under.

Hard-core Areas (Tribal Areas)

These are the areas where malaria control operations over the last four decades have failed to control the disease. Such areas have the following characteristics:

- These are mostly difficult terrain areas, large part of which becomes inaccessible during monsoon and subsequent flooding.
- The population is predominantly tribal.
- They have predominant Pf malaria.
- They have stable malaria with transmission period extending up to 9 months or more.
- These report bulk of deaths due to malaria in the country.

These areas comprise seven North and Eastern States, tribal areas of 87 districts of Andhra Pradesh, Bihar, Gujarat, MP, Maharashtra, Odisa and Rajasthan.

Epidemic Prone Areas

High-risk areas are considered to be prone to malaria outbreaks or epidemics. The periodic fulminating malaria epidemic contributes a large number of malaria deaths. North western plains, semi-arid climatic zone with annual rainfall up to 100 mm and Indo-Genetic plains are identified as major epidemic prone areas. During epidemic, the malaria deaths in these high-risk areas outnumber the malaria deaths reported from the rest of the affected states. These areas have unstable malaria.

Project Areas:

The development projects attract large number of migrant labour population from endemic areas having different strains of malaria parasites as well as non-immune population groups. The prolific increase in vector breeding places and increased man mosquito contact favours high transmission of malaria. Construction activities in metropolis, in and around Delhi, Gurgaon and Faridabad, migrant industrial labour and brick kiln labour are examples of project areas which become vulnerable population for many other problems apart from spreading malaria. Specific control strategies are required for such areas.

Urban Areas

Review of past date indicates that the following 15 cities like Delhi, Chennai, Kolkata, Mumbai, Hyderabad, Bengaluru, Bhopal, Ahmedabad, Jaipur Lucknow, Chandigarh, Vadodara, Vishakhapatnam, Vijayawada and Kanpur are accountable for nearly 80% of cases of urban malaria scheme (UMS) of NMEP. City of Chennai alone contributes half of malaria cases in Tamil Nadu.

.These urban areas have unplanned and rapid growth, with prolific increase in slum population, large size of floating population, poor water management, civic by-laws for control of mosquito population are absent or not implemented and case finding mechanism is either absent or very poor and these is insufficient staff for anti larval activities. These urban areas require different strategies for control of malaria.

Triple Insecticide Resistant Areas

The ubiquitous rural vector, Anopheles has become resistant to the conventional insecticides namely DDT, BHC and Malathion in the Western belt of India, specially Northern parts of Maharashtra and Karnataka and Southern parts of Gujarat. Alternate insecticides such as synthetic pyrethroids are considered for indoor residual spray in these areas.

Based on the Observations and epidemiological situation the expert committee has used the epidemiological parameters to identify the worst affected areas in different malaria paradigms.

Rural Urban Distribution

The health indicators are usually low for rural areas as compared to urban areas. The distribution of diseases vary in urban and rural areas. Density of population is much more in urban areas; urban slums are worse than rural areas in many ways. The plan of action suggested for "high-risk" rural and urban areas for malaria is being implemented under National Programme of Control of Malaria. During the year 2007 in India, rural areas had very high share (92.6%) of malaria in comparison to urban areas (7.4%).

C. HEALTH EVENTS IN TERMS OF PERSON DISTRIBUTION

The descriptive studies describe the *distribution of disease* according to characteristics of the person (host) like age, sex, occupation, literacy, marital status, social class and health behavior, resident or migrant, etc. The *disease pattern* varies with age of a person; diseases of infants, young children, adolescents, youths and adults and old age vary considerably.

Common age classification for the purposes of epidemiology is mentioned as:

Under one year of age, 1–4 yrs, 5–14 yrs, 15–24 yrs, 25–34 yrs, 35–44 yrs, 45–54 yrs, 55–64 yrs, 65 yrs and over.

Age Classification for Special Statistics of Infant Mortality:

For malaria control programme, age classification adopted is 0–1 year, 1–4 years, 5–8 years and 9–14 years and above 15 years. For the purpose of distribution of drugs and study the incidence of fever and malaria in different age groups to calculate infant parasite rate which is an indicator of recent transmission of malaria in the community and it confirms local transmission of malaria during current transmission period.

Infant parasite rate (IPR) =

No. of infants found positive for malaria parasite   × **100**

    Total no. of infants' blood smears examined during survey

Age distribution (Distribution of Disease According to Age)

Malaria affected all age groups in the rural community of this rural block. It means all age groups or whole of population is exposed to occurrence of malaria ***Table 4***

Table 4: Age and sex distribution of malaria cases in a rural block

Table 4: Age and sex distribution of malaria cases in a rural block		
Age groups (years)	*Sex*	*Cases of malaria year 1996*
0–1	M	4
	F	10
1–4	M	116
	F	97
5–8	M	239
	F	195
9–14	M	404
	F	209
15 and above	M	1432
	F	1183
Total		**3989**

Source: Health center PHC Cheri Population round 1,00,000.

Sex distribution (Distribution of Disease According to Sex)

Both sexes were affected; however, incidence of malaria in adult males was of high preponderance as compared to females, probably due to more outdoor exposure and sleeping habits of outdoor (Table 4). *This descriptive observation needs further studies and verification.*

From the data of National Malaria Control Programme, following hypotheses can be developed as:

a. Why falciparum malaria is showing rising trends in India?

b. What makes malaria to stay at high annual incidence of around two million cases?

c. Why there is variation of incidence and distribution of malaria in different states of country?

To answer these questions or to prove/disapprove the hypotheses, we use the knowledge of analytical epidemiology

B.   ANALYTICAL EPIDEMIOLOGY OR STUDY (WHY AND HOW)

The analytical study analyses the relationship between the health status (incidence and prevalence of disease) with other variables or risk factors associated with occurrence and distribution.While descriptive epidemiology describes the health status and its distribution in population. The analytical epidemiology focuses on "determinants" risk factors and reasons for such situation or status in the population. Analytical epidemiology studies cause to effect relationship (why and how of health event).

TYPES OF ANALYTICAL EPIDEMIOLOGY (STUDY)

a. Ecological studies

b. Cross-sectional studies

c. Case control studies

d. Cohort studies

ECOLOGICAL STUDIES

Ecological studies are also known as co relational studies. The focus and unit of analysis in these studies is population or groups of people. These studies provide an indirect evidence or clue of some events. Ecological studies are studies of risk-modifying factors on health or other outcomes based on populations defined either geographically or temporally. Both risk-modifying factors and outcomes are averaged for the populations in each geographical or temporal unit and then compared using standard statistical methods.

Ecological studies have often found links between risk-modifying factors and health outcomes well in advance of other epidemiological or laboratory approaches.

For example:

Cholera study

The study by John Snow regarding a cholera outbreak in London is considered the first ecological study to solve a health issue. He used a map of deaths from cholera to determine that the source of the cholera was a pump on Broad Street. He had the pump handle removed in 1854 and people stopped dying there. It was only when Robert Koch discovered bacteria years later that the mechanism of cholera transmission was understood.

Diet and cancer

Dietary risk factors for cancer have also been studied using both geographical and temporal ecological studies. Multi-country ecological studies of cancer incidence and mortality rates with respect to national diets have shown that some dietary factors such as animal products (meat, milk, fish and eggs), added sweeteners/sugar, and some fats appear to be risk factors for many types of cancer, while cereals/grains and vegetable products as a whole appear to be risk reduction factors for many types of cancer. Temporal changes in Japan in the types of cancer common in Western developed countries have been linked to the nutrition transition to the Western diet.

UV radiation and cancer

An important advancement in the understanding of risk-modifying factors for cancer was made by examining maps of cancer mortality rates. The map of colon cancer mortality rates in the United States was used by the brothers Cedric and Frank C. Garland to propose the hypothesis that solar ultraviolet B (UVB) radiation, through vitamin D production, reduced the risk of cancer (the UVB-vitamin D-cancer hypothesis). Since then many ecological studies have been performed relating the reduction of incidence or mortality rates of over 20 types of cancer to higher solar UVB doses.

Diet and Alzheimer's

Links between diet and Alzheimer's disease have been studied using both geographical and temporal ecological studies. The first paper linking diet to risk of Alzheimer's disease was a multi-country ecological study published in 1997. It used prevalence of Alzheimer's disease in 11 countries along with dietary supply factors, finding that total fat and total energy (caloric) supply were strongly correlated with prevalence, while fish and cereals/grains were inversely correlated (i.e., protective). Diet is now considered an important risk-modifying factor for Alzheimer's disease. Recently it was reported that the rapid rise of Alzheimer's disease in Japan between 1985 and 2007 was likely due to the nutrition transition from the traditional Japanese diet to the Western diet.

36

UV radiation and influenza

Another example of the use of temporal ecological studies relates to influenza. John Cannell and associates hypothesized that the seasonality of influenza was largely driven by seasonal variations in solar UVB doses and calcidiol levels. A randomized controlled trial involving Japanese school children found that taking 1000 IU per day vitamin D3 reduced the risk of type A influenza by two-thirds.

ADVANTAGES AND DRAWBACKS

Ecological studies are particularly useful for generating hypotheses since they can use existing data sets and rapidly test the hypothesis. The advantages of the ecological studies include the large number of people that can be included in the study and the large number of risk-modifying factors that can be examined.

The term "ecological fallacy" means that risk-associations apparent between different groups of people may not accurately reflect the true association between individuals within those groups. Ecological studies should include as many known risk-modifying factors for any outcome as possible, adding others if warranted. Then the results should be evaluated by other methods, using, for example, Hill's criteria for causality in a biological system..

Ecological studies are rapid methods of getting clue for some evidences and based on the initial clues, the study can be enlarged.

CROSS-SECTIONAL STUDIES

CROSS SECTIONAL STUDY:

In medical research and social science, a cross-sectional study (also known as a cross-sectional analysis, transverse study, prevalence study) is a type of observational study that analyzes data from a population, or a representative subset, *at a specific point in time*—that is, cross-sectional data.

These studies are also called "prevalence studies". These studies are done on a part or a sample of population and this sample is representative of the area.

In cross-sectional studies, the "exposure" and the "health effect" are measured simultaneously. In cross-sectional studies, it is not easy to measure the cause and effect relationship.

A cross-sectional study involves looking at people who differ on one key characteristic at one specific point in time. The data is collected at the same time from people who are similar in other characteristics but different in a key factor of interest such as age, income levels, or geographic location. Participants are usually separated into groups known as cohorts. For example, researchers might create cohorts of participants who are in their

These studies are easier to conduct and results are available quickly with affordable cost.

USEFULNES

- These studies provide quick estimate of burden of disease in the community.
- It also identifies individuals/population or groups at risk.
- Variation of disease or event in different geographical areas.

EXAMPLES OF CROSS-SECTIONAL STUDIES

There are innumerable examples. Most studies done (over 90%) are cross-sectional in nature. The major cross-sectional studies conducted in the country are:

1. National family health survey (NFHS-I–III) done once in five years. These studies provide data on key health indicators and family welfare indicators such as fertility, use of contraception, mortality, coverage and quality of maternal and child health services by states.

2. National sample surveys.

3. Sample Registration Survey (SRS) done every year provides state level estimates on birth, death and infant mortality rates.

4. Another example of cross-sectional survey is outbreak investigation and response. Since we have built the story of descriptive epidemiology on one disease, i.e. Malaria, it is worthwhile to discuss briefly utility of cross-sectional surveys in outbreak of malaria.

OUTBREAK RESPONSE

In the event of occurrence of outbreaks, the rapid response is essential. First response comes from local areas and the District.

The response or actions consists of:

a. Stepping up of surveillance activities.
b. Additional laboratory support in the area of occurrence.
c. Ensuring adequate supplies of anti-malaria drugs.
d. Fogging and spray operations.
e. Mass fever treatment if indicated.
f. Deployment of additional manpower and material.
g. Involvement of community.

WARNING SYSTEM FOR EARLY DETECTION AND RAPID RESPONSE TO OUTBREAK

For prediction of outbreaks of malaria, we rely on surveillance system of active and passive case detection. Apart from this, regular monitoring of meteriological data like, rainfall, temperature, humidity, etc. Together with epidemiological situation of malaria are reviewed. Deviation from the normal trends in these variables may indicate increase in mosquitogenic potential, in that situation any lapse in control activities may lead to outbreaks of malaria. For accuracy and better prediction, these data need to be analysed locally at micro-level say a primary health center or a section or a subcentre area. The exercise is not only data-based but also requires area specific information, both meteriological and epidemiological. Rainfall is single most important meteriological data along with epidemiological data for prediction of epidemic of malaria and averting impending outbreak. The exercise is useful for early warning signals.

OUTBREAK OF MALARIA IN DISTRICT, BETUL, MADHYA PRADESH 2000:

A team of National Institute of Communicable Diseases investigated "fever-related deaths" reported from 6 blocks of district Betul in October 2000.

General: Betul District is situated on Satpuda hills in Madhya Pradesh. The central part of district is plain, while the surrounding area is mostly hilly with thick forest. The annual rainfall is about 1043 mm and the temperature is favourable for survival of mosquitoes throughout the year.

Tribals constitute about two-thrids of the population. Of 65 deaths reported from Ist September to 5th October, 27 (42%) occurred in persons having febrile illness. Deaths occurred in all age groups with some preponderance (large) in young adults (Table).

The major presenting symptoms were moderate to high fever with chills and rigors, headache, bodyache, nausea and vomiting. In addition, severe cases had altered sensorium and were brought to health facilities in coma. No haemorrhagic manifestations were observed. The patients were treated with antibiotics and antimalarials. Only a few deaths occurred in admitted cases. The duration of illness was 2–3 day in most of cases.

A house-to-house survey was organized in a village on 11 October where a 9-year-old child had died on 6th October 2000. About 70% of population surveyed was found to have fever in the last two weeks. All age groups were affected and multiple cases were seen in many families. Of 33 blood smears collected from cases 24 (73%) were found positive for Plasmodium falciparum in the laboratories of NICD.

Table 5. Reported deaths in Betul district by various blocks 1st September to 5th October 2000			
Name of block	Total deaths		Fever-related deaths with fever
Chicholi	10	2	20
Bhimpur	24	11	45.8
Shakpur	10	5	50
Ghodadongri	12	3	25
Betul	5	3	60
Amla	4	3	75
Total	**65**	**27**	**41.5**

Source: NICD-outbreak investigation report.

Eight blood samples tested for Hi antibody against JE and dengue viruses were found to be negative for these antibodies. These samples were also negative for antibodies against measles. Isolation of influenza group of viruses was attempted from throat swabs of 10 cases and one CSF sample without any positive results.

It is worthwhile mentioning that 34% of the blood smears collected from 88 cases in the affected areas during 6–9 September were positive for malarial parasites and 80% of them had vivax malaria.

These and other epidemiological data indicated that vivax malaria continued to dominate up to September but gave way to falciparum malaria subsequently (Table 5).

The affected area has always been a focus for malaria. The terrain is rocky and undulating with a number of quarry pits. Optimum humidity and temperature favored increased mosquitogenic conditions. Since most of the persons are engaged in agriculture and forest-based occupations, they usually stay overnight in agriculture fields and forests with bare minimal clothing resulting in exposure to vectors. This increased the potential of malaria transmission in the affected area.

Only one round of spray with 50% DDT was carried out in September. In addition, the coverage was much below the expected level. All the houses were Kutcha and repeated mud plastering was a common practice. Consequently, there was no evidence of residual insecticide deposits on the surface of walls.

Disease surveillance mechanism was poor. Fortnightly visits by the health workers (surveillance staff) as well as visits by the supervisors were totally lacking. Patients were referred to the District Hospital although the Primary Health Centers (PHCs) were not equipped with microscope facilities and medicines to deal with malaria. Radical treatment was grossly delayed due to long interval between disease onset, diagnosis and treatment.

Follow-up visits to the affected areas were made from 14–20 December 2000. Forty-two blood slides were

Table 6. Epidemiological situation of malaria in Betul district 1999–2000

Events	1999	2000
Population (million)	1.44	1.47
Blood slides examined	3,12,440	3,96,019
No. of blood smears positive for malaria parasite	14,133	16,234
Slide positivity rate (%)	4.5	4.1
No. of blood slides positive for P. falciparum	3879	6668
Proportion on falciparum cases	24.4	41.07
No. of deaths due to malaria	0	30

Source: NMW

Collected from fever cases during the follow-up visits. Of the 42 slides collected, 36 (86%) were positive for malaria parasite. Thirty-four of positive slides showed P. falciparum (95%). By this time, at least 120 cases had died as shown in Table 8.24.

Table 7: Distribution of total deaths in Betul by age due to fever

Age groups (years)	No. of deaths	Percentage of deaths
0–5	35	29.2

6–10	9	7.5
11–15	5	4.2
16–30	040	33.3
31–35	21	17.5
>45	10	8.3
Total	**120**	**100**

Conclusion

The District was endemic for malaria. The situation worsened in 2000 when falciparum malaria increased tremendously (Table 8.23) and caused many deaths because of:

- Poor surveillance
- Inadequate insecticide coverage
- The falciparum malaria was persisting which indicated the inadequate local capacity to deal with the situation.

This is an example of cross-sectional study during outbreak which has measured several exposures—like environmental conditions, surveillance operations, insecticidal spray, local practices, supervisory mechanism and spread of disease.

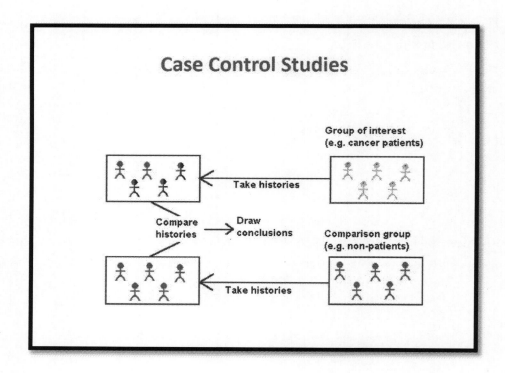

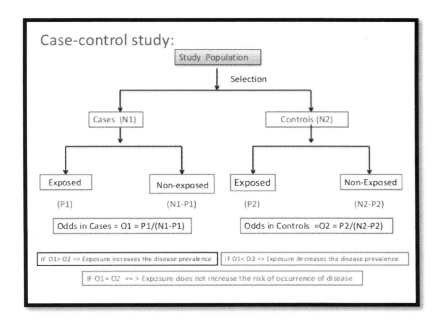

Definition:

The case–control is a type of epidemiological observational study. Porta's *Dictionary of Epidemiology* defines the case–control study as: *"an observational epidemiological study of persons with the disease (or another outcome variable) of interest and a suitable control group of persons without the disease (comparison group, reference group)"*.The potential relationship of a suspected risk factor or an attribute to the disease is examined by comparing the diseased and nondiseased subjects with regard to how frequently the factor or attribute is present (or, if quantitative, the levels of the attribute) in each of the groups (diseased and nondiseased).

The purpose of case control study is to investigate the cause or probable exposure or risk factors for that disease.

Case control studies focus on disease or sick persons. These studies are also simple and economical to carry out. In addition to cases of disease, a suitable control group is also chosen /selected. Control group consists of people who are healthy and not affected by the disease, which is being studied. The occurrence of possible cause/exposure is compared between cases and controls. The case control studies collect data at more than one/different points of time while cross-sectional studies collect data at one point of time.

STEPS IN CASE CONTROL STUDY

The case control study follows the following steps:

- It begins with selection of cases of a disease. To select "case", we must adopt a standard case definition and include case in the study. For example; all adults of 15–49 Years of age who are HIV positive or adults who are positive for malaria parasite included in the study.
- The cases can be selected from a Hospital or from the Community.
- Selection of controls or healthy people: Again, controls can be close relatives of case or the controls can be selected from community or hospital/clinic (attendants coming with patients.)

Controls should match with cases in respect of age, sex, social customs, culture and economic status and belong to the same background from where patient or case is selected. Preferably, controls should be chosen from the same population from where the cases are chosen.

Classical example of case control study is a marriage party of 150 men (Table 8).

Table 8: Association between ice cream consumption and development of diarrhoea and vomiting in the year 2004 in a marriage party

Disease	Exposure (consumption of ice creame)		
	Yes	No	Total
Vomiting and Diarrhea	Yes		
	80	20	100
	No		
	20	30	50
	Total		
	100	50	150

Out of 150 people who took part in marriage party, many suffered due to vomiting and diarrhoea and other escaped. Those who suffered were cases and those who did not suffer acted as controls.

The association of occurrence of vomiting and diarrhea with ice cream consumption can be measured by calculating the odds ratio (OR), which is the ratio of the odd (chances) of exposure amongst cases to the odds of exposure amongst controls.

Odds ratio is sometimes called the cross product ratio.

From the data in Table 8 the odds ratio can be calculated by:

$$(80: 20) + (20: 30)$$

$$= 80 \times 30 / 20 \times 20$$

$$= 6$$

It means that the cases were 6 times more than the controls likely to have consumed ice cream.

Here in this example these were the natural controls who did not consume the ice cream. The association between consumption of ice cream and development of vomiting and diarrhea is causal as the size of the risk ratio is more then 2. The odds ratio is very similar to risk ratio. Here there were natural controls who did not consume ice cream.

In a rural community development block, 2700 births occurred in 100,000 population in the year 1996. Of these 900 births weighed below 2.5 kg and the rest 1800 had birth weight 2.5 kg and above. We wish to test the following hypotheses:

- To ascertain the causes or risk factors of low birth weight in the block.
- Could it be due to moderate or severe anemia in pregnant women, or could it be due to high parity (4 and above) or less birth interval. Are low birth weights common to primi para or to girls marrying in teen ages and having teen age pregnancy? To answer these questions or to test these hypotheses, we do case control study.

DEFINITION OF CASE:

- In this setting, the case is a live birth below 2.5 kg.
- Controls—live birth above 2.5 kg in the same area.

We study the attributes or exposures like anemia, parity, and age of marriage, parity of women who gave birth to these children by interviewing or looking at the records and obtaining the history of these exposures. After ascertaining these exposures in cases and controls the data are compiled and analysis done (Table 8.26).

In this contingency table of 2×2, we depict the respective frequencies or numbers and calculate the odd ratio. The odd ratio of 5.44 indicates that mothers of low birth weight babies have over 5 times more chances of severe anaemia as compared to mothers of babies who have adequate birth weight.

Thus, severe Anemia during pregnancy has causal association with Low Birth Weights.

COHORT STUDIES

A **cohort study** is a particular form of longitudinal **study** that sample a **cohort** (a group of people who share a defining characteristic, typically those who experienced a common event in a selected period, such as birth or graduation), performing a cross-section at intervals through time.

Cohort studies are a **type** of medical **research** used to investigate the causes of disease and to establish links between risk factors and health outcomes. These types of studies look at groups of people. They can be forward-looking (prospective) or backward-looking (retrospective).

The cohort study measures the incidence and this is why cohort studies are also called incidence studies. In cohort study, the focus is on healthy population. The healthy population is divided into two subgroups: One group is that which is exposed to the risk or risk factor which is present in that subgroup and the second subgroup is free from risk or exposure. Both these groups, i.e. exposed and non-exposed should match with each others in terms of age, sex, economic status and other attributes but not for exposure.

Cohort, Cross Sectional, and case-control studies are collectively referred to as Observational Studies. Cross Sectional Studies are used to determine prevalence. They are relatively quick and easy but do not permit distinction between cause and effect. Case Controlled Studies compare groups retrospectively.

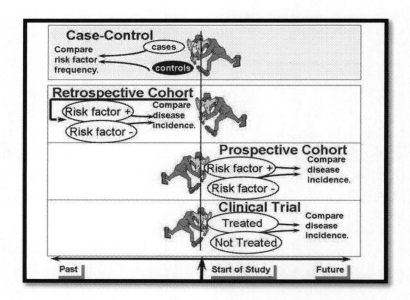

A "cohort" is any group of people with a shared characteristic. For example, Birth Cohort, in this Birth Cohort, what's common to all individuals is their birth year.

In a cohort study, the study participants are followed over time—from weeks to years, depending on the time frame. The goal is to understand the relationship between some attribute related to the cohort at the beginning of the study and the eventual outcome.

In terms of levels of evidence for establishing relationships between exposure and outcome, cohort studies are considered second to randomized controlled trials (RCTs) because RCTs limit the possibility for biases by randomly assigning one group of participants to an intervention/treatment and another group to non-intervention/treatment or placebo.

Cohort studies are observational—meaning the researcher observes what's happening or *naturally occurring*, measures variables of interest and draws conclusions. RCTs, in contrast, are experimental—meaning the researcher *manipulates* one of the variables (assigns treatments, for example) and determines how this influences the outcome.

FIVE STEPS IN A COHORT STUDY:

1. Identify the study subjects; i.e. the cohort population.

2. Obtain baseline data on the exposure; measure the exposure at the start. (The exposure may be a particular event, a permanent state or a reversible state.)

3. Select a sub-classification of the cohort—the unexposed control cohort—to be the comparison group.

4. Follow up; measure the outcomes using records, interviews or examinations. (Note: Outcomes must be defined in advance and should be specific and measurable.)

5. Do the data analysis where the outcomes are assessed and compared.

Table 9: Association Between Low Birth Weight and Severe Anemia in Pregnancy

Exposure			Birth weight	
	Yes		No	Total
	Less than 2.5 kg		More than 2.5 kg	
Anaemia of less than 7gm +	Yes	630	540	1170
−	No	270	1260	1530
Total		900	1800	2700

$$\text{Odds ratio} = \frac{630 \times 1260}{270 \times 540} = 5.44$$

PURPOSE

Cohort study has two purposes:

- To measure the incidence of disease.
- To find out the cause of disease.

ADVANTAGES

- Cohort study provides the best information about the causation of disease and the most direct measurement of the risk of developing disease.
- By Cohort Study multiple outcomes can be observed.
- Cohort studies are easier to conduct. For example, in young children; Study of growth and development and mortality in the first month or first year of life. Notable examples of global cohort studies are Framingham heart study, MONICA study on heart disease and Doll and Hill study on smoking and cancer.

DISADVANTAGES

- The cohort studies require long time period for follow-up of subjects and many of the subjects may be lost to the follow-up.
- The cost involved may be too much.
- If the incidence of disease is low or it is rare very large sample size has to be studied.

DESIGN OF COHORT STUDY

MODEL FIRST (COHORT STUDY OF IMR) (TABLE 10)

During the year 1996 in a rural community development block in 1,00,000 population, 2700 births occurred. Of these 900 were low birth weights and 1800 weighed 2.5 kg or more. These two subgroups of births were followed for one-year period to study the effect of mortality/incidence of mortality in the first year of life. The hypothesis was that incidence of death is much more in babies who are born with low birth weights (Table10).

Table 10: One year follow-up of cohort of 2700 births in a rural block to study incidence of mortality in LBW

The incidence of infant mortality was 120 per thousand live births in low birth weight babies

Birth weight	Number	Survived	Died	Incidence of IMR (kg)	
<2.5	900	792	108	120	
>2.5	1800	1728	72	40	
Total	**2700**	**2520**	**180**	**67**	

while IMR of 40 was observed in babies who had adequate birth weight. The incidence of IMR was there times higher in low birth weights as compared to normal birth weights after a follow-up period of one year. Thus, risk ratio of infant mortality ($I_E \div I_{NE}$) was measured as 120/40 = 3.

The incidence of mortality can be obtained for different periods such as during the first 7days of life, up to 28 days of life and 28 days to less than one year to capture early neonatal, neonatal and post-neonatal component of infant mortality.

MODEL SECOND (COHORT STUDY OF NUTRITIONAL STATUS) (TABLE 11)

This cohort study measured the change of nutritional status of cohort of 570 under six children over a period of one year follow-up with intervention by supplementary and therapeutic nutrition under ICDS.

Out of 187 children who were normal in year 1979, 114 (60.97) continued as normal while 39. 07% deteriorated. Out of 202 grade I malnutrition 29.22% improved, 55.93% remained in the same grade while 14.36% deteriorated. Similarly, out of 118 grade II malnourished children 55.09% improved and 39.84% maintained the same grade while 5.07% deteriorated. Of 41 grade III children, 65.90% improved their nutritional status, 24.38% maintained and 9.72% deteriorated. Of 16 grade IV children all children, i.e. 100% improved their nutritional status (Table 11).

Table. 11: Longitudinal follow-up of under six children to assess the outcome of nutritional status after one year of follow-up in a rural block.

Yr 1979 Baseline			Repeat survey 1980 Survey			
Gr. No	Normal	Grade I	Grade II	Grade III	Grade IV	Not recorded
Normal 187	114 (60.97)	53 (28.34)	16 (8.56)	2 (1.07)	1 (0.53)	1 (0.53)
Gr. I 202	59 (29.22)	113 (55.93)	24 (11.88)	5 (2.48)	0 (0)	1 (0.49)
Gr. II 118	20 (16.95)	45 (38.14)	47 (39.84)	6 (5.07)	0 (0)	0 (0)
Gr. III 41	2 (4.86)	8 (19.44)	17 (41.60)	10 (24.38)	4 (9.72)	0 (0)
Gr. IV 16	2 (12.50)	1 (6.25)	8 (50.00)	5 (31.25)	0 (0)	0 (0)
Not Recorded	0 (0)	0 (0)	6 (100)	0 (0)	0 (0)	0 (0)
Total 570	**197**	**220**	**118**	**28**	**5**	**2**

Model Third (Cohort Study in Leprosy)(Table 12)

This exercise was done in May 2004, for carrying out LEM (leprosy elimination monitoring). Cohort for the MB cases of leprosy registered during the period from 1st May 2001 to 30th

April 2002 was analyzed to determine the total number of cases, total number cured and total number defaulted and total number still on treatment after completion of 12 does of MDT. Similarly, cohort for PB case from 1st January 2002 to 31st December 2002 was chosen for outcome of treatment and case holding.

Similarly, cohort of new sputum smear positive cases of pulmonary TB can be followed up, to determine cure rate, sputum conversion and default rate.

Table 12: Case holding indicators for MB

Case = A person with clinical signs of leprosy (with or without bacteriological examination), who has yet to complete full course of treatment. **Cured** = A patient who has completed a full course of MDT (12 doses for MB). **Defaulter** = A patient who has not taken treatment consecutively for more than 12 months. **Left the control area** = A patient who has left the area where he/she used to come for MDT treatment and has migrated somewhere else. This patient should be removed from the register (and therefore from the prevalence).					
Number of MB cases from 1st May 2001 to 30th April 2002 Registered in area	Number of MB cases cured	Number of MB cases defaulted	Number of MB cases still on treatment after completion of 12 doses of MDT	Left the control area	Died
Total 12	12	3 6	1 2		

Note: MB patients who had received more than 12 doses should be included in both columns (cured and still on treatment after completion 12 doses).

SOURCE OF DATA: Leprosy treatment register and/or patient card for the period from 1st may 2001 to 30th April 2002.

Table : Case holding indicators for PB

Case = A person with clinical signs of leprosy (with or without bacteriological examination), who has yet to complete full course of treatment. **Cured** = A patient who has completed a full course of MDT (6 doses for PB). **Defaulter** = A patient who has not taken treatment consecutively for more than 12 months. **Left the control area** = A patient who has left the area where he/she used to come for MDT treatment and has migrated somewhere else. This patient Should be removed from the

Number of PB cases from 1st JAN 2002 to 31st dec. 2002 Registered in area	Number of PB cases cured	Number of PB cases defaulted	Number of PB cases still on treatment after completion of 6 doses of MDT	Left the control area		Died
Total 40	30	6	6	2	2	

If a single skin lesion (SSL) case is treated with 6 doses of MDT for PB leprosy cases, he/she should be included in the cohort.

Note: PB patients who had received more than 6 doses should be included in both columns (cured and still on treatment after completion of 6 doses).

EXPERIMENTAL EPIDEMIOLOGY

Experimental epidemiology is also known as intervention epidemiology. In this research, the interventions are undertaken which could be treatment, immunization, supplementary nutrition, therapeutic nutrition, specific nutrient like vitamin A and iron and folic acid, salt iodization, insecticidal spray and chlorination of water, etc. Similarly, new drug is tested for its effectiveness. Experimental epidemiology involves experimentation in the groups or community and usually the effects of and interventions are measured in two groups namely: Experimental Group and Control Group. The interventions are strictly determined by laid down protocol or plan. There are important ethical considerations in the conduct of these studies. **There are three designs of experimental or intervention epidemiology or research:**

1. *Randomized controlled trials (a type of Clinical Research)*

2. *Field trials*

3. *Community* trials

RANDOMIZED CONTROLLED TRIAL (RCT)

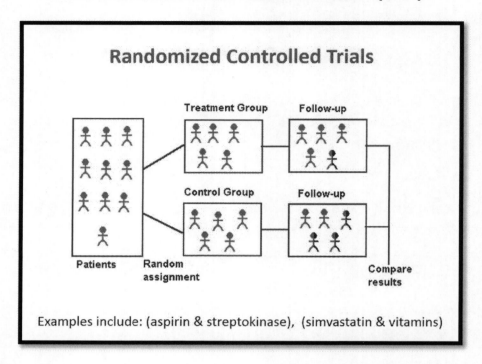

Randomized Controlled Trials

Examples include: (aspirin & streptokinase), (simvastatin & vitamins)

DEFINITION: It can be defined as *"A study design that randomly assigns participants into an experimental group or a control group. As the study is conducted, the only expected difference between the control and experimental group in a randomized controlled trial (RCT) is the outcome variable being studied."*

OBJECTIVE

Objective of Clinical Trail is to study the effectiveness of a new drug or a regimen in 'patients'.

STEPS IN RCT

1. **Plan of Study or Protocol:** First step in RCT is to prepare a plan of study or protocol what you wish to test or study.

2. **Define study population.**

3. **Selection of participants by defined criteria as per plan.**

4. **Randomization of Participants.**

5. **Treatment group and control group.**

6. **Follow-up of these groups.**

7.   Analysis

1. PLANNING OF RCT

Define clear objective of RCT, state the inclusion and exclusion criteria of case (case definition is essential to have valid conclusions), Determine the sample size, place, and period of study. The design of the trial must be written in advance whether it would be single blind, double blind or triple blind method. In single blind method the investigator knows the treatment plan and it is not known to the patients. In double blind trials, the investigator and the participants both do not know the treatment plan. In triple blind trials, the investigator, participants and the person associated with analysis do not know the treatment plan and group allocation. The blinding is useful tool to avoid bias in the study. The plan of study must be approved by ethical committee of the institute.

2. STUDY POPULATION

The study population varies according to the nature of RCT. Most often the patients are chosen from hospital or from the community as per defined criteria as explained below. In choice of patients for domiciliary and home treatment; open cases of tuberculosis were chosen as study population.

3.   SELECTION OF PARTICIPANTS—

Inclusion criteria once we have defined the study population out of open cases of tuberculosis those who fulfilled criteria for inclusion as participants were selected based on some of the criteria like: age groups, severity of disease and treatment taken or not, etc. Thus the participant patients must meet the criteria set by the investigator under the step planning of RCT. Further informed consent of the participant is essential for RCT.

4.   RANDOMIZATION OF PARTICIPANTS

Subjects in a population are randomly allocated into groups. Once you have selected the study population the next step is to allocate the participants of the study into:

a. **Treatment groups**
b. **Control groups**

This should be done without any bias. You can adopt a lottery system, i.e. have predetermined chit or token specifying treatment or control word on it and as the case enters the study, drew a token and categorize the patient to either control or treatment group. Random table numbers can be used for randomization. Randomization is considered to be "sheet anchor" of RCT.

5.   TREATMENT GROUP AND CONTROL GROUP (INTERVENTION):

The treatment group is put on a drug under trial and the control group is given no drug or given a placebo, which resembles with treatment drug in size and color and looks identical with treatment drug.

If one wishes to determine the efficacy of two different drugs then subgroups can be made for allocation of these subgroups to drug A, B or C, etc. The treatment and intervention need to be supervised very closely in the hospital.

6.   FOLLOW-UP

The final outcome in two groups i.e. treatment group and control group is observed with the passage of time or such time interval which has been predetermined. The outcome could be cure or improvement in the condition or worsening or no change in the condition or patient may die. Cure and all other outcomes are determined as per laid down criteria under the plan of study.

7.   ANALYSIS

The final outcomes are compared between the treatment group and control group or between various subgroups. It could be metaanalysis of several RCTs done in different parts of the country.

For example;

A. RANDOMIZED CONTROLLED TRIALS IN TUBERCULOSIS (*Comparison of Home and Sanatorium Treatment*)

This study was undertaken by Tuberculosis chemotherapy center in Madras, as a controlled comparison of Home and Sanatorium treatment for one year and subsequently for another four years to study the emergence of relapse cases in these two groups.

STUDY POPULATION

163 newly diagnosed and previously untreated sputum positive patients of pulmonary tuberculosis from poor section of community in Madras City.

RANDOMIZATION

These 163 cases were randomly allocated for treatment at Sanatorium or Home with the same chemotherapy i.e. INH 200 mg and PAS 10g in two divided doses per day. Patients in home series were given weekly supply of drugs to be administered by them at home with monthly super-vision of their progress at the clinic and were visited at home by a health visitor every fortnight (supervised therapy).

COMPARISON

The patients in the sanatorium series had bed rest, good accommodation, balanced diet and nursing care. Thus, this was the comparison of treatment of patients in best sanatorium conditions with those in usual day-to-day home conditions of poor sections of the community.

RESULTS

At the end of one year, 86% of patients treated at home converted to sputum negative and remained so (bacteriological quiescent) as against 92% in sanatorium patients. Improvement in X-ray and closure of cavity were also of the same order in both the groups.

FOLLOW-UP

After one year, the sanatorium patients returned to their homes and the patients in both series were closely followed up for

another 4 years to study the long-term results. Considering the overall relapse rate of disease in the two groups, it was found that 7% of patients in home series and 10% patients in sanatorium series had bacteriologically relapse over a 4-year period of follow-up.

Conclusion

It was conclusively proved that effect of treatment of patients at home was as good as treatment in an institution both in respect of immediate recovery and subsequent prevention of relapse and that good food, nursing care and isolation did not play any useful role in the treatment of tuberculosis. Domiciliary treatment has the added advantage of not causing any dislocation of the family during the period of treatment for tuberculosis. Supervised domiciliary treatment paved the way for present day DOTS under revised RNTCP and thus DOTS was born in India

A. Randomized Controlled Trials in TB Attack Rates among Close Family Contacts

This study was planned by the Tuberculosis chemotherapy centre to determine the relative risks for contacts of patients treated at home and in the sanatorium.

256 close family contacts of patients treated at homes and 272 similar contacts of patients treated in sanatorium were intensively followed up by X-ray and bacteriological examination for five years. In each family, there was just one infectious case and the contacts in the two series were similar in all other aspects. Efforts of isolation of the index cases could be best in the to series in the first year when the index case of the sanatorium series was isolated in the hospital.

In the first year, 4.9% of the contacts in home series developed tuberculosis compared with 7.6% of contacts of sanatorium patients. Over the whole period of 5 years, 9.8% of contacts of patients treated at home developed tuberculosis as against 14.4% of contacts of patients treated in sanatorium. There was no difference of attack rates in the two groups even when the initially tuberculin negatives and initially tuberculin positives were analysed separately.

An interesting observation of the study was that the majority of cases in contacts occurred in children below 5 years of age and were detected within 3 months of diagnosis of the index case and there was suggestive evidence that in most of them the infection occurred before in index case was diagnosed.

CONCLUSION

There is no special risk to the contacts of patients treated at home with effective chemotherapy, the main risk to them being before the treatment has begun. Hence, isolation of patients in hospital/institution or at home is not required. What we require is effective chemotherapy treatment at the earliest.

B. SOCIOLOGICAL STUDY OF AWARENESS OF SYMPTOMS AMONG PERSONS WITH PULMONARY TUBERCULOSIS

About 2000 patients having evidence of inactive, probably active and active tuberculosis disease in their X-rays whose sputum results were also available (experimental groups) were age and sex matched with an equal number of persons with normal X-ray (control group) in 34 villages and 4 towns of Tumkur district in Karnataka. These persons were interviewed at random by social investigators for symptoms. Only such symptoms that were associated with pulmonary tuberculosis were taken into consideration. Of these cough for one month or more fever for one month or more were analysed statistically. 79% of experimental group and 83% of the control group were satisfactorily interviewed.

RESULTS

Cough was found to be the most important single symptom. 69% of sputum positives and 46% of X-ray positives had this symptom against 9% of the normal.

69% of the sputum positive, 52% of the X-ray positives, 29% of inactive and 15% of the controls had at least one of the above symptoms (cough and fever more than a month).

Analysis also showed that 95% of the bacteriologically positive cases were aware about their symptoms. 72% experienced cough and were worried about their symptoms and 52% of them actually took action at the existing health facilities under pressure of their symptoms.

CONCLUSION

Cough of more than a month was most important symptom in bacteriologically positive cases. It is new built in the programme that individuals or patients who have cough for 2 weeks or more with ro with or other symptoms should have 2 sputum samples examination done for AFB. Usually, at least 2% of adult outpatients in general OPD have cough for 3 weeks or more. Half or more than half of infectious cases in the community are already seeking services and knocking at the door of health services.

C. CLINICAL TRIAL IN LEPROSY

A randomized controlled trial in leprosy has made revolution in treatment and has reduced the duration of treatment with multidrug therapy (MDT).

Outcome of multicentric study in India on efficacy of different treatment regimens have been accepted by WHO Leprosy Elimination Advisory Group (LEAG) in 1997 and 7th WHO expert committee on chemotherapy. The LEAG has endorsed the technical recommendations of the 7th expert committee on chemotherapy of leprosy and has urged all the national Governments to implement the same. Now the duration of treatment of MB has been reduced to 12 months and for PB cases for 6 months.

It is envisaged further to reduce the duration of MB treatment from 12 months to shorter duration 9-11.

FIELD TRIALS

Field trials in contrast to clinical trials focus on healthy populations who are exposed to the risk of development of disease. For example, infants and young children are at risk of developing measles in the community.

Trial of vaccine is conducted on healthy children or healthy population in the field. According to protocol, the study population is defined and participants are chosen and assigned to experimental group and control group and intervention is done. One group is immunized and other is non-immunized. These two groups are followed for a defined period (say one year or longer) and the outcome or incidence of disease occurrence in both groups is recorded and the results are compared in two groups.

In field conditions such a situation already exists, some children are immunized and some do not accept the immunization and are left as unimmunized. This opportunity provides a chance to conduct field trials to determine the efficacy of a vaccine.

Example

The efficacy of measles vaccine is determined by field trials under ideal conditions. This vaccine has high proven efficacy (approx. 90%) and should not be denied to infants. Immunization services with a measles vaccine efficacy of 90% are protecting children as effectively as possible against measles. A vaccine efficacy of less than 80% means there is problem with the vaccine. This could be due to problem with the cold chain, the injection technique or the age at which the health worker is immunizing the children, and you should take action to correct it.

To calculate vaccine efficacy, we need to obtain following informations from the health records.

- The size of study population— the children which are 12–23 months of age, since these children were under one year of age in the previous year.
- The coverage of measles vaccine in children.
- The number of cases of measles in immunized children 12–23 months of age.
- The number of cases of measles in unimmunized children 12–23 months of age.

SIZE OF POPULATION

If a health centre has 30,000 populations and the birth rate of the area is 30/1000, the size of study population (12–23 months children) can be calculated by 30,000 × .03 = 900

Therefore,

Study population of 12–23 months of children = 900 children

Measles immunization coverage in children 12–23 months of age = 40%

No. of measles cases in immunized children 12–23 months of age = 40

No. of measles cases in unimmunized children 12–23 months of age = 486
No. of immunized children in study population

$$= \frac{900 \times 40}{100} = 360$$

No. of unimmunized children in study population = 540
Let us put these data in tabular form   (Table   8.32).

INTERPRETATION

The measles vaccine efficacy of 88% in field trials indicates that high efficacy is being achieved in field conditions. It means it confers protection to nearly 88% of immunized children and occurrence of disease—one in 9 children in immunized against 9 out of 10 in unimmunized children.

Table 13: Efficacy of measles vaccine (field trials)			
Disease	No. of children (12-23 months of age)		
	Vaccinated	Non-Vaccinated	Total
Occurrence Yes	40	486	526
of measles No	320	54	374
disease Total	360	540	900

Attack rate of measles in immunized children = 40 ÷ 320 = 1/9

Attack rate of measles in unimmunized children = 486 ÷ 540 = 9/10

Efficacy of measles Vaccine = Attack rate of measles in unimmunized children (-)Attack rate of measles in immunized children ÷ Attack rate of measles in unimmunized children × 100

= $\frac{9/10 - 1/9}{9/10}$ × 100 = 88 %

s

BCG Vaccine Trials

A field trial of BCG vaccine has reported the efficacy of BCG vaccine ranging from 0 to 80% all over the world. Thus, efficacy of BCG is variable. The reasons for this variation are not clear, but the conclusion is obvious—BCG vaccine will not control TB. It still has vital role in preventing serious disseminated disease in children and that is why it is incorporated in the universal programme of immunization in India and most developing countries.

COMMUNITY TRIALS

In these trials, the treatment groups are communities rather than individuals.

The best example of community trial is supply of iodized salt to the community and reduction of prevalence of the problem of goiter in the community. The goiter prevalence rates were very high in Himachal Pradesh in 1953 as revealed through baseline survey of goiter in the community. A successful trial of providing iodized salt in phased manner indicated marked reduction of problem of prevalence of goiter in experimental population. The control groups in this study were communities in Himachal Pradesh which were not supplied iodized salt.

Some of the areas in Himachal Pradesh started receiving iodized salt as early as 1957 (Kangra Valley) after initial surveys in 1956, however, the national programme on control of goitre commenced in 1962.

Table 14: Results of supply of iodized salt

Area	Prevalence of goiter in 1956	Intervention in 1962	Prevalence of goiter 1968	1994
Kanga valley in HP 40 Districts of India	55%	Iodized salt	32.1 %	7%
	14-69 % (1984-94)	Do	2-40 % in (2003)	

The prevalence of goiter was 55% in 1956 in Kangra Valley, which declined to low level of 32% in 1968 after the supply of iodized salt in Kangra Valley. Following this experiment, national programme on control of goitre was launched in 1962 and subsequently renamed as National Iodine Deficiency Disorders Control Programme (NIDDCP). Recent pilot study (1994) reported TGR (Total Goiter Rate) of 7% in 4 selected blocks of district Kangra which further speaks of success of intervention.

A country wide study carried out by NIN and DGHS in 40 districts to assess the impact of iodization revealed that overall prevalence of total goiter rate declined from 14–69% during 1984–94 to 2–40% in 2003. TGR was > = 5% in 37 out of 40 districts.

TRENDS AND POSSIBILITIES OF RESEARCH AND DEVELOPMENT OF UNANI DRUGS

As we know that for the development or progress of any medicine, it is mandatory to conduct a research on concerning medicine.

Research and Development of Unani medicine is in the hands of the Central Council for Research in Unani Medicine (CCRUM) that has been established by Government of India in 1969.

Research had been carried out on Unani drugs in the last six decades has benefitted the modern medicine fraternity and not enriching the Unani system of medicine. Similarly, we are conducting clinical Studies based exclusively on biomedical diagnosis and to fit Unani treatment into this diagnosis. This leads to trimming and modifying Unani treatment to fit the biomedical research design.

Modern medicine has developed from the logic of modern science which follows the deductive approach; while the Unani medicine is known for its holistic approach. Thus, the application of modern concepts in the direction of clinical trials leads to the inevitable sacrifice of some of the important fundamental principles of Unani medicine. Consequently, the results of such ill designed studies are unlikely to add any value to the Unani system of medicine.

Ongoing research in Unani medicine is focusing more on modern medicine than to the system itself. Predominantly, Research in preventive medicine has been confined to cross-sectional studies in line of modern medicine protocol without taking into consideration the contrasting epistemology and principles of the respective system

Unani system of medicine has not gained much recognition in the contemporary world. The reason is that the quantity and quality of the safety and efficacy data on Unani medicine is far from sufficient to meet the criteria needed to support its use worldwide. The reasons for the lack of research data are not only due to inappropriate health care policies, but also due to lack of adequate or accepted research methodology for understanding and evaluating Unani medicine.

Unani system of medicine is one of the oldest systems of medicine and existence of this system till now itself is an evidence of validity of its principles. The existence and development of any pathy or branch of medicine depends on continuous research study and its proper application. With the same objective, Government of India established a Central Council for Research in Unani Medicine to develop this system in its own theoretical framework. But researches undertaken to revive the system have not been very rewarding except for the translations of some classical texts; which at least made the literature accessible to academicians and researchers. ***The past as well as the current trends have failed to reap desired results primarily due to use of inappropriate protocol designs for scientific research.*** But there are so many possibilities for Research and Development of *Unani* Drugs, if we make an appropriate research designs consisting of suitable factors mentioned in the classical literatures of Unani medicine.

Thus, there is a need for a paradigm shift (a great an important change in the way something is done or thought about) in the research methodology for evaluating of Unani medicine.

Chapter 3: RESEARCH PROBLEM, SOURCES AND ITS SELECTION

DEFINITION: Research Problem can be defined as "A research problem is an interrogative statement which shows relationship between two or more variables". Or a **research problem**, in general, refers to some difficulty which a researcher experiences in the context of either a theoretical or practical situation or wants to obtain a solution for the same. The best research question is one where the answer is hidden.

SELECTION OF RESEARCH PROBLEM:

First step in conducting a research is to identify a suitable problem which should be investigated. For selection of a problem a researcher should take into consideration the pattern and changes which have taken place in the area of subject matter of the study and understand what has already been done and what is yet to be done besides looking into the priorities. This can be done through review of available literature and discussions with peer group. Important sources of literature for review are different journals or periodicals, review articles, dissertations or doctoral thesis on the topic of the research. Web based Computer search is most helpful as a source of information for understanding about available literature but it should be authentic.

While reviewing literature, assessing the quality of research is a prime consideration. Each study reviewed should be evaluated in terms of Methodological quality i.e. extent to which the design and conduct of the study are likely to have prevented systematic errors (bias), precision of results i.e. measure of the likelihood of random errors (usually depicted as the width of the confidence interval around the result), external validity generalized or applicable to a particular target population. Besides review of literature, a pilot study will help in obtaining familiarity with the research problem and to test all aspects of the study design and feasibility. After a careful study on the above aspects, one should clearly define the problem in specific and easily understandable words.

Some points to be followed in the selection of problem as:
1. Subjects which are over done should not be normally chosen, for which it will be difficult to throw new light in such cases.
2. Controversial subject should not be taken as a choice.
3. Too narrow and too vague problem should be avoided.
4. The subject selected for research should be familiar and feasible so that selected research material should be in access.
5. The central research question should be based on sound scientific principles.
6. The research question should be relevant and important.

7. The research problem selected should be feasible, it should fit to the budget and time allotted
8. The research problem should be ethical.
9. The selection of problem must be preceded by a preliminary study.

Characteristics of a good research problem can be summarized as:

- Variables in the problem must be clear
- It should be limited in scope and should be specific
- It must have a goal
- It should be free from Ethical constrains
- It should be researchable, Feasible, Important, Novel and Relevant.

Techniques involved in defining the research problems as:

- Statement of the problem in a general way.
- Understanding the nature of problem.
- Surveying the available literature.
- Developing ideas through discussion.
- Rephrasing the research problem

SOURCES OF RESEARCH PROBLEM FOR THE STUDY: There are many sources for the selection of research problem for the study as:

- Mecdical issues like, Different types diseases
- Social problems like unemployment, crimes, female genital mutilation, etc.
- Theory deduction.
- Funding agencies.
- Past researches and literature review.
- Casual observation.
- Related literature.
- Current social and economic issues.
- Personal interest and experience.

LITERATURE REVIEW

A **literature review** or narrative **review** is a type of **review** article. A **literature review** is a scholarly paper, which includes the current knowledge including substantive findings, as well as theoretical and methodological contributions to a particular topic.

After making the choice of field of study and selecting the problem it is essential to search the literature for research. After selecting the problem literature review will explore the work done on that problem and one can avoid from unnecessary duplication and wastage of money, time and power in short. N*o researcher is supposed to plan a clinical trial without exploring existing \literature on the subject.*

Importance of literature review in Unani system of Medicine

In Unani System of Medicine *(USM)* the literature, which we have is the result of thoughts, observations, experiments and researches of ancient physicians of *USM*. So a researcher of *Unani* System of Medicine must review that literature to select a right path and to strengthen the system**.**

Benefits of Literature Review: It helps to understand the-

- Presence and nature of the problem.
- Planning (Hypothesis, design, variable)
- Interpretation of findings.

Source of literature: The sources for literature are –

a. Classical texts and old manuscripts.
b. Experts in field.
c. Published reports.
d. Previous work done (journals, books, seminars)
e. Seminars and conference
f. Electronic data bases internet
g. Unpublished reports

FORMULATION OF OBJECTIVES AND HYPOTHESIS OF RESEARCH

OBJECTIVES:

Researcher has to clearly identify what is expected to be derived out of the study. These are known as the objectives of the study. This should include both overall objectives as well as the specific objectives. Over all objectives of research are those results which are to be ascertained broadly from the study while the specific objectives relate to the specific research questions the investigator would like to answer within the broad objective. An example of an overall objective in a drug trial would be to assess whether a particular new drug is more effective for a disease as compared to a known drug. Specific objectives would be to answer questions as to effectiveness of the new drug for different stages of disease, or the dose or regimen of drug to be administered etc.

Research can formulate these objectives into certain research hypothesis, which are statements relating to the objectives.

Usually hypothesis is formulated as a tentative statement showing a relationship between certain variable. As for example, in the above drug trail, the hypothesis can be stated as follows:

- The new drug is more effective in curing the disease as compared to the known drug.
- The new drug is effective only in mild cases of disease.
- The new drug has to be administered in higher doses in more severe cases of disease etc.

Chapter 4: HYPOTHESIS

It can be defined as *"A hypothesis is a prediction of what will be found at the outcome of a research project and is typically focused on the relationship between two different variables studied in the research"* or *Hypothesis is a testable statement, an assumption and a tentative explanation of a specific problem undertaken for doing research or Hypothesis is basically a prediction about the solution of the research problem and states the outcome of the study is expected.*

It is usually based on both theoretical expectations about how things work, and already existing scientific evidence. Within social science, a hypothesis can take two forms. It can predict that there is no relationship between two variables, in which case it is a **null hypothesis.** Or, it can predict the existence of a relationship between variables, which is known as **an alternative hypothesis**. In either case, the variable that is thought to either affect or not affect the outcome is known as the independent variable, and the variable that is thought to either be affected or not is the dependent variable.

Researchers seek to determine whether or not their hypothesis, or hypotheses if they have more than one, will prove true. Sometimes they do, and sometimes they do not. Either way, the research is considered successful if one can conclude whether or not a hypothesis is true.

TYPES OF HYPOTHESIS

- Null hypo thesis (H°)
- Alternate Hypothesis (HA)

NULL HYPOTHESIS

A researcher has a null hypothesis when she or he believes, based on theory and existing scientific evidence, that there will not be a relationship between two variables. For example, when examining what factors influence a person's highest level of education within the U.S., a researcher might expect that place of birth, number of siblings, and religion would *not* have an impact on level of education. This would mean the researcher has stated three null hypotheses.

ALTERNATIVE HYPOTHESIS

Taking the same example, a researcher might expect that the economic class and educational attainment of one's parents, and the race of the person in question are likely to have an effect on one's educational attainment. Existing evidence and social theories that recognize the connections between wealth and cultural resources, and how race affects access to rights and resources in the U.S. would suggest that both economic class and educational attainment of the one's parents would have a positive effect on educational attainment. In this case, economic class and educational attainment of one's parents are independent variables, and one's educational attainment is the dependent variable--it is hypothesized to be dependent on the other two.

Conversely, an informed researcher would expect that being a race other than white in the U.S. is likely to have a negative impact on a person's educational attainment. This would be characterized as a negative relationship, wherein being a person of color has a negative effect on one's educational attainment. In reality, this hypothesis proves true, with the exception of Asian Americans, who go to college at a higher rate than whites do. However, Blacks and Hispanics and Latinos are far less likely than whites and Asian Americans to go to college.

FORMULATING A HYPOTHESIS

Formulating a hypothesis can take place at the very beginning of a research project, or after a bit of research has already been done. Sometimes a researcher knows right from the start which variables she is interested in studying, and she may already have a hunch about their relationships. Other times, a researcher may have an interest in a particular topic, trend, or phenomenon, but he may not know enough about it to identify variables or formulate a hypothesis.

Whenever a hypothesis is formulated, the most important thing is to be precise about what one's variables are, what the nature of the relationship between them might be, and how one can go about conducting a study of them.

Usually, in traditional system of medicine like Unani medicine both the starting point and the ending point are known but the connection between them is not. For example, most of the time in traditional medicine we know that medicine X has a marked effect in disease B, the question that arises is; 'How does this occur?' The answer to this common situation is to develop a hypothesis that can be tested using either a forward or backward approach.

When we talk about the two samples from the same population, we would expect two types of results –

a. There is no significant difference between two groups (Null Hypothesis H°)
b. There is significant difference between two groups or variables (Alternate Hypothesis HA)

So, for the clinical research it is essential that Hypothesis should be tested and Null Hypothesis should be rejected and alternate Hypothesis should be sustained /supported

For Example:

Majoon_-e-Ushba has no effect in Fasad- ud- dam, known as (Null Hypothesis-H°)

Majoon-e-*Ushba* has some effects in fasad-ud-dum (Alternate Hypothesis HA)

Here, Alternate Hypothesis should be adopted for the research study and the research study should be conducted to assess the efficacy of the drug (Majoon-e-*Ushba) in the disease as* fasad-ud-dum and the Null Hypothesis-H° should be rejected.

IMPORTANCE OF HYPOTHESIS

- It specifies the area of research
- It tries to bridge theory with reality
- It proves direction by suggesting a tentative outcome.
- It forms an infra structure for drawing conclusion.
- It prevents blind research
- It provides basis for adopting correct research procedures to achieve the goals specified by the hypothesis.

CHARACTERISTICS OF A GOOD HYPOTHESIS: It should be –

- Simple and to the point,
- Specific not vague or casual,
- Conceptually clear,
- Confirming to the available technique of measurement or experimentation or knowledge or to the existing theory and.
- Capable of being empirically tested.

Chapter 5: RESEARCH DESIGN AND TYPES OF RESEARCH DESIGN

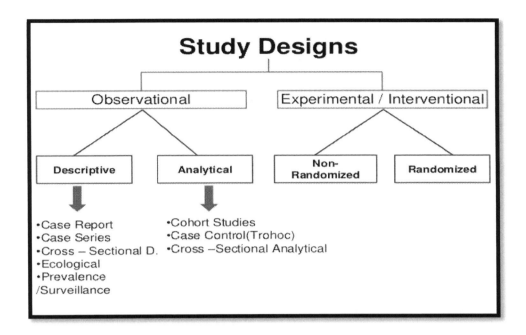

DEFINITION OF RESEARCH DESIGN:

It can be defined as **"a research design is the blue print of the procedures that are developed for conducting the trial".** It is the arrangement of conditions for collection, analysis and measurement of data in most economical manner in terms of both time and money.

A GOOD RESEARCH DESIGN MUST EXPLORE THE FOLLOWING–

- A clear statement of research problem
- Means of obtaining information (procedure/ Technique)
- Population to be studied.
- Objectives of the problem to be studied.
- Nature of the problem to be studied.
- Methods to be used in processing and analyzing data.
- Availability of time and money for research should be there.

The study design varies according to the type of research problem, either an epidemiological study elucidating determinants or etiology of the disease in clinical research. Both these studies are to be designed carefully as they are susceptible to bias that can distort the results and conclusions. Methodologies of epidemiological studies can be cross sectional or longitudinal or case-control or cohort studies. In clinical experimental research, the randomized trials are the most common methodology to test the effectiveness of an intervention or a method of diagnostic evaluation. Randomized trials when performed properly, with an adequate sample size, protects against selection and other biases. In planning of a randomized trial, three basic principles should be kept in mind as:

1. **Principle of Randomization**, meaning that the treatments or interventions are allocated to different units randomly, which provides better estimate of experimental error and takes care of extraneous variability.
2. **Principle of Replication** which means that experiments should be repeated with more than one group or treatment or intervention is applied on many units or subgroups instead of one, which increases the precision of the study.
3. **Principle of controls**, which means that the total experimental group is divided into different homogeneous groups and the treatment or interventions are randomly assigned to these groups and comparisons are done between these groups.

EXPERIMENTS CAN BE CONDUCTED BY ANY ONE OF THE FOLLOWING DESIGNS

(A) PATIENT AS HIS OWN CONTROL:

All patients will not react equally to any drug. This variability amongst different patients to the drug can be overcome by recording the results on the same patient before and after treatment in certain types of experiments. In such cases, a group of patients is selected and the observations on desired characteristics are recorded before treatment for each of the patient. After administering the treatment to the group the results are again recorded and the comparisons are made between the 'initial' and 'after treatment' values. In this case the patients serve as their own controls. In using such a control, the basic assumption will be that the patient will not have variations over a period of time, with regard to response to the drug or severity of the symptom and also that there is no carry over effect from any treatment which the patient might have had previously. Validity of such assumptions can be established by conducting preliminary investigations on small groups, which are known as pilot investigations.

An example of such a design in a drug trail would be the assessment of the effect of a drug in reducing the inflammation by administering a particular drug, where the quantum of inflammation is measured before and after administering a particular drug and assessing the effect of the drug.

(B) CONCURRENT CONTROL:

In experiments on human beings, in many cases the initial effect cannot be estimated or in animal studies the results to be compared between various treatments cannot be obtained without sacrificing the animal under experimentation. Hence in such cases the different treatments are administered to different identical groups. Out of these groups, one group is kept as a control group receiving only a placebo or a previously known drug against which the other groups are compared. It is most important that these groups are to be allocated to different treatments using random allocation technique, to ensure principle of random allocation.

Measurements may be made only at the end of the trail on all the groups where such measurements are known as 'after only with control'. Here the effect of treatment is assessed as the difference in measurements between the groups at the end of experimentation.

An example of such a design is the comparison of effect of different analgesic agents administered in any surgery, where different analgesic agents are administered to different groups and the duration of the effect is measured between the groups.

In the above design, the assumption is that all the treatment groups are identical at the start of experimentation or the initial values do not affect the outcome values. In many instances this assumption may not be valid and in such cases, measurements on each experimental unit has to be made both at the start as well as at the end of treatment, and effect of the treatment is assessed considering the initial and after treatment values of each of the individual units in the control and experimental groups. Such a comparison is known as 'before and after with control'.

A simple example would be when assessing the effect of drugs in reducing the blood sugar level of diabetic patients. Patients may respond to different drugs according to their initial levels. As such assessment is to be made taking the initial levels into consideration. In such experiments above design is to be adopted.

TYPES OF RESEARCH DESIGNS

Research design can be categorized as follows:

1. **Research design in Exploratory and Formulative Research Studies.**
2. **Research design in Descriptive and Diagnostic Research Studies.**

These both exploratory and formulative research studies V/S descriptive and diagnostic research studies described by the following table as:

Types of research designs	Types of research Studies	
	Exploratory / Formulative Study	**Descriptive / Diagnostic Study**
• Overall design	• Flexible design (it must provide opportunity for considering different aspects of problem)	• Rigid design (it must make enough provision for protect against bias)
• Sampling design	• Non probability sampling design	• Probability sampling design (Random Sampling)
• Statistical design	• No preplanned design for analysis	• Preplanned design analysis
• Observational design	• Unstructured instruments for collection of data	• Structured or well thought out instrument for collection of data
• Operational design	• No fixed decision for operational procedure	• Advanced decision about operational procedure

3. Research designs in Experimental Research study (or Hypothesis Testing Research Studies):

In this design, hypothesis is tested for casual relationship between variables (like, Weight, height, Room Temp, age, etc.)

TYPES OF EXPERIMENTAL RESEARCH DESIGN/ TRIAL DESIGN:

These designs are 5 in number:

1) Parallel design
2) Cross over design
3) Factorial design
4) Latin square design

5) Group allocation design

1. PARALLEL DESIGN:

In this study design the subjects are allocated into two groups.

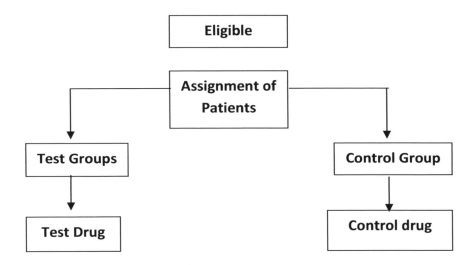

Advantages

- Easy to conduct.
- Takes less time to achieve objective.
- Less chances of dropout because patient is for short duration in trial.
- More suitable for clinical trial phase I & II.

Disadvantages

- Chances of being different of test and control group.
- Expensive.

2. Cross over Design

A research design where the subject gets both treatments in sequence (first control then Testing Vice Versa) is called cross over design. This design represents a special situation where there is not a separate comparison group. Infact each subject serves as their own control.

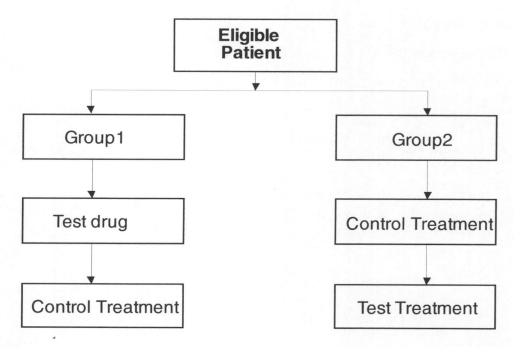

Advantages

- It minimizes variability in drug response because pt acts as its own control.
- It is suitable in reversible disease like HTN, DM.
- The treatment period is too long, the condition is relatively stable and carry over effects are not considered as problem.

Disadvantages

- Patients have to be enrolled for longer duration.
- Not used in self limiting or short duration disease

3. Factorial Design:

In this design several factors are examined simultaneously. In a single study two or more experiment interventions are not only evaluated but also in combination and against a control, e.g. Analgesic Activity of morphine, Ibuprofen in the management of cancer patient as:

- Morphine V/S Placebo.
- Morphine V/S Ibuprofen.
- Ibuprofen V/S Placebo.
- Combined effect of Morphine and Ibuprofen.

Advantages:

- Less No. of subjects and observation.
- No. of factors and level within each factor describes dimensions of factorial design like 2x2, 3x3.

Disadvantages:

- Chances of Interaction if drugs have same mode of action.

4. Latin Square Design:

It is a type of cross over design in which the no. of different Unani drugs (or drug dosages) equals the no. of patients or blocks.

Week\Drug		Datura (1)	OPIUM (2)	Ajwain Khurasani (3)	Tukhme Kahu (4)
Ist	Weak	1	2	3	4
IInd	Weak	2	3	4	1
IIIrd	Weak	3	4	1	2
IVth	Weak	4	1	2	3

Advantages:

- It can efficiently control against the influence of several factors while using relatively few patients.

Disadvantages:

- Assumes that the factors do not interact with each other.
- Randomization is complex.

5. Group Allocation Design (Cluster Randomization):

Cluster randomization is done to control and test groups.

Advantages:

- No need of physician to randomize each individual.

Disadvantages:

- Less efficient.

Professor Fisher enumerated 3 principles for experimental Research studies as:

1. **Principle of Replication:** According to this principle the experiment should be repeated more than once.
2. **Principle of Randomization:** Experiment should be conducted against the effect of extraneous factors by randomization.
3. **Principle of local control:** The extraneous factors (Variables) are made to very deliberately over as a wide range to eliminate from experimental errors.

Chapter 6: ELEMENTS OF RESEARCH (TRIAL) DESIGN, CONTROL, RANDOMIZATION AND BLINDING

A research design should be consist of the following three elements:

1. **Control**
2. **Randomization**
3. **Blinding**

CONTROL IN RESEARCH DESIGN

CONTROL: A study in which a test article is compared with a treatment that has known effects is called control study. The control may receive no treatment, standard treatment or placebo.

Benefits of control group:

- It helps us to understand what would have happened to patients if they had not received the test treatment.
- It helps us in differentiating the results or outcomes caused by test treatment because some results may be caused by other factors such as natural progression of disease.
- It provides sufficient evidence to prove the effectiveness of Unani Medicine used in the prevention, diagnosis, improvement or treatment of an illness.

Control may consist of any of the following:

a. No Treatment
b. Placebo Treatment
c. Well established Treatment (Standard treatment)
d. Different dosages of same Treatment
e. Full Scale Treatment
f. Minimal Treatment
g. Alternative Treatment

Types of Control:

a. Placebo concurrent control
b. No treatment concurrent control
c. Dose response concurrent control
d. Active (positive) concurrent control

e. External control

f. Multiple control group

(a) Placebo Concurrent Control:

In this experimental design the subjects are randomly selected for test or control group. It is better to use one for placebo control to understand mechanism of treatment. Such trial should ideally be conducted "double blind". *Placebos are usually given when we have to record subjective parameters e.g.; in psychological patients- anxiety, cheerfulness, depression etc.*

(b) No Treatment Concurrent Control:

Subjects are randomly selected to test or no treatment group. It is always open. This kind of control is used when it is difficult or impossible to double blind and only when there is reasonable confidence that study end points are objectives, *for example: effect of cupping in LBA.*

(c) Dose Response Concurrent Control:

In this control different dosages of test group are compared against each other. Subjects are randomized to one of several fixed dose groups. *This is to see the dosage at which the efficacy of drug is highest.*

(d) Active (Positive) Concurrent Control:

It is usually double blind but in some cases like trial for cancer it is single blind study.

(e) External Control (Historical Control): Here test group is compared to the patients of external group. This external group can be group of patients, treated early or during the same time.

(f) Multiple Control Groups:

More than one kind of control groups are used in a study. These kind of multiple control groups are useful for active drug comparisons, where the relative potency of two drug is not well established or where the purpose of trial is to develop relatives potency, e.g.; use of both active control and placebo or several doses of test drug and several doses of an active control with or without placebo.

SELECTION CRITERIA OF CONTROLS:

A group of subjects, who are identical to the treatment group in all aspects that affect the outcome except the intervention of interest, is a significant criterion of control for conducting a study in an evidence-based medical research.

The control must be free from the disease under the study. They must be as similar to the cases as possible, except for the absence of the disease under study. As a rule a comparison group is identified before a study is done, comprising of persons who have not been exposed to the disease or some other factor whose influence is being studied. Selection of an appropriate control group is therefore an important prerequisite, for it is against this, we make comparisons, draw inferences and make judgment about the outcome of the investigation.

SOURCES OF CONTROLS

There are some possible sources from which control may be selected are the following:

a. Hospital control:

The control may be selected from the same hospital as the cases, but with different illness other than the study disease. For example, if we are going to study cancer cervix patients, the control group may comprise patients with cancer breast or cancer of the digestive tract.

b. Relatives:

The control may also be selected from relatives (spouses and siblings).Siblings controls are unsuitable where genetic conditions are under study.

c. Neighborhood control:

The control may also be drawn from persons living in the same locality as cases, persons working in the same factory or children attending the same school.

d. General population:

Population control may be taken up or can be obtained from a defined geographic area, by taking a random sample of individual free from the study disease.

MATCHING:

Matching is defined as "the process, by which we select controls in such a way that they are similar to cases with regard to certain pertinent selected variables e.g., age which are known to influence the outcome of a disease and which, if not adequately matched for comparability, could distort or confound the result."

The controls may differ from the cases in a number of factors such as age, sex, occupation, social status, etc. An important consideration is to ensure comparability between cases and controls.

CONFOUNDING FACTOR: A "confounding factor" can be defined as one which is associated both with exposure and disease, and is unequally distributed in study and control groups.

Here two examples are being given to understand the confounding factor properly:

a) In the study of the role of alcohol in the etiology of esophageal cancer, smoking is a confounding factor because it is associated with the consumption of alcohol and it is also an independent risk factor for esophageal cancer. In these conditions, the effects of alcohol consumptions can be determined only if the influence of smoking is neutralized by matching.

b) Age could be a confounding variable or factor, for example, we are investigating the relationship between steroids contraceptive and breast cancer. If the women taking these contraceptives were younger than those in the comparison group, they would necessarily be at lower risk of breast cancer since this disease become increasingly common with the increasing age. This 'confounding' effect of age can be neutralized by matching so that both the groups have an equal proportion of each age group. In other words matching protects against an unexpected strong association between the matching factor (e.g., age) and the disease (e.g., breast cancer)

RANDOMIZATION

The process of assigning study subjects to either the treatment (test) or control group is called randomization.

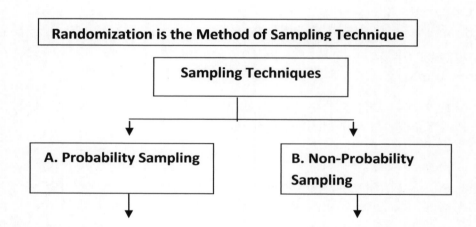

Randomization is the Method of Sampling Technique

Sampling Techniques

A. Probability Sampling

B. Non-Probability Sampling

1. Simple Random Sampling
2. Stratified Random Sampling
3. Systematic Random Sampling
4. Multi Stage Random Sampling
5. Multi Phase Sampling
6. Cluster Sampling
7. Area Sampling

1. Accidental/Incidental Sampling
2. Judgment Sampling
3. Quota Sampling
4. Convenience Sampling
5. Sequential Sampling

A. PROBABILITY SAMPLING:

Probability sampling also called random sampling or chance sampling. Under this sampling design every item of the universe has an equal chance of inclusion in the sample.

1. Simple Random Sampling:

This method is applicable when population is small, homogenous, and readily available. This method is also called unrestricted Random Sampling.

There are two methods of Simple Random Sampling –

    a. Lottery Method

    b. Use of Table of Random Number

a. Lottery Method

This is the simplest and most popular method of obtaining Random Sampling.

In this method various units of population to be studied are written on small slips which are folded and mixed together in a drum thoroughly. Then a blind fold selection is made of no. of slips required to constitute the desired sample size.

Another method – draw out one slip, read it, note its no. and put it again into drum, mix again and take another slip and do same. Discard the slip if repeated.

b. Use of Random Number Table

Give serial number to all subjects, then select at random any page of Random Number Table and pick up the no. in any row and column at random.

    Merits:

- Scientific method
- More representative
- More economical

    Demerits:

- It needs complete list of study population.
- Its sample size is very small, it will not truly represent.

2. Stratified Random Sampling:

It is used in the heterogeneous population and in large sample size. The population is first divided into small homogenous "strata" and then desired sample is drawn from each "strata" by simple random sampling.

If the strata are different in proportion size then a given percentage of subjects are selected from each strata.

Merits:

- More representative
- Greater accuracy
- Administrative convenience

Demerits:

- It is very difficult to divide population into homogenous.
- Sometime different strata may overlap.

3. Systematic Random Sampling:

It is used when complete list of population from which the sample has to be withdrawn is available.

Here we select every K^{th} house or item from sample frame N

$$K = \frac{N}{M} \quad or \quad \frac{Total\ Population}{Desired\ sample\ size}$$

For example, if we want 50 cut of 500 item.

$$K = \frac{500}{50}$$

Every 10th house included in the study.

Merits:

- Simple and convenient
- Time and labor is used in small amount.

Demerits:

- Can't be used in non-homogenous population.

4. Multistage Random Sampling:

It is done in multistage. It is used mainly for nutritional status. In this sampling, random selection is made of primary, secondary and final units.

Example: Nutritional status of India.

Ist stage: Selection of N States from 4 parts.

IInd stage: Selection of N District from each State.

IIIrd stage: Random Selection of N Villages from each District.

Suppose N = 3

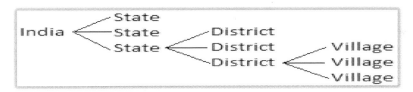

Total N = 3 x 3 x 3 = 27

Merits:

1. Very helpful in large scale survey.
2. Less expensive and less time consume.

5. Multiphase Sampling:

In this technique, **Purposive** knowledge is +-+collected in parts. Some part of information is collected from one sample and other from sub sample.

Example: Tuberculosis survey.

Ist phase: Mx test is done on all cases of population.

IInd phase: CxR is done who are Mx test positive

IIIrd phase: Sputum smear who have + ve C x R finding

Merits:

*   Less cost
*   Less laborious
*   More purposeful

6. Cluster Sampling:

It is the smallest units into which the population can be described are called elements of population and groups of elements are called clusters. Cluster is a randomly selected group from the population. For example, village, ward, factory, slums of town and school children etc.

Clusters are internally heterogeneous while **strata** are internally homogenous. In cluster sampling we use 30 clusters by Random Sampling.

7. Area Sampling:

The total area is first divided into a no. of small non-overlapping areas – called geographical clusters, and then these areas are randomly selected for study.

B. Non Probability Sampling: It includes following types of sampling

1. **Accidental/Incidental/Accessibility/Convenience/Haphazard Sampling:**
   The people who are assembled in one place with common interest or accidentally are surveyed e.g., Prevalence of HTN in persons, seeing IND V/S PAK cricket match.

2. **Judgment/ Sampling:**
   Sample selection is based on the judgment of the person interested with job used frequently in qualitative research work where the desire is to develop.

3. **Quota Sampling:**
   It is stratified Random Sampling minus randomization. The interviewers in stratified sampling are given quota to be filled and the Judgment is made by the interviewers

4. **Convenience Sampling:**
   When political elements are selected on the ease of access, sampling is made from available sources i.e., Telephone directory, automobile registration, cards, stock exchange, directory.

5. **Sequential Sampling:**

6. No. of samples lots are drawn one after another from a depending upon the results of earlier samples.

   Need of Randomization in Experimental Research:

   - It is essential to control various known and even unknown biases at the beginning of trial, during the trial and randomization is very helpful to achieve this goal.
   - In randomized trial, people receive the intervention in question on a random basis.
   - Successful Randomization allows for valid statistical interpretation of raw result.
   - It is the best way to prove efficacy of a test drug
   - Avoids systematic differences between groups with respect to known or unknown baseline variables that could affect outcome e.g., Investigator bias.
   - It produces comparable groups.
   - Assures validity of Statistical tests of significance.

BLINDING:

It is a method of control experimentation in which the subjects or researcher or both are not informed of treatment which is being given.

Types:

1. Open trial / Non blind trial.
2. Single blind trial.
3. Double blind trial.
4. Triple blind tial

NON BLIND TRIAL / OPEN STUDY:

Open study is one where both the patients and doctor are aware of the treatment given. It is used where awareness about treatment, patient and investigator does not affect results. It is also used in surgery, Acupuncture, Regimental Therapy or Manual therapy, e.g., where the trial blinding is not feasible.

SINGLE BLIND STUDY:

Here the patient is not aware about the treatment given to him but the investigator knows about the treatment.

DOUBLE BLIND STUDY:

Neither the patient nor investigator is aware about the treatment. It is done to avoid bias. Ideally all randomized clinical trials should be double blind design.

TRIPLE BLIND STUDY:

Patient, doctor and data analyst are not aware about the treatment. This clinical trial is done under a monitoring committee which can evaluate the responses in a more objective fashion.

BALANCING

In comparative or matching research involving two or more treatments, the equivalence of the patient groups is of critical importance. In the past, equivalence has either been imposed by matching or balancing, or has been assured statistically by randomization. Matching and balancing, while useful in many contexts, nonetheless have important limitations, as does simple randomization. In recent years, a new tool has been developed that represents a compromise between balancing and randomization. This method, urn randomization, gives clinical investigators new options for improving the credibility of studies at a relatively modest cost. Urn randomization is randomization that is systematically based in favor of balancing. It can be used with several covariates, both marginally and jointly, producing optimal multivariate equivalence of treatment groups for large sample sizes. It preserves randomization as the primary basis for assignment to treatment and is less susceptible to experimenter bias or manipulation of the allocation process by staff than is balancing. Disadvantages include the fact that it is more difficult to implement, and that it violates the simple probability model of simple randomization. A number of research studies on addictions, including client-treatment matching trials, have used urn randomization. A summary of the mechanics of urn randomization is presented, and guidelines for its use in treatment studies are discussed.

MATCHING (STATISTICS)

Matching is a statistical technique which is used to evaluate the effect of a treatment by comparing the treated and the non-treated units in an observational study or quasi-experiment (i.e. when the treatment is not randomly assigned). For example, matching in case control study; Matched case-control study designs are commonly implemented in the field of public health. While matching is intended to eliminate confounding, the main potential benefit of matching in case-control studies is a gain in efficiency.

Chapter 7: PLACEBO

A pharmacologically inert substance used in a clinical trial is called a placebo. Sometime people report relief in their condition even when they are given inert substance in the form of drug. It is called as 'placebo effect'. Placebos are also called 'dummy treatment' and are used to facilitate blinding in a clinical trial. They should be similar in every way- appearance, taste, smell, etc to the actual experimental treatment.

A trial in which one group receives the investigational treatment and the control group receives a placebo is known as a classical placebo-controlled trial. According to World Medical Association (WMA), in general it is ethically unacceptable to conduct placebo - controlled trials if a proven therapy is available for the condition under investigation.

SELECTION OF SUBJECTS FOR THE STUDY

Various characteristics of the study population are very important in assessing the outcome of any intervention. Experiments conducted on particular type of patients will not help in generalizing the results of the study. As such, selection of the study population has to be decided on the basis of objectives envisaged under the proposed research. The inclusion and exclusion criteria of subjects appropriate to the research question need to be defined and adhered to rigidly. Inclusion criteria are important for indicating external validity. Exclusion criteria are applied not to include subjects/ patients who might make evaluation of the study end point difficult or for whom participation in the study may not be safe. Any violation of this ultimately leads to bias and invalid results. These inclusion and exclusion criteria will affect the generalization of the study results (i.e.,applicability of its findings to other populations). The subjects for the study may consist of persons suffering from a disease of different grades such as mild, moderate or severe or different clinical stages of the disease while selecting subjects for the study. There is a need to adopt a strict diagnostic criterion either based on histo-pathological confirmation of disease or clinical diagnosis or radiological findings.

ESTIMATION OF ADEQUATE SAMPLE SIZE

Since investigations are always conducted on samples and later generalized to the populations, the size of the sample for the study plays a crucial part in these generalizations. Sample size has to be adequate enough to assure a given probability of detecting a statistically significant effect of given magnitude if one truly exists.

The sample size estimation or calculation involves knowledge of the following basic features:

- It is necessary to have an approximate idea of the prevalence or incidence rate in any epidemiological observational study. In a clinical trial this corresponds to the smallest difference in the parameter assessment that can be expected between the treatment and the group as an outcome of the intervention. Smaller these estimates large samples are required to estimate the parameters with desired accuracy.

- Different group of population are not similar in prevalence or incidence rates of diseases or every unit in the population do not respond in a similar way to a particular intervention. Information on the variability, in these rates or outcome parameter within the population is essential for estimating the sample size. This variability is expressed as standard deviation of the parameter. Large is the variability, bigger would be the desired sample size. The information on the above two aspect has to be obtained by previously published reports or by pilot investigation.

- Experimenter has to decide as to what precision he would like to have in the parameters he would be estimating from the research. In an epidemiological study this would be the error in estimated prevalence or incidence rate as compared to true values in the population. In clinical experiments this refers to the precision of estimated differences in the parameters between the groups, as compared to the true difference in the population. As for examples, if the true difference in the cure rate between two drugs is say 30 what precision one would be satisfied in the estimated difference in the cure rate as estimated from his sample? Is he satisfied if the estimated difference in the cure rate is between 28 to 32%, i.e. an error of 2% on either side? This error limit has to be decided keeping the gravity of the decisions one would take from the research findings.

- Level of probability of the chance factor in bringing out the difference for the required precision. In other words, with what probability the desired precision is maintained in the estimates, otherwise known as significance level.

- Sample size is calculated taking the power of a statistical test, which will be used for testing the significance of the differences, usually taking it is 80%. Practicability, availability of subjects for investigation and cost of investigations, are to be taken into consideration while determining the sample size. Precision of estimation and probability of maintaining the desired precision can be adjusted considering the practical aspects into consideration, while calculating the sample size. Investigations carried out on inadequate sample size may fail to reveal statistically significant results, unless the true effect is large.

SAMPLE SIZE CALCULATIONS

Sample size calculations or sample size justifications is one of the first steps in designing a clinical study. The sample size is the number of patients or other investigated units that will be included in a study and required to answer the research hypothesis in the study. The main purpose of the sample size calculation is to determine the enough number of units needed to detect the unknown clinical parameters or the treatment effects or the association after data gathering.

If the sample size is too small, the investigator may not be able to answer the study question. On the other hand, the number of patients in many studies is limited due to practicalities such as cost, patient inconvenience, and decisions not to proceed with an investigation or a prolonged study time. Investigators should calculate the optimum sample size before data gathering to avoid the mistakes because of too small sample size and also wasting money and time, because of too large sample size. Besides, sample size calculations for research projects are an essential part of a study protocol for submission to ethical committees or for some peer review journals. It is very important to determine the sample size according to the study design and the objectives of the study. Making mistakes in the calculation of the size of sample can lead to incorrect or insignificant results.

Assumptions for sample size calculation

In order to calculate the sample size, there are some assumptions like variability, type I and type II errors and the smallest effect of interest.

Outcome's variability

The variability in the outcome variable is the population variance of a given outcome that is estimated by the standard deviation. Investigators can use an estimate obtained from a pilot study.

The type I and type II errors

The type I error is the rejection of a true null hypothesis and type II error is the failure to reject a false null hypothesis. In other meaning, a type I error is corresponding to the level of confidence in sample size calculation, which is the degree of uncertainty or probability that a sample value lies outside a stated limits and type II error is in corresponding to power, which means the ability of a statistical test to reject the false null hypothesis. Power analysis can be used to calculate the minimum sample size so that investigator can detect an effect of a given size.

Effect size

The effect size is the minimal difference between the studied groups that the investigator wishes to detect or the difference between estimation and unknown parameter which investigator wants to estimate. Therefore, one can makes a statement that it does not matter how much the sample estimation differs from true population value by a certain amount. This amount is called minimum effect size.

There are some examples of sample size calculation in research studies like cross-sectional studies, case-control studies and clinical trial:

SAMPLE SIZE CALCULATION IN CROSS-SECTIONAL STUDIES

In cross-sectional studies the aim is to estimate the prevalence of unknown parameter(s) from the target population using a random sample. So an adequate sample size is needed to estimate the population prevalence with a good precision.

To calculate this adequate sample size there is a simple formula, however it needs some practical issues in selecting values for the assumptions required in the formula too and in some situations, the decision to select the appropriate values for these assumptions are not simple.

The following simple formula would be used for calculating the adequate sample size in prevalence study:

n = Z 2 P (1-P) d2

Where

n is the sample size,

Z is the statistic corresponding to level of confidence,

P is expected prevalence (that can be obtained from same studies or a pilot study conducted by the researchers), and

d is precision (corresponding to effect size).

The level of confidence usually aimed for is 95%, most researchers present their results with a 95% confidence interval (CI). However, some researchers want to be more confident can chose a 99% confidence interval.

Researcher needs to know the assumed P in order to use in formula. This can be estimated from previous studies published in the study domain or conduct a pilot study with small sample to estimate the assumed P value. This assumed P is a very important issue because the precision (d) should be selected according to the amount of P. There is not enough guideline for choosing appropriate d. Some authors recommended to select a precision of

5% if the prevalence of the disease is going to be between 10% and 90%, However, when the assumed prevalence is too small (going to be below 10%), the precision of 5% seems to be inappropriate. For example, if the assumed prevalence is 1% the precision of 5% is obviously crude and it may cause inappropriate sample size. *A conservative choice of precision would be one-fourth or one-fifth of prevalence as the amount of precision in the case of small P*. In the following table, we presented sample size calculation for three different P and three different precisions. For P = 0.05, the appropriate precision is 0.01 which resulted to 1825 samples. For P = 0.2, the best precision would be 0.04 which resulted to 384 and when P increases to 0.6, the precision could increases up to 0.1 (or more), yields to 92 samples. The investigators should notice to the appropriate precision according to assumed P. The wrong precision yields to wrong sample size (too small or too large).

Table 1:

Sample size to Estimate Prevalence with different precision and 95% of confidence

Precision	Assumed Prevalence		
	0.05	0.2	0.6
0.01	1825	6147	9220
0.04	114	384	576
0.10	18	61	92

SAMPLE SIZE CALCULATION IN CASE-CONTROL STUDIES:

The case-control study is a type of epidemiological observational study. It is often used to identify risk factors that may be associated to a disease by comparing the risk factors in subjects who have that **disease (the case)** with subjects who do not have the **disease (the control).**

The sample size calculation for unmatched case control studies (the number of cases and controls) needs these assumptions; the assumed number of cases and controls who experienced the risk factors from similar studies or from a pilot study (also researchers can use the assumed odds ratio; OR), the level of confidence (almost 95%) and the proposed power of the study (would be from 80%).

There are software or guide books that provide the investigators with the formula or the sample size calculated in tables according to different assumptions. But researchers should remember that, in the presence of a significant confounding factor, researchers require a larger sample size. Since the confounding variables must be controlled for in any analysis, a more complex statistical model must be made, so a larger sample is required to achieve significance.

SAMPLE SIZE CALCULATION IN CLINICAL TRIALS:

In a clinical trial, if the sample size is too small, a well conducted study may fail to answer its research hypothesis or may fail to detect important effects and associations. The minimum information needed to calculate sample size for a randomized controlled trial includes the power, the level of significance, the underlying event rate in the population and the size of the treatment effect sought. Besides this, the calculated sample size should be adjusted for other factors including expected compliance rates and, less commonly, an unequal allocation ratio.

There are some recommendations for different phases of clinical trials based on their sample size; in phase I trial that involve drug safety on human volunteers. Initial trials might require a total of around 20-80 patients. In phase II trials that investigate the treatment effects, seldom require more than 100-200 patients.

For example

If an investigator wants to estimate the sample size in a study where the cure rate of a particular drug compared against a known drug for any disease, minimum number of cases in each group to be investigated is calculated as follows.

For example, from a pilot study it is known that the response rate in the new drug is 80% and the previously known drug was 40%, then the sample size is estimated as follows.

P1 the expected response in the new treatment group = 80% or 0.80

P2 the expected response in the previously known drug = 40% or 0.40

$Q1 = (1 - 0.80) = 0.20$

$Q2 = (1 - 0.40) = 0.60$

ZA is the value of the standard normal variate corresponding to a significance level of 0.05 taken as 1.96

ZB is the value of the standard normal variate corresponding to the desired level of power of the test, taken as 1.24 for a power of 80%

$$n = [\ (p1q1 + p2q2)\ (za + zb)^2\ ]$$
$$/\ (p1 - p2)^2$$
$$= [\ (0.80 \times 0.20) + (0.40 \times 0.60)\ ]$$
$$(1.96 + 1.24)^2$$
$$(0.80 - 0.40)^2$$
$$= [\ (0.16) + (0.24)\ ]\ (10.24)$$
$$(0.40)^2$$
$$= (0.40)\ (10.24)$$
$$(0.16)$$
$$= (4.096) / (0.16)$$

= 26 cases are required to be investigated in each group

SELECTION OF VARIABLES FOR THE STUDY

On the basis of the defined objectives and hypothesis, list of relevant variables has to be formulated. While making a list, it is important to decide the parameters of assessment and the variables required for calculating these parameters. Based on the objectives, the list should include co-varieties, back round variables and independent or causative variables. It is necessary to keep in mind the feasibility of collecting the data in a reliable and accurate manner on the listed variables. The variables to be collected during the study depend on the availability of tools and equipment. The variables thus selected must be objectively defined. As far as possible, it would be better to adopt the definitions provided by agencies like world health organization for defining various terms.

BLINDING DURING TRIALS

To avoid bias due to experimenter's or patient's knowledge on the type of treatment being administered, it is desirable that the treatment received by the patient may not be revealed to both the investigator and patient. Even the person analyzing the results may be influenced by the treatment schedule to the patient. To take care of these errors usually blinding of the treatment is done. Blinding can be done by not informing the patient as to what treatment has been administered. This type of blinding is known as single blind trial. In order to avoid experimenter bias, both the experimenter as well as the patient is kept unaware of the treatment schedule. This type of blinding is known as double blinding trial. If the person analyzing the results of the experiment is also kept unaware of the treatment schedule then it is known as triple blind trial. Blinding allows the subject's follow-up and evaluation to be performed in an objective manner and not to be influenced by group assignment.

Advance knowledge on type of analysis to be performed. An advance idea about tabulation and statistical analysis procedures are some of the important factors which are to be kept in mind at the planning stage of the investigation. If the analysis procedures are not comprehended at the time of planning of a research study, one may end-up with a situation that the data collected may not be amenable to desired analytical procedures or interpretations.

CONTROLLING ERROR IN THE STUDY

Usually two types of errors can occur in the course of an investigation. First type of error is the response error which will come up if the sample is not completely covered due to either non cooperation or mortality of I units during the course of investigation, which results in loss to follow up. This error can be reduced by preservant efforts of the investigator to reduce the non co-operation or by proper planning of the sample size allowing for non-responses due to mortality, or loss to follow up etc. The second type of error may be due to faulty techniques and or errors in measurement and recording. These can be reduced by standardization of techniques and proper training of personnel. Errors can also occur due to wrong statistical methodologies applied for analyzing the data.

FACTORS (ERRORS /BIAS) AFFECTING RESEARCH RESULTS

The most epidemiolical studies rely on part or sample of population, to arrive at true population value, sample value should reflect true value of population, which might not be so. Errors in epidemiological studies affect the sample value; hence, these errors should be minimized, by observing the principles or rules of the study

There are many potential errors associated with health services research, but the main ones to be considered are bias, confounding, and chance.

1. Bias is the deviation of results from the truth, due to systematic error in the research methodology. Bias occurs in two main forms:

   (a) Sampling bias: The sample selected may be a biased sample and it may not be representative of true characteristics of population. Selection bias occurs when there are systematic differences between the characteristics of people selected for a study and characteristic of those who are not.

If the non-respondents are replaced by other individuals this results in selection bias. Selection biases are common in randomized controlled trials (RCT). In a school health survey for prevalence of disease the sick children may be absent or stay at home on the day of survey or if one is studying the factory workers the sick might not have come at work place, unless follow-up visits are assured the results may be biased. In HIV sentinel surveillance, selection bias has been removed by including all consecutive new cases of STDs in the sample.

   (b) Observer/information bias: which occurs when there are systematic differences in the way of information is being collected for the groups being studied.

2. A confounding factor is some aspect of a subject that is associated both with the outcome of interest and with the intervention of interest. For example, if older people are less likely to receive a new treatment, and are also more likely for unrelated reasons to experience the outcome of interest, (for example, admission to hospital), then any observed relation between the intervention and the likelihood of experiencing the outcome would be confounded by age.

Similarly, If one is studying the association of diet with occurrence of cardiovascular disease and the smoking is not being accounted for, the interpretation is biased one.

Common confounding factors are—age, social class and habit in epidemiological studies. confounders can be removed by adopting the procedure of randomization, matching controls with experimental subjects and adhering to criteria of selection of cases and controls and by giving due weightage to confounding factors at the time of analysis.

3. Chance is a random error appearing to cause an association between an intervention and an outcome. The most important design strategy to minimise random error is to have a large sample size.

These errors have an important impact on the interpretation and generalisability of the results of a research project

4. Biological Variations

The individual biological variations are well known since we study the part of population and that part of population may have different biological characteristics and may not be true representative of total population. The biological variations are related to age, sex, genetic makeup and heredity, race and ethnicity.

5. Measurement Bias

The measurement of a disease may be inaccurate or may not be valid or in other words the measurement do not measure correctly what they intend do measure. Defective collection of information, it is called response error. There could be defective measurement or defective instrument (Proforma, Questionnaire) or defective diagnostic criteria. Laboratory results may differ from one lab to another. Therefore, standardization of technique of measurement or instrument is essential to avoid measurement bias. The instruments like blood pressure apparatus. weighing machine and laboratory test must be standardized.

Internal. quality control by the testing laboratory itself is desirable and external quality control helps to establish reliability and validity of a test. HIV positive samples detected by one laboratory are cross checked at reference laboratory to enhance the quality control. Training of laboratory personnel helps avoid measurement errors apart from calibration of instruments.

6. PARTICIPATION BIAS

If HIV testing is not unlinked/anonymous or if testing facility is located far way from clinic site then individual may not participate in study and this way participation bias results.

7. RESEARCH DESIGN: If it is not according to Research types research result may be wrong for example, there is a need of an experimental design and are using Survey type design.

8. METHODOLOGICAL BIAS.

9. REALIST REVIEW OF LITERATURES.

10. REVIEW EMPIRICAL DATA.

Chapter 8: TOOLS AND TECHNIQUES IN RESEARCH INTERVIEW, QUESTIONS

These include-

- Data collection
- Analysis of Data
- Testing of Hypothesis
- Statistical analysis
- Documentation
- Records and reports
- Need of retention of record
- Reporting the results of clinical trial
- Consort statements

DATA COLLECTION:

Data: The information selected by a researcher

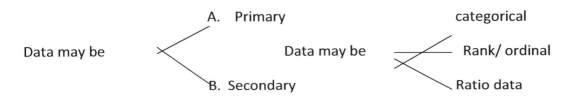

A. Primary Data: Primary data is one which is collected as fresh and collected for the first time and thus happen to be original in character.

Methods of Collection of Primary Data:

(a) Observation method.

(b) Interview method.

(c) Questionnaires.

(d) Collection of data schedule:

(e) Other methods are as:

- Warranty cards
- Distributers audit
- Pantry audit
- Consumer panels

- Using Mechanical device
- Through Projective Techniques

(f) Depth Interview

(g) Content analysis

(A) OBSERVATIONAL METHOD

It is most commonly used method especially in studies related to behavioral sciences. In this method the information is sought by way of investigates own direct observation without assessing respondents.

Advantages:

- Subjective bias is eliminated.
- Information collected denotes what is currently happening.
- It is independent of respondent's will.

Limitations:

a. Expensive
- Limited information is collected.

- Sometimes unforeseen factors may interfere with observational task.

Types of Observation Method: It includes -

(1) Structured Observation: If the observation is characterized by a careful definition of units to be observed, style of recording the observed information, standardized condition of observation, selection of pertinent data of information – then it is structured observation.

(2) Unstructured Observation: When observation is carried out through out of their characters in advance then it is called unstructured_observation.

(3) Controlled and uncontrolled observation on:

When observation is in natural setting then it is uncontrolled and when it is according to pre arranged plans, involving experimental procedures then it is controlled observation.

Controlled observation is used in experimental researches while uncontrolled observation is used in exploratory researches.

(B) INTERVIEW METHOD

An interview may be defined as a conversation of interviewers and interviews with the purpose of eliciting certain information.

Interview method involves oral verbal stimuli and oral – verbal responses.

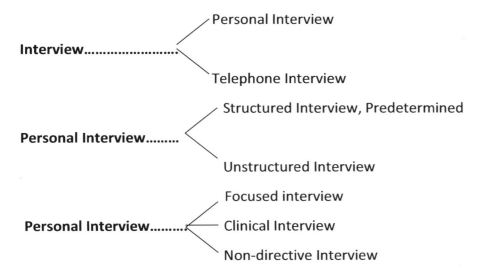

Interview.......................
- Personal Interview
- Telephone Interview

Personal Interview.........
- Structured Interview, Predetermined
- Unstructured Interview

Personal Interview.........
- Focused interview
- Clinical Interview
- Non-directive Interview

Merits of personal Interview:

- It is widely used method.
- More and in depth information is collected.
- Yield almost perfect sample of general information.
- Flexibility to restructure questions.
- Can record verbal answer.
- Personal information can be obtained.
- Samples can be controlled.
- Language can be adopted as per the knowledge of the interviewee.

Demerits of personal Interview:

- Very expensive and time consuming.
- Possibilities of bias are more.
- High profile person's approach is not easy.
- Systematic errors may be found.
- May over stimulate the respondent he may give imaginary information just to make the interview interested.

Telephone Interview:

It is not widely used method. It is useful in industrial surveys.

Merits:

- Flexible
- Faster method.

- Cheaper than personal.
- Recall is easy.
- Higher rate of response.
- No field staff required.
- Representative and wider distribution of sample is possible.

Demerits:

- Little time is given for interview.
- Survey is restricted to respondents who have only telephones.
- Extensive geographic of coverage is restricted by cost consideration.

(C) QUESTIONNAIRES

A questionnaire consists of no. of questions printed in a definite order or a form. The questionnaire is directly given to respondent or sent by E-mail or by post. It is used by research workers, private and public organizations.

Merits:

- Low cost required.
- Free from bias of interviews.
- Respondents have enough time to answer.
- Those respondents can be included in the study that is not easily approachable.
- Large sample can be covered.

Demerits:

- Low rate of return of duly filled questionnaire.
- It can be used when respondent is educated and co-operative.
- Control over questionnaire may be lost.
- There is inbuilt inflexibility.
- Difficult to know about respondent truthness.
- Method is slowest of all.

Aspects of questionnaire:

    a. General form
    b. Question sequence.
    c. Question formulation and wording.

General form:

It may be structured or unstructured.

A structured questionnaire has definite, concrete and predetermined questions and questions are presented with exactly the same wording and in same order to all respondent thus we can say that a highly structure questionnaire is one in which all the questions and answers are specified and comments in the respondents own words are held to the minimum when their characteristics are not present in questionnaire, it is termed as unstructured.

Questions sequence:

The question sequence must be clear and smoothly moving, means relation of one question to another should be readily apparent to the respondent. Questions are put in such a way that easiest question should be in beginning and first questions sshould be important one to influence the respondent.

Questions formation and wording:

Each question must be very clear without any misunderstanding. They should be easily understood, simple and concrete. Question may be MCQ or open ended.

Features of good questionnaire:

- Questions should be comparatively short & pin point.
- They should be in logical sequence from easiest to hard.
- Technical terms should be avoided.
- Questions may be dichotomous (yes/no), MCQ or open ended.
- There should be some control questions to gain reliability of respondents.
- Questions affecting sentiments of respondent should be avoided.
- Adequate space for answer should be provided.
- There should be provision for identification of uncertainty like "do not know".
- Physical appearance of questionnaire should be good.
- Pilot study should be under taken for pre-testing the questionnaire.
- It should cover all the aspects related to the problem for which questionnaire is structured.

(D) COLLECTION OF DATA SCHEDULE

Schedule: Means Performa containing a set of questions. It is slightly different from questionnaire. Scheduled are being filled in by enumerators who are specially appointed for the purpose. Enumerator goes to the respondents, put the question from schedule and record their reply in space. Enumerator explains the aim and objective of the study to gain their co-operation.

(E) OTHER METHODS OF DATA COLLECTION

It includes-

- **Warranty Cards**: It is used by dealers of consumer durables to collect information regarding
- **Product:** Information is printed in the form of questions in warranty card and requested to send after filling.
- **Distributor or Store Audits:** Audit to distributor store.
- **Pantry Audit:**
- **Consumer Panel:** Extension of pantry audit.
- **Used of Mechanical devices:** Like SMS, E-Mail, Eye camera, pupil metric camera, psycho galvanometers, motion picture camera and audio meter.
- **Projective Techniques:** These are used by psychologist in motivational research and attitude survey. Few tests are used as :
  - ❖ Word Association Test
  - ❖ Sentence Completion Test
  - ❖ Story Completion Test
  - ❖ Verbal Projection Test
  - ❖ Play Techniques
  - ❖ Quizzes, test and examinations
  - ❖ Sociometry
  - ❖ Pictorial Techniques Like,
    - Thematic Appreciation Test (TAT)
    - Rosenzwieig Test
    - Rorschach Test
    - Holtzman Inkblot Test (HIT)
    - Tomkin's Horn Picture Arrangement Test

SCALES (OF MEASUREMENT) — It is a system of differentiating one type of observation from the other. When names are used (opposed to grades) for differentiation, the scale is called nominal. Signs and symptoms are generally measured on nominal scale. Textual grades such as mild, moderate, serious, are measurements on ordinal scale. Numeric measurements such as body mass index are on metric scale.

RATING SCALE DEFINITION:

Rating scale is defined as a closed-ended survey question used to represent respondent feedback in a comparative form for specific particular features/products/services. It is one of the most established question types for online and offline surveys where survey respondents are expected to rate an attribute or feature. Rating scale is a variant of the popular multiple-choice question which is widely used to gather information that provides relative information about a specific topic.

Researchers use a rating scale in research when they intend to associate a qualitative measure with the various aspects of a product or feature. Generally, this scale is used to evaluate the performance of a product or service, employee skills, customer service performances, processes followed for a particular goal etc. Rating scale survey question can be compared to a checkbox question but rating scale provides more information than merely Yes/No.

Types of Rating Scale

Broadly speaking, rating scales can be divided into two categories as:

      a. **Ordinal and**

      b. **Interval Scales.**

An ordinal scale is a scale which depicts the answer options in an ordered manner. The difference between the two answer options may not be calculable but the answer options will always be in a certain innate order. Parameters such as attitude or feedback can be presented using an ordinal scale.

An interval scale is a scale where not only is the order of the answer variables established but the magnitude of difference between each answer variable is also calculable. Absolute or true zero value is not present in an interval scale. Temperature in Celsius or Fahrenheit is the most popular example of an interval scale. Net Promoter Score, Likert Scale, Bipolar Matrix Table are some of the most effective types of interval scale.

There are four primary types of rating scales which can be suitably used in an online survey:

- Graphic Rating Scale
- Numerical Rating Scale
- Descriptive Rating Scale
- Comparative Rating Scale

(F) DEPTH INTERVIEW

It is conducted to discover the underlying motives and desires and used in motivational researches.

(G) CONTENT ANALYSIS

It is used to analyze the content of documentary material like books, magazines, newspapers, and recorded material.

B. SECONDARY DATA: Secondary data is one which has already been collected by someone else and which has already been passed through the statistics.

Methods of collection of secondary data:

They can be collected from the following:

- Various publications government and other bodies.
- Books, magazines, newspapers,
- Reports and publications of various associations.
- Public records and statistics.

ANALYSIS OF DATA: Analysis refers to breaking a whole into its separate components for individual examination. Data analysis is a process for obtaining raw data and converting it into information useful for decision-making by users. Data are collected and analyzed to answer questions, test hypotheses or disprove theories.

Statistician John Tukey defined data analysis in 1961 as: "Procedures for analyzing data, techniques for interpreting the results of such procedures, ways of planning the gathering of data to make its analysis easier, more precise or more accurate, and all the machinery and results of (mathematical) statistics which apply to analyzing data."

TESTING OF HYPOTHESIS:

Hypothesis testing is used to infer the result of a hypothesis performed on sample data from a larger population. The test tells the analyst whether or not his primary hypothesis is true. Statistical analysts test a hypothesis by measuring and examining a random sample of the population being analyzed.

Above these three factors/ things have been discussed in B part of this book.

STATISTICAL ANALYSIS: Statistical analysis is an essential technique that enables a medical research practitioner to draw meaningful inference from their data analysis. Improper application of study design and data analysis may render insufficient and improper results and conclusion. Converting a medical problem into a statistical hypothesis with appropriate methodological and logical design and then back-translating the statistical results into relevant medical knowledge is a real challenge

Chapter 9: COMPUTER PROGRAMMES USED IN RESEARCH STUDY IN DATA HANDLING

These include- **MINITAB AND SPSS:**

MINITAB (SOFTWARE)

CONTENTS:

- A brief Introduction of Minitab
- Basic Features of Minitab
- Minitab Assistant
- Basic Statistics
- Graphics
- Regression
- Reliability/Survival
- Application in Research methodology

A brief Introduction of Minitab

In a Statistical Approach in the Research and development, Minitab is powerful software for the data handling by the help of a computer. It is Software that can reduce the extra time to analysis data on papers and other basic tools. The Minitab Assistant includes analyses to compare independent samples to determine whether their variability significantly differs. The multi comparison can be performed by this tool in a single time.

Minitab can access a complete set of statistical tools, including Descriptive Statistics, Hypothesis Tests, Confidence Intervals, and Normality Tests which are the powerful tools for the basic statistics. It can uncover the relationships between variables and identify important factors affecting the quality of your products and services in the case of Regression and ANOVA.

Minitab is a powerful tool in giving the rate to the goodness of any measurement system. If your measurement systems are adequate, assess how well your processes meet specification limits; create sampling plans, and more. In order to design the experiments this program can find the settings that optimiz e your processes using Factorial, Response Surface, Mixture, and Taguchi design.

It is a complete tool having control charts which monitor the processes over time and evaluate their stability. It is reliable to determine a product's lifetime characteristics using a wide range of tools including Distribution Analysis and Accelerated Life Testing.

It is easy to import data on other basic software like MS Excel just in a smart way by Minitab. In the case of mismatches, properly represent missing data, remove extra spaces, and make column lengths equal when importing data from Excel and other file types.

Basic Features of Minitab

It is comprehensive set of powerful methods and graphs to analyze your data. The Minitab is having the following features as

- Minitab Assistant
- Basic Statistics
- Graphics
- Regression
- Analysis of Variance
- Statistical Process Control
- Measurement Systems Analysis
- Design of Experiments
- Reliability/Survival
- Power and Sample Size
- Multivariate
- Nonparametric
- Equivalence Tests
- Tables
- Simulations and Distributions

Minitab Assistant

It gives step by step guidance; an interactive decision tree leads you to the right statistical tool by posing a series of questions you need to answer, such as the type of data you're working with and the objective of your analysis. You can have expert support in this tool, when you face a question you can't answer, the Assistant provides the information you need to respond correctly, such as the definitions of important terms and illustrated examples that help you understand how the question relates to your own data.

Basic Statistics

Minitab can access a complete set of basic statistical tools, including Hypothesis Tests, Confidence Intervals, Descriptive statistics, One-sample Z-test, one- and two-sample t-tests, paired t-test, One and two proportions tests, One- and two-sample Poisson rate tests, One and two variances tests, Correlation and covariance, Outlier test and Poisson goodness-of-fit test.

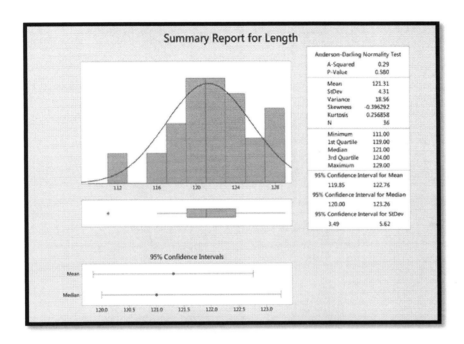

Figure: Basic statistical Approach

Graphics

Minitab can easily create professional-looking graphics, Scatter plots, matrix plots, box plots, dot plots, histograms, charts, time series plots, Bubble plot, Contour and rotating 3D plots, Probability and probability distribution plots. It is also having dit attributes such that axes, labels, reference lines. Minitab interactively recreate custom graphs with new data, Easily place multiple graphs on one page and Automatically update graphs as data change. It is also have Brush graphs to explore points of interest. It is easy to export the data to another extension of graphics such that TIF, JPEG, PNG, BMP, GIF and EMF etc.

Regression

The Minitab uncovers the relationships between variables and identifies important factors affecting the quality of your products and services. Which includes Linear regression, Binary, ordinal and nominal logistic regression, Nonlinear regression, Stability studies, Orthogonal regression, Partial least squares, Poisson regression. It also plots the result based on residual, factorial, contour, surface, etc. It is having stepwise and best subsets Response prediction and optimization.

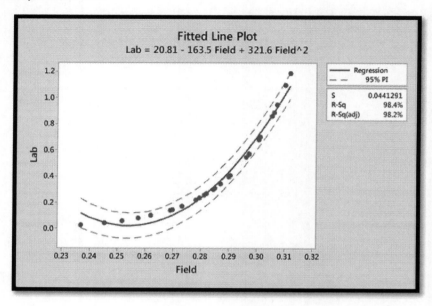

Figure: Regression Analyses

Reliability/Survival:

It is used in Parametric and nonparametric distribution analysis, Goodness-of-fit measures, ML and least squares estimates, exact failure, right-, left-, and interval-censored data, Accelerated life testing, Regression with life data, Reliability test plans, Threshold parameter distributions, Repairable systems, Multiple failure modes, Probit analysis, Weibayes analysis, Hypothesis tests on distribution parameters. It may have plots like distribution, probability, hazard, survival and Warranty analysis.

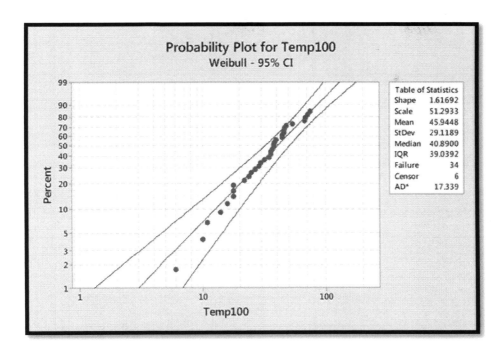

Figure: Reliability analysis

Application in Research methodology

Minitab is powerful software having an integration of wide use of statistical techniques in the research work to reduce the complexity of the calculations and data handling related to the statistical approach. The Minitab having all the Statistical analysis in the features which having Basic Statistics, Graphics, Regression, Analysis of Variance, Statistical Process Control, Measurement Systems Analysis, Design of Experiments, Reliability and Survival, Power and Sample Size, Multivariate, Nonparametric, Equivalence Tests, Tables and Simulations and Distributions.

The Minitab having an assistant in its feature which is a programmed as an expert for solves each problem in the guidance. The guidance is in the step by step process. The Minitab Assistant gives the interactive decision flow leads you to the right statistical tool by posing a series of questions you need to answer, such as the type of data you're working with and the objective of your analysis.

Assistant provides the information you need to respond correctly, such as the definitions of important terms and illustrated examples that help you understand how the question relates to your own data.

Minitab is well suited for instructional applications, but is also powerful enough to be used as a primary tool for analyzing research data.

SPSS (SOFT WARE)

CONTENTS:

It includes -

- About SPSS
- Features of SPSS
- Base Edition
- Complex Sampling and Testing Add-on
- Custom Tables and Advanced Statistics Add-on
- Forecasting and Decision Trees Add-on
- Basic Statistics Used in SPSS
- Descriptive statistics
- Bivariate statistics
- Prediction for numerical outcome
- Prediction for identifying groups

About SPSS:

Instead of using multiple tools and resources, work within a single integrated software suite for faster results. The SPSS is a complete package of statistical techniques used in the data handling of research. In research methodology it is a very powerful tool as it reduces the complexity.

The SPSS Statistics is a software package used for logical batched and non-batched statistical analysis. Long produced by SPSS Inc., it was acquired by IBM in 2009.The current versions (2015) re officially named IBM SPSS Statistics. Companion products in the same family are used for survey authoring and deployment (IBM SPSS Data Collection), data mining (IBM SPSS Modeler), text analytics, and collaboration and deployment (batch and automated scoring services).

The software name originally stood Statistical Package for the Social Sciences (SPSS), reflecting the original market, although the software is now popular in other fields as well, including the health sciences and marketing.

SPSS is a widely used program for statistical analysis in social science. It is also used by market researchers, health researchers, survey companies, government, education researchers, marketing organizations, data miners, and others. The original SPSS manual (Nie, Bent & Hull, 1970) has been described as one of "sociology's most influential books" for allowing ordinary researchers to do their own statistical analysis. In addition to statistical analysis, data management (case selection, file reshaping, creating derived data) and data documentation (a metadata dictionary was stored in the data file) are features of the base software.

The many features of SPSS Statistics are accessible via pull-down menus or can be programmed with a proprietary 4GL command syntax language.

Command syntax programming has the benefits of reproducibility, simplifying repetitive tasks, and handling complex data manipulations and analyses. Additionally, some complex applications can only be programmed in syntax and are not

accessible through the menu structure. The pull-down menu interface also generates command syntax: this can be displayed in the output, although the default settings have to be changed to make the syntax visible to the user. They can also be pasted into a syntax file using the "paste" button present in each menu. Programs can be run interactively or unattended, using the supplied Production Job Facility.

Features of SPSS

- **Base Edition**

It provides a wide variety of analytics capabilities including descriptive statistics, linear regression, and presentation quality graphing and reporting. You can access multiple data formats without any size constraints. Advanced data preparation capabilities enable you to eliminate labor-intensive manual checks. You can leverage bivariate statistics procedures, factor and cluster analysis as well as bootstrapping, and extend your capabilities with R/Python

- **Complex Sampling and Testing Add-on**

It helps you to compute statistics and standard errors from small or complex sample designs. You can predict numerical and categorical outcomes from non-simple random samples, and account for up to three stages when analyzing data from a multistage design. Also enables you to access regression with optimal scaling including lasso and elastic net. Additional features include categorical principal components analysis, multidimensional scaling and unfolding, and multiple correspondence analyses.

- **Custom Tables and Advanced Statistics Add-on**

It enables you to summarize and display your analyses in production-ready tables, exportable to Microsoft or PDF. You can present survey results using nesting, stacking and multiple response categories, and manage missing values. Also provides univariate and multivariate analytical techniques and models to improve the accuracy of your analyses.

111

Includes non-linear and general linear models and mixed model procedures as well as logistic, 2-stage least squares regression and survival analysis.

- **Forecasting and Decision Trees Add-on**

Enables you to develop forecasts and predict trends using time-series data. It includes ARIMA and exponential smoothing forecasting capabilities. Now you can automate model parameters, and test your data for intermittency and missing values. Also features decision trees, based on four tree-growing algorithms, to help you present categorical results and discover relationships between groups. As well, you can create neural network predictive models and RFM analysis to test marketing campaigns.

Basic Statistics Used in SPSS

Statistics included in the base software are as follows

- ❖ Descriptive statistics
- ❖ Bivariate statistics
- ❖ Prediction for numerical outcomes
- ❖ Prediction for identifying groups

- ❖ **Descriptive statistics**

Descriptive statistics are statistics that quantitatively describe or summarize features of a collection of information. Descriptive statistics are distinguished from inferential (or inductive statistics), in that descriptive statistics aim to summarize a sample, rather than use the data to learn about the population that the sample of data is thought to represent. This generally means that descriptive statistics, unlike inferential statistics, are not developed on the basis of probability theory. Even when a data analysis draws its main conclusions using inferential statistics, descriptive statistics are generally also presented. For example, in papers reporting on human subjects, typically a table is included giving the overall sample size, sample sizes in important subgroups (e.g., for each treatment or exposure group), and demographic or clinical characteristics such as the average age, the proportion of subjects of each sex, the proportion of subjects with related co morbidities etc.

Some measures that are commonly used to describe a data set are measures of central tendency and measures of variability or dispersion. Measures of central tendency include the mean, median and mode, while measures of variability include the standard deviation (or variance), the minimum and maximum values of the variables, kurtosis and skewness.

112

❖ Bivariate statistics

It includes Means, t-test, ANOVA, Correlation (bivariate, partial, instances), Nonparametric tests which is used in the SPSS. For a data set, the terms arithmetic mean, mathematical expectation, and sometimes average are used synonymously to refer to a central value of a discrete set of numbers: specifically, the sum of the values divided by the number of values. Analysis of variance (ANOVA) is a collection of statistical models used to analyze the differences among group means and their associated procedures (such as "variation" among and between groups), developed by statistician and evolutionary biologist Ronald Fisher. In the ANOVA setting, the observed variance in a particular variable is partitioned into components attributable to different sources of variation.

In its simplest form, ANOVA provides a statistical test of whether or not the means of several groups are equal, and therefore generalizes the t-test to more than two groups. ANOVAs are useful for comparing (testing) three or more means (groups or variables) for statistical significance. It is conceptually similar to multiple two-sample t-tests, but is more conservative (results in less type I error) and is therefore suited to a wide range of practical problems.

❖ Prediction for numerical outcome

In statistics, linear regression is an approach for modeling the relationship between a scalar dependent variable yand one or more explanatory variables (or independent variables)

❖ Prediction for numerical outcome

The case of one explanatory variable is called simple linear regression. For more than one explanatory variable, the process is called multiple linear regressions. (This term is distinct from multivariate linear regression, where multiple correlated dependent variables are predicted, rather than a single scalar variable.)

In linear regression, the relationships are modeled using linear predictor functions whose unknown model parameters are estimated from the data. Such models are called linear models. Most commonly, the conditional mean of y given the value of X is assumed to be an affine function of X; less commonly, the median or some other quintile of the conditional distribution of y given X is expressed as a linear function of X. Like all forms of regression analysis, linear regression focuses on the conditional probability distribution of y given X, rather than on the joint probability distribution of y and X, which is the domain of multivariate analysis.

Linear regression was the first type of regression analysis to be studied rigorously, and to be used extensively in practical applications, This is because models which depend linearly on their unknown parameters are easier to fit than models which are non-linearly related to their parameters and because the statistical properties of the resulting estimators are easier to determine.

❖ **Prediction for identifying groups**

Factor analysis is a statistical method used to describe variability among observed, correlated variables in terms of a potentially lower number of unobserved variables called factors. For example, it is possible that variations in six observed variables mainly reflect the variations in two unobserved (underlying) variables. Factor analysis searches for such joint variations in response to unobserved latent variables. The observed variables are modeled as linear combinations of the potential factors, plus "error" terms. Factor analysis aims to find independent latent variables. Followers of factor analytic methods believe that the information gained about the interdependencies between observed variables can be used later to reduce the set of variables in a dataset.

Factor analysis is not used to any significant degree in physics, biology and chemistry but is used very heavily in psychometrics personality theories, marketing, product management, operations research and finance. Users of factor analysis believe that it helps to deal with data sets where there are large numbers of observed variables that are thought to reflect a smaller number of underlying/latent variables. It is one of the most commonly used inter dependency technique and is used when the relevant set of variables shows a systematic inter-dependence and the objective is to find out the latent factors that create a commonality.

DEVELOPMENT OF A STUDY PROTOCOL

A protocol is an overall plan of act to be followed for a particular clinical trial. It is the written mechanism that describes how the clinical trial design will be implemented. So, for the development of a protocol various experts like clinical pharmacologist, pharmacists, biostastician, physician and other relevant health workers are required.

Following points should be included to make a protocol:

1. The title of the trial, name, address and contact. No. of research team should be mentioned
2. There should be a clear statement on the objectives of the study.
3. Details of investigational products or intervention should be mentioned.

4. Justification of purpose of trial based on available information on safety and efficacy should be mentioned.
5. The composition of formula of test drug should be studied with justification of route of administration.
6. The type of trial (controlled), trial design (parallel group / cross over), technique (double blind, Single Blind), randomization (methods procedure), description of primary and secondary end point.
7. Inclusion and exclusion criteria should be mentioned.
8. No. of trial subjects needed is achieve trial object should be mentioned.
9. Control group (placebo control or standard control) should be mentioned.
10. Subjective and objective parameters required laboratory investigation should be mentioned.
11. The treatment schedule and durations of the trial should be mentioned.
12. It should be clearly mentioned that other treatment during the trial will be given or not.
13. Procedure for identification of subject code list, treatment record, randomization list and case record form (CRF) should be adopted.
14. Information of establishment of trial code, where it will be kept and when, how and by whom it can be broke in emergency.
15. Qualification and experience of investigators.
16. Facilities and site of the study.
17. Methodology of evaluation of result.
18. Information to be given to trial subjects.
19. Relevant communication with appropriate regulatory authorities.
20. Information to the staff involved in trial.
21. Medical care to the patients after trial.
22. List of references used in Literature Review.

PROTOCOL

RECOMMENDED FORMAT FOR EXPERIMENTAL AND CLINICAL RESEARCH BY W H O

SUMMARY OF THE PROTOCOL

The summary of the protocol should be no more than 300 words and at the most a page long consisting of font size 12 with single spacing. It should summarize all the central elements of the protocol, for example, the rationale, objectives, methods, populations, time frame, and expected outcomes. It should stand on its own, and not refer the reader to points in the project description.

GENERAL INFORMATION

- Protocol title, protocol identifying number (if any), and date.
- Name and address of the sponsor/funder.
- Name and title of the investigator(s) who is (are) responsible for conducting the research, and the address and telephone number(s) of the research site(s), including responsibilities of each.
- Name(s) and address (ess) of the clinical laboratory(ies) and other medical and/or technical department(s) and/or institutions involved in the research

RATIONALE & BACKGROUND INFORMATION

The Rationale specifies the reasons for conducting the research in the light of current knowledge. It should include a well documented statement of the need/problem that is the basis of the project, the cause of this problem and its possible solutions. It is the equivalent to the introduction in a research paper and it puts the proposal in context. It should answer the question of why and what: why the research needs to be done and what will be its relevance. The magnitude, frequency, affected geographical areas, ethnic and gender considerations, etc of the problem should be followed by a brief description of the most relevant studies published on the subject.

REFERENCES (OF LITERATURE)

References can also be listed at the end of the protocol.

STUDY GOALS AND OBJECTIVES

Goals are broad statements of what the proposal hopes to accomplish. They create a setting for the proposal. Specific objectives are statements of the research question(s). Objectives should be simple (not complex), specific (not vague), and stated in advance (not after the research is done). After statement of the primary objective, secondary objectives may be mentioned.

STUDY DESIGN

The scientific integrity of the study and the credibility of the study data depend substantially on the study design and methodology. The design of the study should include information on the type of study, the research population or the sampling frame, and who can take part (e.g. inclusion and exclusion criteria, withdrawal criteria etc.), and the expected duration of the study

(The same study can be described in several ways, and as complete a description of the study as possible should be provided. For example, a study may be described as being a basic science research, epidemiologic or social science research, it may also be described as observational or interventional; if observational, it may be either descriptive or

116

analytic, if analytic it could either be cross-sectional or longitudinal etc. If experimental, it may be described as a controlled or a non controlled study. The link below provides more information on how to describe a research study

METHODOLOGY

The methodology section is the most important part of the protocol. It should include detailed information on the interventions to be made, procedures to be used, measurements to be taken, observations to be made, laboratory investigations to be done etc. If multiple sites are engaged in a specified protocol, methodology should be standardized and clearly defined.

Interventions should be described in detail, including a description of the drug/device/vaccine that is being tested. Interventions could also be in the realm of social sciences for example, providing training or information to groups of individuals.

Procedures could be biomedical (collection of blood or sputum samples to develop a diagnostic test), or in the realm of social sciences (doing a questionnaire survey, carrying out a focus group discussion as part of formative research, observation of the participant's environment, etc.).

In the case of randomized controlled trial additional information on the process of randomization and blinding, description of stopping rules for individuals, for part of the study or entire study, the procedures and conditions for breaking the codes etc. should also be described.

A graphic outline of the study design and procedures using a flow diagram must be provided. This should include the timing of assessments.

SAFETY CONSIDERATIONS

The safety of research participants is foremost. Safety aspects of the research should always be kept in mind and information provided in the protocol on how the safety of research participants will be ensured. This can include procedures for recording and reporting adverse events and their follow-up, for example, we have to remember that even administering a research questionnaire can have adverse effects on individuals.

FOLLOW-UP

The research protocol must give a clear indication of what follow up will be provided to the research participants and for how long. This may include a follow up, especially for adverse events, even after data collection for the research study is completed.

DATA MANAGEMENT AND STATISTICAL ANALYSIS

The protocol should provide information on how the data will be managed, including data handling and coding for computer analysis, monitoring and verification. The statistical methods proposed to be used for the analysis of data should be clearly outlined, including reasons for the sample size selected, power of the study, level of significance to be used, procedures for accounting for any missing or spurious data etc. For projects involving qualitative approaches, specify in sufficient detail how the data will be analysed.

QUALITY ASSURANCE

The protocol should describe the quality control and quality assurance system for the conduct of the study, including GCP, follow up by clinical monitors, DSMB, data management etc.

EXPECTED OUTCOMES OF THE STUDY

The protocol should indicate how the study will contribute to advancement of knowledge, how the results will be utilized, not only in publications but also how they will likely affect health care, health systems, or health policies.

DISSEMINATION OF RESULTS AND PUBLICATION POLICY

The protocol should specify not only dissemination of results in the scientific media, but also to the community and/ or the participants, and consider dissemination to the policy makers where relevant. Publication policy should be clearly discussed- for example who will take the lead in publication and who will be acknowledged in publications, etc.

DURATION OF THE PROJECT

The protocol should specify the time that each phase of the project is likely to take, along with a detailed month by month timeline for each activity to be undertaken.

PROBLEMS ANTICIPATED

This section should discuss the difficulties that the investigators anticipate in successfully completing their projects within the time frame stipulated and the funding requested. It should also offer possible solutions to deal with these difficulties.

PROJECT MANAGEMENT

This section should describe the role and responsibility of each member of the team

ETHICS

The protocol should have a description of ethical considerations relating to the study. This should not be limited to providing information on how or from whom the ethics approval will be taken, but this section should document the issues that are likely to raise ethical concerns. It should also describe how the investigator(s) plan to obtain informed consent from the research participants (the informed consent process).

INFORMED CONSENT FORMS

The approved version of the protocol must have copies of informed consent forms (ICF), both in English and the local language in which they are going to be administered. However translations may be carried out after the English language ICF(s) have been approved by the Ethical Research Committee. If the research involves more than one group of individuals, for example, healthcare users and healthcare providers, a separate specifically tailored informed consent form must be included for each group. This ensures that each group of participants will get the information they need to make an informed decision. For the same reason, each new intervention also requires a separate informed consent form.

BUDGET

The budget section should contain a detailed item-wise breakdown of the funds requested for, along with a justification for each item.

OTHER SUPPORT FOR THE PROJECT

This section should provide information about the funding received or anticipated for this project from other funding organizations.

COLLABORATION WITH OTHER SCIENTISTS OR RESEARCH INSTITUTIONS

LINKS TO OTHER PROJECTS

CURRICULUM VITAE OF INVESTIGATORS

The CV of the Principal investigator and each co-investigator should be provided. In general each CV should not be more than one page, unless a complete CV is specifically requested for.

OTHER RESEARCH ACTIVITIES OF THE INVESTIGATORS

The Principal investigator should list all current research projects that he/she is involved in, the source of funding of those projects, the duration of those projects and the percentage of time spent on each.

FINANCING AND INSURANCE

Financing and insurance if not addressed in a separate agreement and where relevant should be described.

ASSESSMENT OF A GOOD PROTOCOL

The protocol should adequately answer the research question. The research design must be sound enough to yield the expected knowledge. It should provide enough detail (methodology) that can allow another investigator to do the study and arrive at comparable conclusions. Here, the proposed number of participants is reasonably justified and the scientific design is adequately described.

Chapter 10: THESIS PROTOCOL

Thesis protocol means to make a plan for thesis or research work. Thesis protocol is considered an official document submitted to the university before doing thesis work or Research Work and its needs to resonance with the same.

STEPS NECESSARY TO PREPARE A THESIS PROTOCOL:

1. Identify a research problem: Problem is a gap between ideal and present situation. Research problem refers to some difficulty to which a researcher experiences and wants to obtain a solution for the same, i.e. a question or issue to be examined.

2. Prioritize the problems in the view of internal and external criteria of selection:

a. Internal criteria

- Researcher's interest
- Researcher's competence
- Researcher's own resonance
    -- Human resources
    -- Money
    -- Time

b. External criteria

- Research ability of the problem
- Importance and urgency
- Novelty of the problem
- Feasibility
- Facilities
- Social relevance
- Public health importance

3. Define the problem in the form of 'Title of the Research': Problem statement should be clear, precise, self-explanatory and include: What, How, When and Where.

4. Make Hypothesis: H_0 null hypothesis and H_a alternative hypothesis (Descriptive studies are needed to generate hypothesis, so there is no need to assume a hypothesis).

5. Define the Research Objectives: Research objectives are the statements of the questions that are to be investigated with the goal of answering the overall research problem.

Characteristics of objectives:

      a. Research objectives should be clear and achievable.

      b. Generally, they are written as statements, using the word "to" For example, 'to discover_____', to determine_____', 'to establish_____', 'to find out _____', 'to assess_____', etc.)

      c. Objectives should be achieved at the end of the study.

6. Collect Review of literature: Literature review is the documentation of a published and unpublished work in the areas of specific interest to the researcher. It helps the following:

      a. Knowing the work done before in the same field

      b. Making researchable hypothesis

      c. Getting the population parameters regarding the problem identified

      d. Understanding the methodology of the research for problem identified

      e. Getting data for comparison with observations of the proposed research.

7. Define study area

8. Selection of study design

9. Define study universe with inclusion and exclusion criteria

10. Calculate adequate sample size

11. Select appropriate sampling technique

12. Prerequisites of study include- Study tools, orientation trainings, consent of other department involved, etc.

13. Planning for data collection, compilation, data entry and analysis

14. Ethical clearance and Consent from:

    i.   Institutional Research Review Board

    ii.   Ethical Committee of the Institute

   iii.   Observational Units

RECOMMENDED FORMAT OF THESIS-PROTOCOL IS AS FOLLOWING:

Name of page/s	Content	Proposed pages
Title page	Title, submitted to, submitted by, under guidance of	1
Certificate from institution	As per institutional format	1
Introduction	Importance and justification	1-2
Review of literature	Brief review of literature	2-4
Purpose of study	Public health importance	1
Hypothesis	Assumptions about study	1
Aims and objectives	Researchable statements	1

Methodology	Study area, study design, study period, study universe, study population including, inclusion and exclusion criteria, sample size, sampling technique, define variables, prodcedure outcome variables and outcome analysis	3-10
Flow Chart	Showing study design	1
Seed article	Almost similar study reference, of which data is used for calculation of sample size	1
References	Almost similar study references (10-15)	1-2
Consent from		1
Study tool	Proforma/schedule	1-5

Other Desirable Technicalities

a. Four copies to be submitted to the research review board
b. A4 size paper
c. Line spacing : Double space
d. Margins : At least 2.5 cm on both sides
e. Font : Times New Roman or Arial
f. Font Size : 127
g. Pattern : Justified

h. As far as possible in active voice and in future tens
i. After approval, 11 copies will be submitted to the university.

STRUCTURE OF THE THESIS PROTOCOL

Page No. 1

1. Title page: This page includes:

    i.   Title of thesis (write in title case or capital letters)
    ii.   Submitted to 'Name of the University'
    iii.   Submitted for what? i.e. Degree (with discipline) for which the thesis is being submitted
    iv.   Years of scheduled examination of candidate.
    v.   Submitted by 'Name of Candidate'
    vi.   Under guidance of 'Name and Designation of Guide'

It is very important that it should be perfectly matched with final thesis report **(Annexure 1).**

Page No. 2

2. Letter to the university forwarded from guide and principal: Letter of university should be attached taking permission from the university about proposed study with personal details. This letter should be written through proper channel and duly forwarded and recommended by guide and principal of the Institute **(Annexure-2).**

Page No. 3 and 4

3. Introduction: It is to establish the purpose of proposed research. This is accomplished by discussing the relevant available *literature (with references) and answer following step-by-step.

  a. What is the research problem?
  b. Why is it an important problem?
  c. What had been done so far in this connection?
  d. Where is the lacuna which requires further explanation/research?
  e. How will this proposed study help in solving lacuna/problem?
  * Latest review articles or systematic reviews on the related topic

Page No. 5

4. Purpose of study: Here public health importance of the proposed study will be quoted, i.e. how this study will be beneficial to the population.

Page No. 6

5. Hypothesis: Research hypothesis is a predictive statement that relates an independent variable to a dependent variable.

Hypothesis should be stated in the form of:

- **Null hypothesis (H_0):** It is the default hypothesis that 'there is no significant difference in outcomes of both groups'.
- **Alternate hypothesis (H_a):** It is Hypothesis other than the default hypothesis that 'there is significant difference in outcomes of both (or if>2 groups then various) groups.

Page No. 7

6. Aims and objectives: What is to be found out from doing this proposed research should be narrated prior to precede for research?

Aim: Overall goal of the proposed study.

124

Objectives: Research objectives are the statement of the questions that are to be investigated with the goal of answering the overall research problem.

Aim: To study the utilization of intranatal services in field practice area of RHTC, Naila.

Objectives:

    a. To find out proportion of institutional deliveries among total deliveries in field practice area of RHTC, Naila.

    b. To determine the factors associated with institutional deliveries in field practice area of RHTC, Naila.

    c. To determine the factors associated with home deliveries in field practice area of RHTC, Naila.

Page No. 8

7. Methodology:

    a. **Study area :** Where the proposed study will be carried out/ Whether in community, laboratory or in hospital; if it is in the community then geographically define the area and if it is in the hospital then which hospital, whether in wards or operation theather or OPD specify the exact location.

    b. **Study period:** When the proposed study will be carried out. Write down the proposed starting date to estimated date of completion.

    c. **Study design:** Write down the study design of proposed study. To find out the study design, following questions should be answered:

        i. Whether the study is community based or hospital based?

        ii. What is the direction of study?

        iii. What is the method of selection of subject? (Random or non-randon: Preference is to given to random technique)

        iv. Whether control group is to be taken or not?

        v. Whether the effect of some intervention is to be studied or not?

        vi. Whether there is comparison between groups or not?

    (According to answers of these questions, study design is to be selected with the help of 'Research Methodology and Biostatistics' or with statistician.)

    d. **Study universe:** Population frame from where the study population will be selected. This target population of your study should be defined.

    e. **Study population:** Study population is to be selected from study universe as per the inclusion and exclusion criteria.

        • **Inclusion criteria:** Inclusion criteria will define the population/subjects to be included in the proposed study, e.g. to study the utilization of intranasal services females who have delivered child within a month period will be included in study on recall basis.

125

- **Exclusion criteria:** Exclusion criteria should also be well defined to exclude the subjects from above screened population, e.g. in above example; among females screened as per inclusion criteria, females seriously ill, not able to recall and do not want to participate in the proposed study will be excluded.

f. **Selection of control:** It is recommended in analytical and experimental studies. Control population should also be defined taking into consideration of confounding factors.

g. **Sample size:** Adequate sample size should be calculated to get the result applicable to universe with minimum resources. Calculation of sample size will be done as per followings:

    I.   Allowable beta error (conventionally 0.2) or Power = 1- Beta error =0.8

    II.   Allowable alpha error (conventionally 0.05)

    III.   Type of study design selected

    IV.   Population parameters available

    V.   Type of outcomes

    VI.   Type of analysis will be done

  Finally to estimate the total number of subjects to be included in the study, non-response rate,   dropout rate should also be taken into consideration.

h. **Sampling technique:** Appropriate sampling technique should be chosen to avoid selection bias. Appropriate sampling technique should be random via giving every subject equal chance to appear in the study population and none of them should have zero probability. There are the different types of random sampling techniques which may be selected as per the type of study. It should be cleared how the randomization will be done in study.

  Blinding: Blinding is being unknown about the group to which individual belongs to while   assessing the outcome. It can further reduce personal biases and it strongly recommended in interventional studies.

i. **Working definition:** Variables to be assessed should be well defined to make understand the meaning of variable and its grouping. It becomes more necessary to make study variables uniform, if more than one investigator is there; in such a case orientation training may be organized prior to data collection to keep uniformity of observations.

j. **Procedures involved:** Various procedures involved in the study should also be detailed prior to study, e.g. procedure for intervention, procedure for withdrawal, procedure for randomization, procedure for blinding, procedure for data collection (study tool), procedure for outcome measurement (measurement tools), outcome analysis procedure, etc.

k. **Outcome variables:** Outcome variable are the variables (value of which vary with individual) that are selected to know the outcome of the study. These variables should be valid, i.e. should measure the outcome it is supposed to measure.

For example:

- To measure the utilization of intranatal services 'proportion of institution delivery' is a valid indicator.
- To find out the effect of Yoga on hypertension 'mean blood pressure' before and after the yoga is a valid indicator.
- To compare the effect of two medicines on diabetes' 'serum blood sugar level' in both the group is a valid outcome variable, etc.

Outcome may be primary and secondary:

Primary outcomes are in main thirst areas on which the hypothesis and objectives are decided. Sample size in calculated on the basis of these primary.

Secondary outcomes are other possible outcome of interest.

Outcome analysis: Outcome analysis is done to get the inferences. It should be done in such a way that answer to the objectives should be obtained out of this for inferences, level of significance should also be pre-defined (conventionally 0.05).

67

This analysis depends on type of data, type of outcome variables and type of inference (as per aims and objectives) needed. So help of statistician or statistical software may be required.

1. **Flow chart:** Whole procedure of study (study design) is shown in schematic flow chart for better understand at a glance.

2. **Seed article:** Reference almost similar to proposed study should be written in order of preference as it appears in the text. Standard method should be choosen to write down references like:

3. **References:** References, referred in the proposed study should be written in order of preference as it appears in the text. Standard method should be choosen to write down references like:

    Simikhada B, teijlingen E, Porter M, Simkhada P. Factors affecting the utilization of antenatal care in developing countries: systematic review of the literature. J Adv Nurs. 2007;61:244-260.

    USAID 2007. Focused antenatal care : providing integrated, individualized care during pregnancy. http://www.accesstohealth.org/toolres/pdfs/ACCESStechbrief_FANC.pdf

4. **Consent form:** Consent should be 'Informed Consent Form' and it should be in local language or in language study subjects can understand. It should be signed by every subject (observation unit) taking part in the study after giving consent to be included

in study. Before presenting it to the subject for sign, it should be conformed that consent form has information about.

    a. Study design

    b. Population parameter available

    c. Types of outcomes

    d. Title of the research

    e. Investigator's name and designation

    f. Procedure of the research

    g. Expected duration of the subject's participation

    h. Benefits that might be expected to the subject or to others

    i. Any foreseeable risk or discomfort to the subject resulting from participation in the study.

    j. Any compensation /reimbursement /insurance cover for participation or risk involved.

    k. Contact number of person responsible in case of emergency

    l. Extent to which confidentiality of records could be maintained

    m. Freedom of the individual to participate or to withdraw from research any time without penalty or loss of benefits.

5. **Schedule/Performa:** It is data collection tool. It should have following parts:

   Introductory schedule: In this schedule, general information about the subject should be written including address and mobile number.

   Specific schedule: In this schedule, specific information as per pre-decided aims and objectives about the subject should be written. It should have reasonable and analyzable data information. If study is intervention study, then more than one specific schedule is required, i.e. pre-intervention specific schedule and post-intervention schedule.

Annexure: Some additional information may be given in the form of annexure.

Chapter 11: THESIS REPORT

Thesis is also an official document submitted to the university before appearing in university examination of MD/MS. It should be in resonance with the thesis protocol previously submitted to the university.

Following steps are considered before writing a Thesis Report:

- After Institutional Research Review Board and ethical clearance, study should be conducted with proper consent of subjects.
- Data should be collected as per previously planned in protocol.
- Data should be entered in Microsoft Excel Worksheet/SPSS worksheet in the form of master chart.
- *Data thus collected in the form of master chart should be grouped or classified as per aims and objectives.
- *These collected data then should be analyzed to get inferences with help of computer and statistical software as and when required.

Structure of the thesis and other technicalities: Structure is same as in thesis protocol except:

- Thesis should be written in past tense.
- Explanatory approach should be used.
- Observations, discussions, conclusions and recommendations are also added to it.

*Observations: Observations will take following steps:

- After collection of data in the form of master chart, grouping and classification of data will be done as per aims and objectives.
- Observation will be drawn from master chart ready for analysis.
- Observation will be drawn in the form of tables, graphs and charts as describe elsewhere.
- Inferences drawn from tables and charts are also included in observations.
  * With the help of computer application in thesis.

Discussion: It is discussing of the observations of the present study with national/state norms and with findings of other authors in detail.

Conclusions: Final conclusion drawn from the observations and discussion is summarized here.

Recommendations: Recommend desirable actions as per observation and conclusions.

Recommended format of thesis is as follows:

Name of page/s	Content	Proposed pages
Title page	Title, submitted to, submitted by, under guidance of	1
Certificate from institution	As per institutional format	1
Introduction	Importance and justification of research problem	5-10
Review of literature	Brief review of literature	15-35
Purpose of study	Public health importance	1
Hypothesis	Assumptions about study	1
Aims and objectives	Researchable statements	1
Methodology	Study area, study design, study period, study universe, study population including, inclusion and exclusion criteria, sample size, sampling technique, define variables, prodcedure outcome variables and outcome analysis	10-25
Flow Chart	Showing study design	1
Observations	Tables, chart and graphs with their inferences	15-35
Discussion	Comparison of observations of present study with observations of other studies	15-35
Conclusions	Finally concluded from observations	3-7
Recommendations	Recommendations as per observations and conclusions	5-10
References	Almost similar study reference (50-100)	6-12
Annexure-	Certificates from RRB of institute	1
	Certificates from ethical committee	1
	Consent form	1
	Study tool-proforma/schedule	1-5
	Master Chart	

Total Pages: 80-180

Annexure of thesis Protocol/Report
- Title page
- Letter to university
- Flow Chart

- Inform consent

PLAN OF DISSERTATION
A STUDY OF TEMPERAMENTAL DISTRIBUTION OF PATIENTS ATTENDING NIUM HOSPITAL

BANGALORE

By

Mahboob Ali

Dissertation submitted to the

Rajiv Gandhi University of Health Sciences, Karnataka, Bangalore

In partial fulfillment

of the requirements for the degree of

MAHIRE TIB

(M.D. Unani)

in

Tahaffuzi wa Samaji Tib

(Preventive and Social Medicine)

Under the guidance of

Dr. Mohd Zulkifle and **Dr. Abdul Haseeb Ansari**
Department of Tahaffuzi wa Samaji Tib

National Institute of Unani Medicine

Bangalore (Karnataka)

To,
The Registrar
Rajiv Gandhi University of Health Sciences, Bangalore, Karnataka

THROUGH PROPER CHANNEL

Subject: Submission of plan of dissertation entitled **"A Study of Temperamental Distribution of Patients Attending NIUM Hospital, Bangalore"**

Respected Sir,

I am enclosing herewith eleven copies of my plan of dissertation on the subject cited above for **MAHIRE TIB (M.D. Unani)** Examination, 2010. My particulars are as follows:

Name   :   **Dr. Mahboob Ali**

                                            Post- Graduate Student in **Tahaffuzi wa Samaji Tib**

                              (Preventive and Social Medicine)

                    National Institute of Unani Medicine, Bangalore, Karnataka.

University   :   Rajiv Gandhi University of Health Sciences, Bangalore, Karnataka

Enrolment Number   :   07UHOOZ

Date of Admission   :   2.10.2007

Name of guide   :   **Dr. Mohd. Zulkifle**

                                            Associate   Professor,   Department   of   **Tahaffuzi   wa Samaji Tib**

Recommended and forwarded by

Dr. Mohd. Zulkifle

Associate Professor, Department of Tahaffuzi wa Samaji Tib

(Preventive and Social Medicine), National Institute of Unani

Medicine, Bangalore, Karnataka.

I shall be highly obliged if you kindly convey the approval of the plan of dissertation at the earliest.

Thanking You

                                                                        Yours Faithuflly
                                                                        Dr. Mahboob Ali

Flow chart

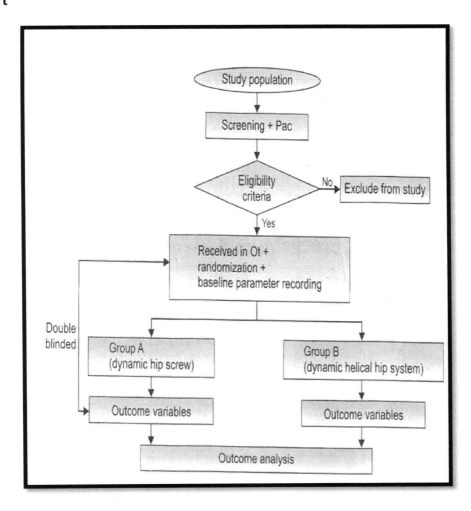

Informed Consent Form

Name of study ---

Date of study --

Number of study--------------------------------

Full name of subject / participant ---

Date of birth --
--------Address---
----

1   I have been fully informed about all the facts and activities of research study
2   My participation in this study is on my willing and I have a right to quit myself from the study any time without giving any reason for that.
3   I agree to participate in the above research study.

Signature of researcher   Signature of patient

                                                            Address:

Address: Registration no:

DOCUMENTATION

The basic concept of record keeping and handling of data is to record, restore, transfer and wherever necessary convert efficiently and accurately the information collected on the trial subjects into data that can be used to complete the study report.

The study would not be considered valid unless an intact data set is developed. The good clinical practice (GCP) has laid down specific guidelines for documentation of clinical trial data. Monitoring the quality of data is very important. All steps involved in data management should be documented in order to allow step-by-step retrospective assessment of data quality and study performance for audit purposes.

RECORDS AND REPORTS

- Records should be accurate, complete, legible and timely pertinent to data reported in case record form (CRF) and other required reports.
- Data reported on CRF should be derived from the source of document.
- All corrections to CRF should be dated, initiated, explained and should not obscure the original entry.
- The investigator should retain records of the changes and corrections.

NEED OF RETENTION OF RECORD

All study related material or essential documents should be retained for 3 years after completion of study. Upon request of monitor it should be made available.

REPORTING THE RESULTS OF CLINICAL TRIAL

A clinical trial report can be defned as presentation of tangible output of the efforts of research. It carries statements on issues on which the study was focused, procedure adopted, stages covered, findings and conclusion.

The purpose of a report is to convey to the interested persons the entire results of the study in sufficienit details and to arrange as to enable each reader to comprehend the data and to determine the validity of the conclusion.

The purpose can be summarized as:

- To disseminate knowledge.
- To present the valid conclusion.
- To validate the generalization.
- To provide guidance to future research.

Characteristic of good reports:

- General appearance / attractiveness
- Balanced language
- No repetition of facts
- Accuracy of data
- Statement of scientific facts
- Current applications
- Description of the difficulties and short comings

The CONSORT Statement:

The Consolidated Standards of Reporting Trials (CONSORT) statement is an important research tool that takes evidence based approach to improve the quality of reports of randomized trials.

CONSORT: It comprises a checklist and flow diagram to help improve the quality of reports of randomized controlled trials. It offers a standard way for researchers to report trials.

In sum, the CONSORT statements is intended to improve the reporting of a randomized controlled trial (RCT), enabling reader to understand to trial's conduct and to assess the validity of result.

The **CONSORT** checklist items pertain to the content of the Title, Abstract, Introduction, Methods, Results and Discussion.

THE REVISED CONSORT CHEKLIST INCLUDES 22 ITEMS AS:

- Title and abstract
- Introduction background
- Methods Participants
- Interventions
- Objectives
- Outcomes
- Sample size
- Randomization sequence generation
- Randomization allocation concealment
- Randomization implementation
- Blinding (masking)
- Statistical Methods
- Results, participants flow
- Recruitment
- Baseline data
- Numbers analyzed
- Outcomes and estimations
- Ancillary analyzer
- Adverse events
- Discussion / interpretation

- Generalization
- Overall evidence

LAYOUT OF THE RESEARCH REPORT:

Layout comprises of:

A. Preliminary pages

B. Main text

C. The end matter.

A. Preliminary pages consists of:

    1. Title and date

    2. Acknowledgement in the form of "Preface" or " Forward"

    3. Tables of contents

    4. List of tables and illustrations

B. Main text comprises of following:

    I. **Introduction:** it includes;

        1. Need of study

        2. Objectives of research

        3. The brief summary of relevant research done before and how does this study differ

        4. Hypothesis of study

        5. Methodology-

            a. Study design

            b. Expert manipulations in case of expert study

            c. Means of data collection

            d. Subjects of study

            e. No. of subjects

            f. Method of selection of subjects

    II. Statements of findings and recommendations:

Statements of findings in non-technical language in summarized form.

    III. Result:

        a. Detailed presentation of finding in the form of tables and charts.

        b. Statistical summarizes and reductions of data

        c. Clear statement of the problem, the

        d. Procedure by which he worked on the problem

        e. Conclusion at which he arrived

        f. Basis for his conclusion

IV.   Implication of the result:
   a.   A statement of the inferences drawn from the present study.
   b.   The conditions of the present study which may limit the extent of legitimate generalization of the inferences drawn from the study
   c.   The relevant questions that remained unanswered or new questions raised by the study along with the suggestions for that kind of research that would provide answer for them.

V.   Summary;
   Conclusion of report with the brief summary about research problem, the methodology, major findings and conclusions drawn from the research.

C.   **End Matter:**
   a.   Appendices should be enlisted in respect of all technical data such as questionnaire, sample information mathematical derivations.
   b.   Bibliography of the sources consulted
   Index

WRITING A RESEARCH REPORT WITH REFERENCES

Research report is a major component of the research study. Even the most brilliant hypotheses, highly well designed and conducted research study are of little value unless they effectively communicate to others.

Following steps should be kept in mind during writing a research report:

Logically analysis of the subjects matter:

It can be developed in two ways:

Logically: Made on the basis of mental connections and association between one thing and another by means of analysis.

Chronologically: It is based on a connection of sequence in time or occurrence

Preparation of the final outline:

Outlines are the framework upon which long written works are constructed. These are the logical organization of the material and a reminder of the points to be stressed in report.

Preparation of the rough draft: Researcher now sits to write down all, what he has done in the contest of his research study i.e., the procedure he has adopted for collecting the material for his study and limitations faced by him, techniques of analysis of data adopted, various suggestions he wants to offer regarding the problem.

Rewriting and polishing of the rough draft:

This is the most different part. The researcher should see the unity and cohesion of the material; he should check the mechanics of writing grammar, spellings and usage.

Preparations of final Bibliography:

It contains all those works which the researcher has consulted.

The bibliography should be arranged alphabetically in two parts;

- Names of books and pamphlets
- Names of magazines, News paper and article

Method of writing for Bbooks, Compendia(a type of book), Bulletins and Pamphlets:

I.   Name of author, last name first.
II. Titled in italics.
III. Place, Publisher and date of publications.
IV. No. of volumes

E.g.: Kothari, C.R., RM Methods and Technique, New age international Pvt. Ltd. Publisher Ansari Road, Daryaganj, New Delhi-110002, 1995.

Method of writing for Magazine, Journal and News paper:

Name of author, last name first

Title of article in *quotation mark*

Name of periodical in italics

The volume and volume number

Date of issue.

The paginations

Writing the final draft:

This constitutes the last step. The final draft should be in a concise and obligative style and in simple language, avoiding vague expressions such as "it seem" "there may be" etc. While writing the final draft, the researcher must avoid abstract terminology and technical jargon. A research report should not be dull.

It must be remembered that every report should include following point;

An attempt to solve some intellectual problems

The repot must contribute the sole of a problem and

The repot must add to the knowledge of both the researcher and the reader.

GUIDELINES FOR RESEARCH

ICMR Guidelines for Research:

There are few rules or principles that should be followed in a research study. These are:

1. **Principle of essentiality:** The use of human beings is considered to be absolutely essential after considering all alternative in the light of existing knowledge in the proposed area of research and has been approved by the responsible body of persons, who are external to that particular research, that the said research is necessary for the advertisement of knowledge and for the benefit of all members of the human species.

2. **Principle of voluntariness, informed consent and community agreement:** Following points are very important and should be cleared during research;

    i. That the research subjects are made fully aware of the research, its impact and risks on the research subjects and others.

    ii. The research subject has the right to abstain from further participation in the research irrespective of any legal or other obligations.

    iii. The written consent to be taken from the volunteers and if they are not capable of giving consent, then the consent should be obtained by someone who is empowered and under a duty to act on researcher's behalf.

3. **Principle of non-exploitation:** During the research or experiment the research subject's social and economic status literary or educational levels attained by researcher. Subjects should be fully informed about the dangerous arising in and out of the research. The research subjects should be compensated either through insurance cover or any other appropriate means to cover all foreseeable or unforeseeable risks by providing remedial action and treatment after the research or experiment.

4. **Principal of privacy & confidentiality:** The identity and records of the human subjects of the research or experiment are kept confidential as far as possible, and are disclosed only if it is essential for the purpose of therapeutics or other interventions and after ensuring that he does not suffer from any form of hardship, discrimination or stigmatizm as a consequence of having participated in the research or experiment.

5. **Principal of precaution & risk minimization:** Due care & caution is taken at all stages of the research & experiment to ensure that the research subjects are put to the minimum risk, suffer from no irriversible adverse effects.

6. **Principal of professional competence:** Research is conducted at all times by competent & qualified persons & who are aware of the ethical consideration in respect of such research or experiment.

7. **Principles of accountability & transparency:** The research or experiment will be conducted in a fair, impartial and transparent manner after full discloser is made by those associated with research or experiment of each aspect of their interest in research. Full and completely records of the research are maintained in order to make such records available for scrutiny by the appropriate legal and administrative authority.

8. **Principle of maximization of the public interest and of distributive justice:** The research of experiment and its subsequent applicative use are conducted and used to the benefits of all human kind and not just those who are socially better off.

9. **Principles of institutional arrangements:** There shall be a duty of all persons connected with the research to ensure that all the procedures, research reports, materials and data connected with the research are duly preserved and archived.

10. **Principles of public domain:** The research and further research, experimentation or evaluation from such research is brought into the public domain so that its results are generally made known through scientific and other publication.

11. **Principal of totality of responsibility:** It is the professional and moral responsibility to follow all the principles, guidelines laid down in respect of the research or experiment of all those who are directly or indirectly involved in the research.

12. **Principal of compliance:** There is a general and positive duty on all persons conducting , associated or connected with any research entailing the use of a human subject to ensure that both the letter and spirit of these guidelines or directions which are specially laid down and which are applicable for that area of research are scrupulously observed and duly compiled.

ETHICAL ISSUES IN RESEACH

Ethical consideration is an important issue in the finalization of all studies. Before a research study is started, the consent of the subjects to participate in the study must be obtained in details about the ethical guide lines (to be followed in Bio-Medical Research on human subjects) that have been published by Indian council of medical research, New Delhi 2.

SOME ETHICAL ISSUES RAISED IN RESEARCH I NCLUDE-

a. **Ethical issues in clinical research primarily involves like, protection of rights, safety, and well-being of the research participants:**

All National and International guidelines lay emphasis on the code of conduct to be followed by researchers and the other stakeholders in clinical research to uphold this basic commitment to safeguard the rights and safety of the research participants who play a central role in research without whom-either themselves, their data, or their biological samples-no research is possible. However, reviewing and constant monitoring of the research activities to ensure adherence to the principles laid down in these guidelines or policies or legislations are the main concerns of the Ethics Review Committees (ERC/EC), whether institutional or independent, which are entrusted with the responsibility of protecting the rights and safety of the research participants. Although all the guidelines are based on the cardinal principles of autonomy, beneficence and justice. The ethical issues to be tackled are increasing day by day with the advancement of new technologies, wide range of research activities, and globalization of clinical research.

b. **THE fundamental ethical concern raised by clinical research is whether and when it can be acceptable to expose some individual to risk and burdens for the benefits of others:**

Risk-benefit analysis is the main responsibility of ethics committees which give final approval for implementation of any research proposal, thereby taking care of the principles of non-malfeasance and beneficence. Medical research often involves exposure to minor pain, discomfort, or injury from invasive medical procedures, or harm from possible side effects of drugs. All of these should be considered "risks" for purposes of EC review. Some of the adverse effects that result from medical procedures or drugs can be permanent, but most are transient. Procedures commonly used in medical research usually result in no more than minor discomfort (e.g., temporary dizziness, the pain associated with acupuncture, etc).

c. **Compensation for participating in research as well as research-related injury is a major bone of contention these days:**

Embedded in the principle of justice, participation in research should be accessible to everyone, regardless of socioeconomic status. Hence, recruitment of participants is a major issue in ensuring that burden of research and benefit of that research is borne by the same group of individuals and there is no exploitation of any vulnerable group because of their socioeconomic, ethnic, or cultural status. Compensation in the form of reimbursement ensures that research costs are not borne by participant and thereby removing financial implications from participants' consideration to enroll. Recognizing that a fair level of benefit is a complex function of participants' inputs compared to the inputs of others, and the extent to which third parties benefit from those inputs, it is difficult to see how one might fill in the details of this scenario to show that the typically minimal, or non-existent compensation offered to research participants is fair. At the same time, addressing the potential for exploitation by offering payments to research participants would introduce its own set of ethical concerns.

Thus, clinical research poses many such ethical dilemmas from the time of formulation of research hypothesis to the final implementation of the research and its conduct till completion including post research issues that have to be clearly understood by all the stakeholders in research to carry out their responsibilities in protecting the rights of the participants. However, in the absence of a well-structured Bioethics education in the country, there is a pressing need for continuous capacity building exercises at all levels. Awareness about national and international guidelines and regulations and putting in place appropriate laws in the country will go a long way in ensuring public confidence about the safety and well being of the research participants.

ESSENTIAL CRITERIA FOR A CLINICAL RESEARCH STUDY:

For conducting a research study, it should be consisting of following points:

1. Selection of research problem or Research question
2. Literature review for the study
3. Development of Hypothesis
4. Development of protocol for the study
5. Development of study design/ Development of sample design
6. Appropriate data collection and quality control
7. Analysis of data
8. Testing of Hypothesis
9. Statistical analysis
10. Documentation
11. Reporting of results

This part of this book covers almost all above mentioned points which are mandatory for a research study.

Chapter 12: HOW TO WRITE A RESEARCH PAPER?

Writing a scientific paper is a great obstacle for many people, or perhaps for most people. But it is really not all that hard. Papers may be clinical or experimental. The paper tells the story of the project from inception, through the data-collection process, statistical analysis, and discussion of the results. The process of writing the paper should be analogous to the research process. There are some vital components in a research paper that should be covered at any cost.

The vital components of a research paper:

- The essential parts
- The Title, Authors, Institution
- Abstract
- Background (Introduction)/Rationale
- Hypothesis/Question
- Aim
- Endpoints
- Subjects(in-exclusion)
- Design
- Intervention
- Measurements
- Analysis(+statistical power)
- Results
- Tables and Figures
- Discussion
- Conclusion
- References

We all know that it is customary to write a scientific paper in sections: introduction, methods, results with tables and figures, discussion, conclusion and references. The backbone of your paper is the link between the three vital elements: the hypothesis or research questions, the design of the study and the analysis. A particular hypothesis can only be addressed by a particular design, which brings in a specific way of analyzing and presenting the data. The most common reason for rejection of papers is some kind of discrepancy between these three issues.

Let us go through each of the sections now one by one. First, carefully check the journal's instructions to authors on the requirement regarding content and layout.

144

Title Page:

A good title is important for several reasons. The title alerts the readers to the topic of your paper. A well written or phrased title creates curiosity and draws readers to investigate the substance of

your paper. However, the main function of the title is to describe your research. Title should describe the research succinctly; long titles provide no advantage. 15 words should suffice (the limit at the *JCI*- Journal of Clinical Investigation). No jargon should be used in the title because you want to attract the readers to your article or paper. If people can't understand your title, they will not read your paper. Avoid using excess punctuations: i.e., no colons, excess commas (parenthetical). The title should let the reader know if your paper is a human, animal or bench study. As an example, if your title is "Moisture Output of 2 Humidification System," it is incomplete. Give more information; for example," Moisture Output of 2 Humidification Systems for Use with Mechanically Ventilated Patients," or "Comparison of the Moisture Output of 2 Humidification Systems with a Lung Model." The title tells the reader what to expect in the paper and thus whether the paper really pertains to his literature-search. If you are looking for data on humidification studies with mechanically ventilated patients, the first title is more germane to your topic. Briefly, but clearly, explain the paper's content in the title.

Introduction: Introduction is an important part of research paper. It should deal with the rationale of your study. It is your most important chance to convince the reader that what you did makes a lot of sense. Start the introduction by providing the background for the field-how does it link to your particular signalizing cascade/polymorphism/technique of interest and what was heretofore unknown-alongside your hypothesis for how you will fill that gap in knowledge.

It includes:

- General background about the disease
- The specific dilemma
- Whys still unresolved?
- My idea to resolve it : sell it as the obvious approach
- Hypothesis or question Aim

The general problem: Which health problem forms the motive of your study? Give a few facts about it. Highlight its relevance. Even if your biomedical study is basic science, it should be embedded into some kind of health problem.

The specific focus: which part of the problem will you be focusing on? Why is this issue so important? What will be the gain when this is solved? Make plausible the idea that this is within reach.

Why still unresolved? Mention whether, and how, others have approached this previously. Why has this not been (fully) successful? Why have others (partly) failed?

Your idea: indicate why you believe that the specific problem can be solved. Explain why your idea is good and probably better than what has been attempted previously. Sell your proposal. After reading this your idea should be an obvious thing to do. Provide any data supporting your idea.

Provide an explicit hypothesis (or a primary and a secondary hypothesis). Second best is to list a few explicit research questions.

Finally, mention the aim/objectives and outcome measures of the study. That is: testing the hypothesis in this material, in such a way, by measuring these (primary and a secondary) outcomes

You may close this section by very briefly giving the implications of rejecting or not rejecting the hypothesis. Similarly, highlight the implications of positive and negative answers to the research questions.

Methods Section:

The methods section should describe in detail how the study was performed. Ideally, after reading your methods section another researcher could duplicate your study. Remember when writing the methods section, it should be clear how your methods will answer the questions the research question and refute or support your hypothesis.

Usually it starts with Subjects, then Design, followed by Measurements and Analysis. You may also start with Design.

Subjects (Material)

- This includes the patients, animals, the tissue, etc.
- Give the required number (based on the sample size estimation in the Analysis section). The actual number that you ended up with comes in the results section.
- Indicate how the subjects were selected, from what source, by whom and in what way. In the case of patients, give details of the recruitment procedure.
- Give explicit inclusion and exclusion criteria. For human subjects think of demographic, clinical, habitual and functional criteria, medication usage, biochemical criteria, etc. If applicable give the rationale and criteria for control group(s).

- If needed, give criteria for predefined subgroups (these should be logical subgroups, derived from the reasoning in the introduction)
- Define criteria for drop-outs.
- Confirm approve by a human or animal ethics committee, and in the case of humans confirm written informed consent.

Design

- Check current guidelines for presenting, e.g. randomized control trials (CONSORT Guidelines) and observational studies (STROBE Guidelines).
- For clinical studies: give the registration number of the study in an International Clinical Trial Registry.
- Give an exact description of the study design: descriptive, observational, cross-sectional, interventional, follow-up, retrospective, prospective, randomized controlled trial, cohort study, case-control, etc.
- Uncontrolled, controlled, placebo-controlled, cross-over, parallel, matched pair. Open, single-blind (who was blind?) or double-blind. Give method of randomization and method of matching.
- Mentioned exactly what was performed, when, how often, and in which sequence. Don't forget what was done prior to and after the study. A figure of the design is always helpful.
- Give the procedure of study monitoring.

Methods of measurement

- This should list each and every measurement of the study.
- Give your rationale for the measurement in view of the study objectives.
- Give apparatus, settings, calibrations, resolution and detection limits if applicable.
- Indicate that detailed standard operating procedures (SOPs) were used. If needed, mention key elements from the SOPs.
- Give variable(s) for each measurement, and the units in which you will present those.
- Provide references about the validation of the methods (accuracy, precision, repeatability), preferably from your own lab.

Analysis

- Check adequate recommendations on how to present the analysis and statistics.

- Indicate whether any of the variables required transformation of the units (e.g. log transformation).
- Mention the structure of the study, and who was responsible for it. Indicate when and who broke the code of the study, and who had access to it. Indicate who carried out the statistics, using which software and version.
- Provide statistics for each hypothesis/ research question. Remember that the tests have to be appropriate to your study design.
- Clearly indicate what was analyzed between groups and what within groups.
- Define the minimally relevant effect size (e.g. the minimally important clinical difference) and the type 1 and type 2 error by either single or double sided testing.
- Present sample-size estimation or power calculation for the analysis and the number of subjects/animals/etc.
- Indicate and explain whether the analysis was performed by "intimation to treat" or "per protocol"
- Mention what was done with missing data or drop-out.
- Was interim analysis planned? If so, why? Was it done? Give detailed consequences of this.

Results

The results section presents facts. Do not repeat the rationale of measuring things, nor discuss the findings here. Even though this section is highly factual, it should remain readable. So, present your findings in clear paragraphs based on the steps in the Analysis. A good way to start writing the Results sections is to construct the tables and figures first. This also splits the thinking from the writing. If the tables and figures highlight your major findings clearly, then writing results will be very easy.

- Results section includes: Base line (sub) groups cross sectional table 1, Main questions figures/ tables data in text readable, secondary questions idem, Unexpected observations very short
- Start the Results with the sample size that was actually obtained. You may use a figure (trial profile), showing the numbers of subjects included (and excluded) at each step of the section procedure.
- Present a base line analysis of your subjects/ material, by giving the vital (demographic, clinical) information in table1. Mention the most striking features in the text.

- Present the result by addressing the hypothesis (or research questions) in a stepwise fashion, separated into logical paragraph. Be concise and clear, and refer to tables and figures.
- Concentrate on primary outcomes first. Secondary outcomes come later.
- Avoid repetition of data between text, tables and figures. However, if highlighting major findings is necessary, a little overlap is acceptable.
- The reader will be interested in the main findings. These must stand out, even for those not reading the result from the beginning to the end.
- Do not bore the reader by constantly repeating the same structure of sentences. Hence, even, the result should read like a logical story-but be thrifty with adjectives.
- Also, be conservative in presenting (planned) subgroup analysis. Follow recent guidelines on presenting subgroup analysis.
- You may end with unexpected findings, and the results of unplanned analysis. These kinds of results are mostly hypothesis generating, and should be limited to the absolute minimum. Otherwise, you be accused of "fishing".

Discussion

There are many ways of writing the Discussion section. Most of consider the Discussion section as the most difficult part of the paper because there are so many issues to be dealt with. Again the best approach is to separate the thinking from the writing. The first step is to distinguish the paragraphs of the discussion. These should be:

- Red line and take-home message.
- Comparisons with previous literature.
- Strengths and weakness.
- Interpretation and mechanism.
- Clinical relevance.
- Conclusion.

Be aware that each paragraph must have a clear head and tail. The first sentence of each paragraph should guide the reader, by indicating what this paragraph will be about. The final sentence of each paragraph should provide the message, and ideally should form a bridge to the next paragraph. How long should the discussion be? One rule of thumb is that it should be about 3.5 double-spaced pages (and should not exceed 4 pages). Hence, being concise is more important than being complete and exhaustive.

The following system of writing a discussion section may not be the best. However, we do know that it always works well. It comes from Ed Daniel from McMaster University, who taught one of us (P.J. Sterk) how to write a discussion on the back of an envelope. And be aware, there is no one with a broader scientific perspective than Ed!

Again, separate the thinking from the writing. After preparing your flow chart, and subsequently writing the discussion part by part, you will be ready within one or two days!

Red line of the findings and take-home message:

- Provide the main results in one or two sentences: the main findings only.
- Indicate what one can infer from them.
- Give the implication of the result: this suggests this or that with regard to mechanisms and/ or the clinical problem.

Comparison with previous studies in the literature:

- Indicate what is novel in your study.
- If your results confirm previous studies: say so.
- More importantly, indicate why your study extends any previous observations.
- Always start with your own findings, and connect these to current literature if available (never the other way around!)
- Discuss only observations, no mechanisms or interpretations here.
- Finally, provide the message of this paragraph: our result is new, different, better, more detailed, etc.

Strengths and weakness:

- Try to start off with a few strong points in the methods of your study. Do not exaggerate
- In any study there will have been choices in the methods that that might have introduced weakness. You should raise points, otherwise the reviewers will.
- Think of issues related to: selection of subjects, design, and methods of measurements, analysis. Go through your protocol and pick out a few potential weak points.
- What would be factors introducing random errors (noise) and systemic errors (bias) leading to variability in the data? If appropriate (negative results), mention the statistical power here.
- Try to emphasize that some of your choices in the protocol had implicit strengths apart from the (less important) weakness.
- You may separate this paragraph in two. On the other hand, don't be too extensive (don't throw yourself away).

- We hope that you can finish by saying that the potential errors have not been that serious. They cannot be the explanation of your (negative finding).

Interpretation in terms of mechanisms:

- How can you explain your findings?
- Which pathophysiological / immunological /etc. mechanisms are likely to form the basis of your findings?
- Address these mechanisms one by one you may need to separate this paragraph into two or even three.
- Again: explain your own findings, and only if it really cannot be avoided explain the findings of others.
- What has been solved by your study, and what has not?
- Speculation is allowed but be very clear on this: mention the word speculation if you do.
- The final sentence, again, present the main message with regard to interpretation of your data. This or that mechanism is likely to be (or not to be) involved.
- And if there are still open questions here, mention.

Clinical interpretation:

- What is the clinical relevance of your findings? Even biochemical basic science studies should have a link to a medical problem.
- Do your results contribute improving, detection, diagnosis, monitoring or treatment of disease?
- What should physicians do differently in this respect from now on?
- Speculation is allowed, but says to.
- What is still missing in this area?

Conclusion:

- This paragraph can be short, because main message has already been addressed in the first paragraph.
- You cannot repeat the first paragraph of the discussion, so you have to use a slightly different wording or emphasis here.
- Be very concise, but crystal clear. This section should contain the take-home message.
- Hence, summarize the main findings in one or two sentences, and most importantly provide the implication(s) of your findings in relation to the specific and general

health problem that you started with. This head and tail closes the circle of the paper. After giving your message, you may emphasize the obvious things to do next.

What does go into the abstract?

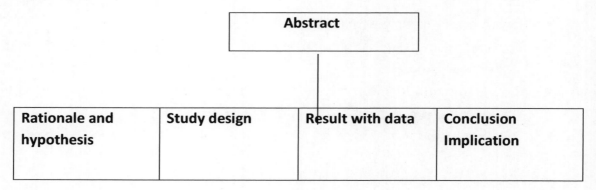

Abstract: The structure of the abstract follows the main sections of your paper. You should check the journal's rules for it. The best way of writing the abstract is to use four paragraphs, rationale, methods, results and conclusion (figure).

- The rationale addresses the relevance of key problem in one or two sentences. It should provide your hypothesis or main research question.

- The methods section is often somewhat longer. Give the essential subject characteristics, the type of design, and the primary outcome parameters. One sentence on the analysis can be very helpful.

- The results section should provide the main outcome of your study, related to the primary hypothesis or research question. Select one or two quantitative results with confidence intervals or p-values (some journals do not appreciate the latter in the abstract).

- The conclusion section essentially presents two aspects. First, one or two sentences on the main finding. Second (and importantly) one sentence on the implication of this. The implication should have relevance to the key problem as mentioned in the rationale (head and tail).

Chapter 13: BIOSTATISTICS

1. **SCOPE AND UTILITY OF BIOSTATISTICS**

2. **DESCRIPTIVE STATISTICS:**

    A. **Analysis of Data:**

        I.   Data collection, tabulation, and presentation of data.

        II.   Measure of central tendency: Mean, Median Mode.

        III.   Measure of dispersion: Range, Standard deviation.

    B. **Probability:**

        I.   Definition and laws of probability

        II.   Types of probability distribution

        III.   Randomized samples

    C. **Sampling:**

        I.   Types and sample size

        II.   Randomized Sampling

3. **INFERENTIAL STATISTICS:**

    A. **Tests of significance:**

        I.   't' test

        II.   'z' test

    B. **Test of variance:**

        I.   ANOVA one way

        II.   ANOVA two way

4. **VITAL STATISTICS:**

    A. **Rate and Ratios**

    B. **Standardization of population**

    C. **Risk factors**

SCOPE AND UTILITY OF BIOSTATISTICS

DEFINITION OF BIOSTATISTICS:

Biostatistics can be defined as "the Statistical processes and methods applied to the collection, analysis, and interpretation of biological data and especially data relating to human biology, health, and medicine is called **biostatistics".**

IMPORTANCE OF BIOSTATISTICS:

Statistics are an essential part of medical research, according to HowStuffWorks. Researchers use statistical tests to determine results from experiments, clinical trials of medicine and symptoms of diseases. The use of statistics in medicine provides generalizations for the public to better understand their risks for certain diseases, such as links between certain behaviors and heart disease or cancer. A wide range of professions within the medical field use statistics, according to Wikipedia. Descriptive statistics show the portion of a population with a disease, for example. Inferential statistics help determine causes to diseases. Those in the pharmaceutical, forensic and biological sciences all use statistics to relay information about health and medicine.

SCOPE AND UTILITY OF BIOSTATISTICS

Biostatistics is the application of statistics to a wide range of topics in biology. It encompasses the design of biological experiments, especially in medicine, pharmacy, agriculture and fishery; the collection, summarization, and analysis of data from those experiments; and the interpretation of, and inference from, the results. A major branch is medical biostatistics, which is exclusively concerned with medicine and health.

- **Following Points Are Included as Scope of Biostatistics as:**
- Methods of collection of Data
- Classification and analysis of Data
- Summarizing the Data
- Interpretation of Data
- Testing the significance of Data
- Presentation of Data

DESCRIPTIVE STATISTICS

A. **ANALYSIS OF DATA:** It includes following factors as

I.   Data collection, tabulation and presentation of data.
II.   Measures of central tendency: Mean, Median and Mode.

III.   Measures of dispersion: Range , quartile deviation , standard deviation.

WHAT IS DATA?

Data is a set of values of subjects with respect to qualitative or quantitative variables. Data and information or knowledge is often used interchangeably; however data becomes information when it is viewed in context or in post-analysis. While the concept of data is commonly associated with scientific research,.

Research data is any information that has been collected, observed, generated or created to validate original research findings. Although usually digital, research data also includes non-digital formats such as laboratory notebooks and diaries.

TYPES OF DATA:

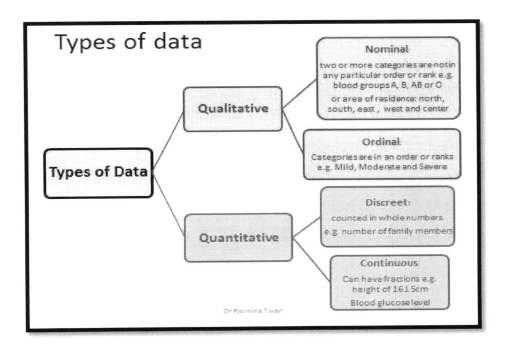

DATA COLLECTION:

There are so many sources in the medical field from where Data can be collected by various methods as:

1. Census

2. Surveys conducted by medical Institutions (SPM Department) and by Government (population survey)
3. Medical records in the Hospital
4. Registration of vital events
5. SRS (Sample registration System)
6. Epidemiological surveillance of certain diseases like TB, Leprosy, Malaria etc.

PRESENTATION OF DATA:

This refers to the organization of **data** into tables, graphs or charts, so that logical and statistical conclusions can be derived from the collected measurements. **Data** may be presented in 3 Methods: - Textual - Tabular or - Graphical.

Bar charts, histograms, pie charts, and box plots (box and whiskers plots). Two common types of graphic displays are bar charts and histograms. Both bar charts and histograms use vertical or horizontal bars to represent the number of data points in each category or interval.

In the presentation of data, the following points should be kept in mind:

a. They should be accurate and complete.
b. When we make them concise, they should not lose their details.
c. They should be simple and meaningful and at the same time they should create interest in the reader.
d. Below the table or picture, few points of explanation may be needed most of the times.
e. They should be helpful in further analysis.

METHODS OF PRESENTATION OF DATA

1. **Tabulation**
   a. Simple table
   b. Frequency distribution tables — Qualitative Data / Quantitative Data

2. **Charts and diagrams**
   a. Illustration of quantitative data
      i. Histogram
      ii. Frequency polygon
      iii. Line chart or line diagram
      iv. Frequency curve
      v. Cumulative frequency diagram (Ogive)

156

b. Illustration of qualitative data
  i. Bar diagram –
   - Simple bar diagram
   - Multiple bar diagram
   - Component bar diagram
  ii. Pi diagram or sector diagram
c. Pictogram or picture diagram
d. Map diagram or spot map
e. Scatter or dot diagram

TABULATION

Tabulation is the first step before the data is used for analysis or interpretation. By tabulation, the data becomes simple from a lot of collection of statistical data.

In tabulation of data, the following principles should be followed:

a. The tables should be numbered, table 1, table 2 etc.

b. Title of the table must be brief and self-explanatory

c. The heading of the columns or rows should be clear and concise. Example: Ht in cm, wt in kg, age in years etc.

d. The data must be presented according to size or importance.

e. If percentages or averages are to be compared they should be placed as close as possible to the actual numbers in the data.

f. The table should not be too large or too small. 10-20 rows are allowed in a table. Ideal is 15 rows.

g. The class interval should be the same throughout the table except in case of age (here grouping 5 yearly class intervals are advised or 10 yearly class intervals may be used. Other groups are below 1 year (to get infants), 1-4 years (to get under 5 years), 5-10 (to get under) 15 years data).

For example:

Table 1

Example for age groups

< 1

1-4

5-9

10-14

15-24

35-44

45-54

55-64

65% above

Table 2

Example for Hb%

< 6 gm

6-8 gm

9-11 gm

12-14 gm

15 gm and above

h. Groups should be tabulated in ascending or descending order from the lowest value in the range to highest value

i. If certain data is omitted or excluded deliberately the reasons for the same should be given

Tables 3 (Simple table):

Population of major countries in the world:

Country	Population in millions
China	1350
India	1000
USA	250
Indonesia	200
Russia	150
Brazil	150

Table 4 (Frequency distribution table):

Population of a village by age and sex distribution:

Age	Male	Female	Total
0-4	200	180	380
5-14	600	800	1400
15-44	1000	1200	2200
45-60	800	900	1700
60 and above	300	400	700
Total	**2900**	**3480**	**6380**

Characteristics of frequency distribution table:

- The data may be qualitative or quantitative.
- Computation of qualitative data is easy.

Table 5:

Number of TB cases admitted and mortality due to TB in admitted cases

Attributes	Males	Females	Total
TB Cases	40	45	95
Deaths due to TB	15%	8.89%	10.53%

COMPUTATION OF QUANTITATIVE DATA

Steps in organizing frequency distribution table-

a. Determine the range.
b. Divide this by 15 to estimate the approximate size of the class intervals.
c. List the intervals, beginning at the bottom. Let the lowest interval begin with a number, which is a multiple of the interval size.
d. Tally the frequencies.
e. Summarize these under a column labeled "f" (frequency).
f. Total this column and record the number of cases at the bottom.

Example: The following are the weight in kg of 48 medical students. Construct the frequency distribution table.

50, 61, 70, 71, 63, 34, 75, 80, 45, 56, 57, 58, 60, 62, 72, 78, 48, 50, 63, 64, 67, 52, 53, 54, 55, 56, 57, 70, 71, 72, 73, 64, 65, 66, 67, 62, 63, 65, 52, 60, 54, 56, 58, 57, 61, 81, 82, 80

Wt. in kg	Tally marks	F
80-84	IIII	4
75-79	II	2
70-74	IIII II	7
65-69	IIII	5
60-64	IIIIIIII II	12
55-59	IIIIIIII	9
50-54	IIII II	7
45-49	II	2
Total		**48**

Table 6: Now we write the table separately

Wt. in kg	F
80-84	4
75-79	2
70-74	7
65-69	5
60-64	12
55-59	9
50-54	7
45-49	2
Total	**48**

CHARTS AND DIAGRAMS (GRAPHS)

In all work with graphs we use two axes. The vertical axis is always labeled as the "Y" axis. It is also "Ordinate". The values taken along this axis are called ordinate values.

The horizontal axis is always labeled as "X" axis. It is also called "Abscissa". The X axis and the Y axis meet at right angles at a point called origin (O).

In most of the graphs X axis is longer than Y axis. Usually a rotio of 3:2 or 4:3 will result in a good graph. (Example: X axis is 25 cm long and Y axis and Y axis is 10 cm long). On X axis we will mark different groups, scores, class intervals and on Y axis we will usually take frequencies (i.e., number of observation).

If the highest frequency on Y-axis is 8, we need to mark more than 8 units (i.e., 9 units) on Y axis. This same ways on X-axis the highest frequency is 14, we need to mark more than 14 units (i.e., 15 units)

Example: Suppose we take weight of 48 individuals from 45-48 kg with class interval of 5.

Here we are having frequency on X-axis is 8. So, we need to draw 9 units on X-axis.

Here the frequencies on y-axis are 6. So, we need to draw 7 units on Y axis.

Here the class interval in Y-axis is 2. We have taken frequencies here. The class interval in X-axis is 5. Here we have taken weight in kg.

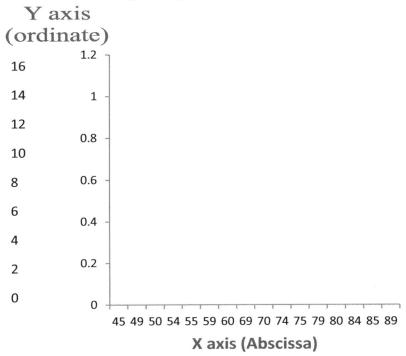

HISTOGRAM

If we draw frequencies of each group or class interval (wt. in kg like 45-49, 50-54, 55-59 etc.), in the form of columns or rectangles such a diagram is called histogram. Histogram is useful in presentation of quantitative data. Now we draw histogram using the data in Table 6

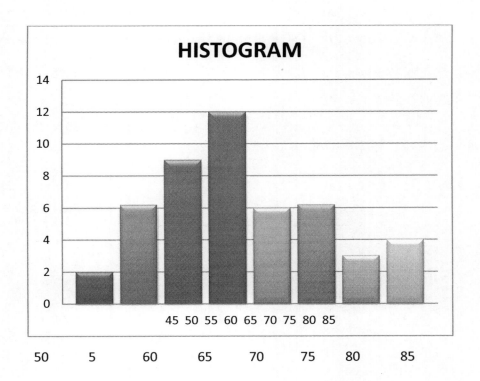

HISTOGRAM

Wt in Kg

Advantages of histogram:

1. Easy to understand

Disadvantages:

1. Only one histogram can be placed clearly on one set of axis
2. More time consuming to construct than a frequency polygon

FREQUENCY POLYGON

This is the most commonly used graphic device to illustrate statistical distribution.

Construction of frequency polygon: Here also we mark frequencies on Y-axis and groups or class intervals (weight) on X-axis. We will draw the same values in table 6 for frequency polygon also.

162

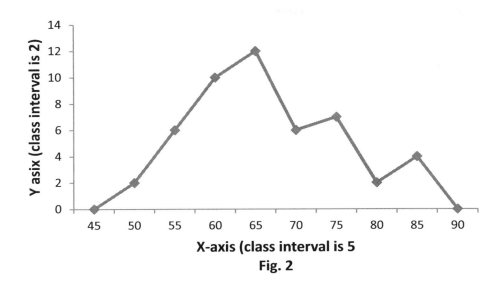

X-axis (class interval is 5

Fig. 2

Steps in drawing frequency polygon are:

a. First we take the first group having 45-50 kg. This group is having frequencies. We need to take mid point of this group (i.e., 47.50). So, place a point corresponding to 47.50 on X-axis and 2 on Y-axis.

b. The same way, mid point of next group (50-55) is 52.5. This group is having 7 frequencies. So, we place a point corresponding to 52.5 on X-axis and 7 on Y-axis (as shown in diagram).

c. The same way all frequencies are marked on the corresponding mid points of the groups.

d. Then with a ruler we connect these points with straight lines.

e. Rather than leaving the graph suspended in space, we assume that there is another interval above and below which is having frequency of zero (O). So the mid points of group 40-45 and 85-90 (i.e., 42.5 and 87.5) are assumed having frequency of zero. The group is now allowed to meet X-axis on both ends.

Advantages of frequency polygon

1. It is very easy to construct and very easy to interpret.
2. It is useful in portraying more than two distributions on the same graph paper with different colors. So, It is very useful to compare two or more than two distributions.

Example: Weights of school children in Indian School and British school

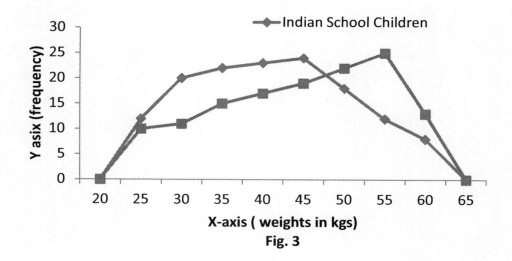

Fig. 3

LINE CHART OR LINE DIAGRAM

This is a frequency polygon presenting variation by line. In frequency polygon, the two ends of the graph are allowed to touch X-axis. Here it is not so.

It shows the trend of an event occurring over a period of time (rising, falling, and stationary) such as prevalence of TB, leprosy cases, AIDS cases, population trends etc.

The class interval may be a month, a year or 5 years. Here there is no rule that both X-axis and Y-axis should start from zero and the graph is not needed to touch X-axis.

Example: Line diagram showing frequency of some diseases:

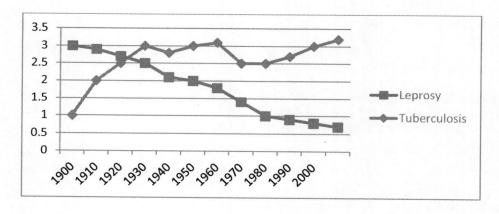

Fig. 4

164

FREQUENCY CURVE

When the number of observations are very large and groups are more (i.e., small class intervals) the frequency polygon tends to lose its angulations and it forms a smooth curve known as frequency curve (or normal curve).

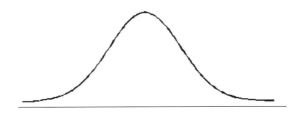

Fig. 5. Normal Curve

Such curves will follow normal distribution of individuals in large samples.

Example:

Weight of children

Height of students

Pulse rate etc.

CUMULATIVE FREQUENCY DIAGRAM (OGIVE)

In setting up the cumulative frequency or cumulative percentage, we follow the general rules of building graphs. So, the cumulative frequency is always placed on Y-axis (vertical-axis). The values on Y-axis will range between 0-100 in case of cumulative percentages.

Here (not like frequency polygon) we place the plotting points on the upper limits of each of intervals.

CONSTRUCTION OF OGIVE:

Ogive is a graph of the cumulative relative frequency distribution. So, to draw Ogive we should convert ordinary frequency distribution into relative cumulative frequency.

Here cumulative frequency means "Total number of persons in each particular range from lowest value to that particular value". It is obtained by cumulating the frequency of previous classes including the class in question.

Example: Construct cumulative frequency diagram for the following data.

Table 7.

Ht in cm	Frequency of each group	Cumulative class frequency
175-180	40	200
170-175	50	160
165-170	60	110
1600-165	30	50
155-160	16	20
150-155	04	4
	200	

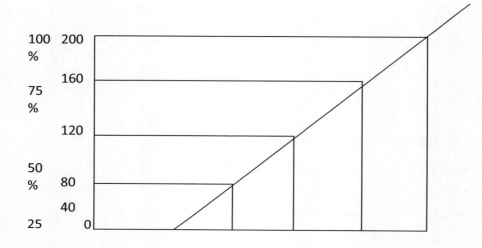

Now, the cumulative frequencies are plotted corresponding to the group limits of the characteristics. On joining the points by a smooth free hand curve, the diagram made is called "Ogive".

Applications of ogive

a. By using ogive we can locate any percentile that will divide the series into two parts.

b. **Quartiles:** There are three different points located on the entire range of variable (here it is height in cm). These are Q1, Q2, Q3.

Q1 or lower quartile will have 25% observations falling in its left and 75% observatinos on its right side.

Q2 is the median, i.e., 50% values lie on either side.

166

Q3 is the upper quartile, will have 75% observations falling on its left side and 25% observations on its right side.

By using these quartiles we can calculate semi inter quartile range and interquartile range (Q3-Q1).

c. **Quintiles:** Four in number. Divide the distribution into 5 equal parts. So, 20th percentile or 1st quintile will have 20% observations falling to its left and 80% to its right.

d. **Deciles:** Nin in number. Divide the distribution into 10 equal parts. First decile (10th percentile) will have 10% values to its left and 90% values to decile its right. 5th decile is the median, contains 50% values on either side.

Uses:

a. Location of a percentile that divides the frequency distribution into two parts.
b. Preparation of standards, such as 1st quartile Q1, (25% values) median or second quartile (50% values) etc.
c. Comparison of one percentile values of a variable of one sample with that of another sample, drawn from same population or different population.
d. To study growth in children
e. As a measure of dispersion (interquartile range and semi interquartile range) also it is sometimes useful.

BAR DIAGRAM:

Bar charts are a popular media of presenting statistical data because they are easy to prepare and understand (which indicates the frequency of a character). Spacing between any two bars should be more than half of the width of the bar.

There are three types of Bars:

      a. Simple bar diagram
      b. Multiple bar chart or compound bar
      c. Compound bar

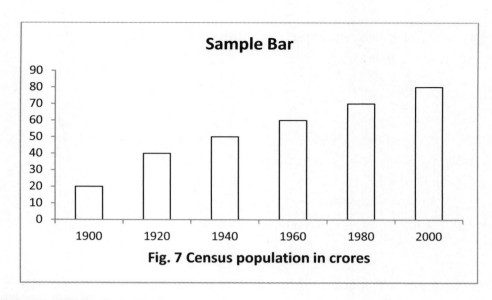

Fig. 7 Census population in crores

PIE DIGRAM (SECTOR DIAGRAM)

This is another way of presenting discrete data qualitative in nature.

Example: Blood grouping, Age groups, social groups in population, causes of mortality and morbidity etc. The frequencies of the groups are showing in a circle. Degrees of angle denoted the frequency and the area of sector.

Total area of the pie diagram should be 100%. So, size of each angle is calculated by multiplying the class percentage with 3.6 (i.e., 360/100 = 3.6).

So, the formula is:

$$\frac{Class\ frequency}{Total\ observation}\ x\ 360$$

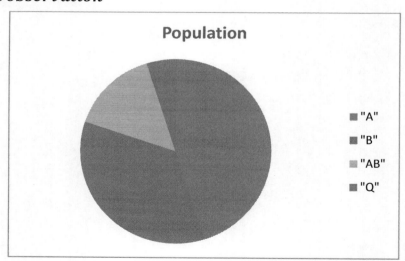

Fig. Blood groups of 100 students shown in pie diagram

It is often necessary to indicate the percentages in the segment. Most statisticians believe that it is not superior to component bar diagram.

PICTOGRAM

A pictogram, also called a pictograph, or simply picto, and in computer usage an icon, is an ideogram that conveys its meaning through its pictorial resemblance to a physical object

This is the popular method of presenting data to illiterate people (that is those who cannot understand the orthodox charts).

Example: Health status of different countries as per doctors available per 1000 Population of the countries of the world.

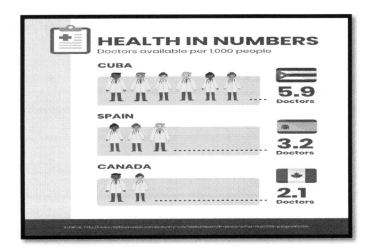

SCATTER DIAGRAM OR DOT DIAGRAM

It is a graphic presentation of data. It is used to show the nature of correlation between two variables (Character X & Y), in the same persons or groups (such as height and weight up to 20 years of age). So, it is also called correlation diagram.

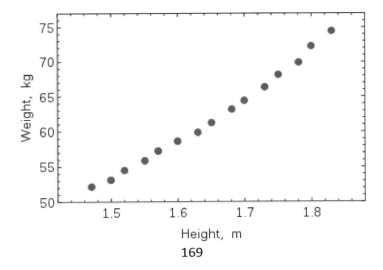

MAP DIAGRAM OR SPORT MAP

These maps are prepared to show geographic distribution of frequencies such as IMR, MMR, etc.

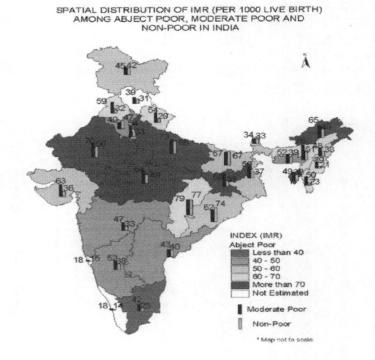

SPATIAL DISTRIBUTION OF IMR (PER 1000 LIVE BIRTH) AMONG ABJECT POOR, MODERATE POOR AND NON-POOR IN INDIA

Exercises

I. Weights of 50 medical students is given, Tabulate the data in appropriate class intervals using tally mark system (wt are given in kg) 51, 53, 52, 39, 58, 48, 45, 62, 66, 67, 42, 48, 43, 44, 45, 45, 52, 54, 50, 49, 38, 38, 39, 32, 34, 36, 33, 34, 36, 38, 42, 43, 48, 49, 50, 51, 52, 30, 30, 31, 32, 45, 45, 47, 46, 48, 49, 58.

Present these data in the forms of histogram, frequency polygon

II. Population of different countries are given, Draw a bar diagram.

a.	India	100 crores
b.	China	132 crores
c.	Indonesia	21 crores
d.	USA	28 crores
e.	Pakistan	15 crores
f.	Sri Lanka	1.8 crores

III. Prepare pie diagram for the following data

Type of leprosy	No of cases
Lepromatous leprosy	50
Border line lepromatous	42

Border line	34
Border line tubercoloid	28
Tuberculoid type	39
Indeterminate type	29

CHAPTOR ---

AVERAGES

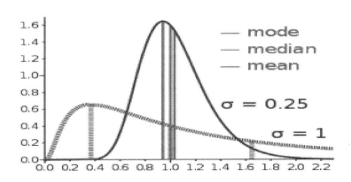

AVERAGES

The word average implies 'a value in the distribution around which the other values are distributed'. It gives a mental picture of central value.

Usually three averages are considered. These are Mean, Median and Mode. Of these three measures of central tendency the mean is the most commonly used one. It is the one that is basic to many other statistical calculations.

1. Arithmetic Mean: It is the another term for 'arithmetic average'.

Definition: "Mean is the sum of scores divided by the number of cases" (i.e., individual observations are first added together and then divided by number of observations).

$$\text{Mean or } (\bar{X}) = \frac{\sum X}{N} = \frac{\textbf{Summation of individual values}}{\textbf{Numer of observations}}$$

Example: Incubation period of 7 polio cases are 8, 6, 5, 8, 6,4, and 5. Calculate mean of these values

$$\text{Mean } = \frac{8+6+5+8+6+4+5}{7} = \frac{42}{7} \qquad \textbf{6}$$

So, Mean is 6

CALCULATION OF MEAN FOR GROUPED DATA

When number of observations is large, first the scores are entered into a frequency distribution table. Later the mean is calculated from the grouped data.

In this method, we use an 'arbitrary reference point ('x') to calculate mean.

STEPS:
Frequency distribution table is set up

We take the midpoint of one of the intervals as the 'arbitrary reference point' (we can take any interval mid-point as arbitrary reference pint, it does not make any difference). Here we have taken the mid-point of interval (50-54) which is 52 as the arbitrary reference e point.

Second column is set up. This column is labeled **(x)** and can be read as deviations from the 'Arbitrary reference point'.

Since we have taken arbitrary reference as 52 (i.e., interval of 50-54) opposite this group we place 'zero' **(0).** The interval of 55-59 deviates one interval from the arbitrary reference point and one is entered for this interval in column 2. This is continued upwards until each interval has a value.

Since we have taken arbitrary reference point as 52 (i.e., interval of 50-54) opposite this group we place zero we place 'zero' (0). The interval of 55-59 deviates one interval from the arbitrary reference point and one is entered for this interval in column 2. This is continued upwards until each interval has a value.

We do the same thing for intervals below the reference point also. But, here we place minus (-) sign in front of each of our deviations.

COMPUTATION OF MEAN FOR GROUPED DATA:

Weight in kg	1 Frequency (f)	2 X'	3 ƒX'
65-69	6	3	18
60-64	5	2	10
55-59	10	1	10
50-54	8	0	0
45-49	9	-1	-9
40-44	8	-2	-16
35-39	7	-3	-21
	53		-8
	N		Σ fX'

Now, we multiply each f (frequency) by x' (deviation from arbitrary reference point) and enter the product fx' in 3rd column.

Sum of this column gives $\sum fx'$

Now the mean is computed by suing this formula: $\overline{X} = M' + \frac{\sum fx'}{N}$ **(i)**

Here:

M'	= Arbitrary reference point (52)
i	= The size of the class interval (5)
$\sum$	= Summation
f	= Frequency
x'	= Deviation from arbitrary reference point
N	= Number of Values

We have already calculated $\sum fx' = (-8)$

So, $\overline{X} = 52.5 + \frac{-8}{53}$ **(5)**

= 52.5 − 0.7555

= 51.745

Now we work out the problem again by selecting the mid-point of another interval as 'arbitrary reference point'. Now, it is 37, the mid-point of 35-39.

Table 8

Weight in kg	Frequency (f)	X'	f X'
65-69	6	6	36
60-64	5	5	25
55-59	10	4	40
50-54	8	3	24
45-49	9	2	18
40-44	8	1	8
35-39	7	0	0
	53		151
N			$\sum$ fX'

$$\overline{X} = M' + \frac{\sum fx'}{N} \times i$$

$$= 37.5 + \frac{151}{53} (5)$$
$$= 37.5 + 14.245$$
$$= 51.745$$

STEPS:

a. We begin by selecting mid-point of the bottom interval as our reference point and place '0' for this interval for the x' column. The next interval is given a value of 1 and this is continued up to the top interval, which receive a value of 6.

b. The f x' value is computed for each interval

c. Then f x' values are summed. We get $\sum$f x' (151)

d. Mean is calculated by using the above formula. Answer is 51.245 (which is same as previous value).

So, if we used any group'smid-point as arbitrary reference point, we get the same answer.

If we start from bottom interval or from upper interval we get $\sum$f x' large values. If we start from middle interval $\sum$f x' will be small value and convenient to calculate.

AVERAGING MEANS

Sometimes we are given the means of two or more samples. We wish to find the mean of all measure combined into one group, i.e., grand mean (or mean of means). This is also called weighted mean.

Example:

Average ESR values of 10 patients is 60/hour

Average ESR value of another 60 patients is 50/hour

Average ESR values of another 30 patients is 40/hour.

Calculate average ESR value of all patients (i.e., 100 patients).

Answer:

We wish to find out the weighted means ($\bar{X}$) of three groups combined.

STEPS ARE:

a. Calculate weights contributed by each group

Table 9

N	ESR Value	Weights of each group
10	60	600
60	50	3000
30	40	1200
100		4800

b. Summation of these three gives total value of the three groups.

174

c. Calculate the weighted mean, ie., $\frac{4800}{100}$ = 48/hour

Example 2: Calculation of weighted mean of the grouped data (another method) weights of 53 students was given as grouped data. Calculate mean (using the same values as in Table 8)

Table 10

Weights in Kgs	f ((frequency)	Xg (mid point of each group)	fXg (weights contributed by each group)
65-69	6	67	402
60-64	5	62	310
55-59	10	57	570
50-54	9	52	416
45-49	9	47	423
40-44	8	42	336
35-39	7	37	259
N = 53			∑f Xg = 2716

Formula = $\frac{\sum f\, Xg}{N}$ = $\frac{2716}{53}$ = 51.245

Effect of adding a constant to or subtracting constant to each measure in a distribution:

When we want to calculate mean from large size observations without using calculator, the following is useful:

'If we add or subtract a constant to each measurement in a distribution (called coding) after doing calculation and decoding, the basic result does not change".

Example 1: Calculate the mean of the following data:

750, 710, 680, 660, 620, 580, 540.

Here coding means subtracting 500 from each measurement and decoding means adding 500 to the mean (we get) of coded data.

Table 11

X	X-500
750	250
710	210
680	180
660	160

620	120
580	080
540	040
$\sum x = 4540$	$1040 = \sum(x - 500)$

$$\bar{X} = \frac{4540}{7} = 648.6 \ (i)$$

$$\bar{X} - 500 = \frac{1040}{7} = 148.6 \ (ii)$$

$\bar{X} = 148.60 + 500$

$\bar{X} = 648.6$

Example 2: Calculate Mean for the following data.

0.5. 1.5, 2.5, 2.5, 1.5, 0.5

X	X-500
0.5	1
1.5	2
2.5	3
2.5	3
1.5	2
0.5	1
9.0	$12 = \sum(x - 0.5)$

Mean = $\frac{12}{6}$ = **2.0**

Decoding: 2 − 0.5 = 1.5, so mean is 1.5

Example 3: Calculate mean of the following data

(-320, -250, -350, -280, -300, -260, -320)

Table 13

X	X-500
-320	30
-250	100
-350	0

176

-280	70
-300	50
-260	90
-320	30
-2080	**370 = ∑(x +350)**

∑x = - 2080

$$\bar{X} = \frac{-2080}{7} = -297.14$$

$$\bar{X} + 350 = \frac{370}{7} = -52.857$$

$$= 52.857 - 350 \qquad \bar{X} \qquad = -297.14$$

MEDIAN

Definition: Median is defined as the point in a distribution with an equal number of cases on either side of it, ie., the individual measures can be arranged from low to higher value, the middle observation is 'median'.

If there are two observations in the middle both should be added together and divided by 2 to get median.

Example 1:
Calculate the median for the following data.
7, 8, 4, 5, 6, 3, 10, 8, 5. Arranging ascending order
3, 4, 5, 5, 6, 7, 8, 8, 10

Here there are 9 values; middle one is the 5thvalue, that is 6. So median is 6.

Example 2: Calculate median for the following data
6, 7, 8, 10, 1, 1, 3, 2, 1, 8, 8 arranging the ascending order
1, 2, 3, 6, 7, 8, 8, 8, 10, 11

Here there are 10 values. In the middle we are having 2 values, i.e., 5th and 6th values. So, we add 5th value (is 7) and 6th value (is 8)

177

Then divide by 2 to get median.

As, $\frac{7+8}{2}$ = **7**

So median is 7.5

COMPUTATION OF MEDIAN FOR GROUPED DATA:
Example 1: Calculate the median for the following grouped data.
Table 14

Weight in kg	F
80-84	1
75-79	2
70-74	4
65-69	4
60-65	5
55-59	10
50-54	8
45-49	8
	42

By definition median means mid-point of the distribution.

Here N = 42; So, the median is $\frac{42}{2}$ = **21.**

Now, we have to locate the place of 21 in this grouped data. We start by counting up from the bottom unit, we come as close to 21 cases as possible. This brings up to the point at the top of the interval 50-54. This point being 54.5.

There are 16 cases below this point. So, we need another 5 cases. In the next interval (i.e., 55-59) there are 10 cases. In this we need 5 cases (to get 21).

So, it is:
$$\frac{5}{10}$$

Here the class interval is 5. Now we need to multiply the distance in the length of interval, which is in this case 5. So, It will be

$$\frac{5}{10} \: x \: 5 = 2.5$$

So, the mean is 54.5 (middle value of 54 and 55) + 2.5 = 54.5 + 2.5 = 57

B. We can also calculate the median from above. But, we have to minus it. We start by counting down from above unit we come as close to 21 as possible.

This brings to the point below the interval 60-64.This point being 59.5. We have 16 cases up to that interval. So, we need another 5 cases from the group of 55-59 which is having 10 cases.

Here the class interval is 5.

So, it will be $\frac{5}{10}$ x 5 = 2.5

So, Median is 59.5 – 2. 5 = 57

MODE

Definition: Most frequency occurring observation is a series.
Example: Calculate Mode of the following values:
6 , 7, 8, 10, 12, 3, 2, 1, 8, 8. Arranging in ascending order:
1, 2, 3, 6, 7, 8, 8, 8, 10, 11
Frequently occurring value is 8. So, Mode is 8.
Calculation of mode for grouped data
Formula is

$$Mo = I_1 + \frac{f_0}{f_o + f_2} \: x \: i$$

Where
I_1 = Lower limit of modal class (55-59) i.e., 55
f_1 = Frequency of mid class ie 10
F_0 = Frequency before the modal class i.e., 8.
F_2 = Frequency after modal class ie 5

"Modal class means the class interval having highest frequency (value)
We will apply the formula given in the table (page 35)

Mode = $55 + \dfrac{8}{8+5}$ **(5)**

= 55 + 3.08

= 58.08

Mode is 58.08

Advantages and Disadvantages of Mean, Median and Mode

Mean

Advantages:

It is easy to calculate and understand.

It is most commonly used in statistics.

Disadvantages:

It may be unduly influenced by an abnormal value in the distribution.

Example: Calculate the mean for the following data:

1, 5, 6, 3, 4, 5, 4, 35

Mean = $\dfrac{68}{8}$ = 7.87

If we delete the abnormal value 35, the mean is $\dfrac{28}{7}$ = 4

That is more appropriate

Median
Advantages:
Median is not influenced by abnormal value from the above date.

1, 3, 4, 4, 5, 5, 6, 35

Median is $\dfrac{4+5}{2}$ = 4.5

Here the median is not influenced by abnormal value.

Mode
Advantages:

Easy to understand

Not affected by abnormal value.

Disadvantages:

It is often not clearly defined.

Most of the time, two or more modes may present. In the above statistics there are two modes. So, it is called 'Bi-modal' distribution.

MEASURES OF DISPERSION

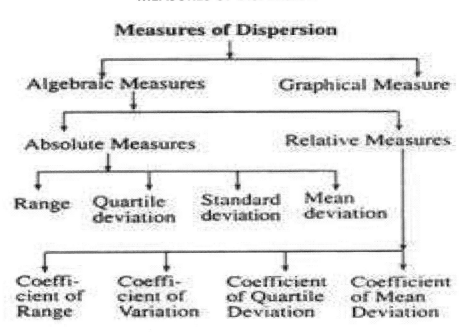

In statistics, dispersion (also called variability, scatter, or spread) is the extent to which a distribution is stretched or squeezed. Dispersion is contrasted with location or central tendency, and together they are the most used properties of distributions.

Dispersion is defined as the breaking up or scattering of something. An example of dispersion is throwing little pieces of paper all over a floor. Another example of dispersion is the colour rays of light coming from a prism which has been hung in a sunny window.

Common examples of measures of statistical dispersion include:

variance, standard deviation, and interquartile range.

A measure of statistical dispersion is a nonnegative real number that is zero if all the data are the same and increases as the data become more diverse.

Most measures of dispersion have the same <u>units</u> as the <u>quantity</u> being measured. In other words, if the measurements are in metres or seconds, so is the measure of dispersion.

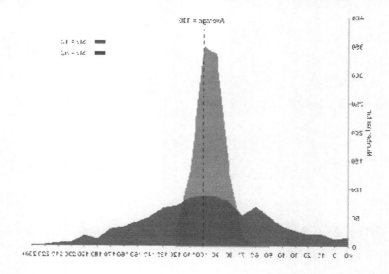

Example of samples from two populations with the same mean, but different dispersion

The blue population is much more dispersed than the red population.

Example

Suppose we have two distributions of scores, each with a mean of 50.

1) 5, 10, 30, 50, 70, 90, 95,

2) 40, 42, 45, 50, 55, 58, 60

In the first distribution the scores are dispersed highly, i.e., from 5 to 95 (range is 95 − 5 = 90).

In the second distribution the scores dispersed minimum, i.e., 40 - 60 (range is 60 - 40 = 20).

Thus, to give a better picture of a distribution we need both a measure of central tendency and measure of variability or dispersion.

Here we will discuss about measure of variability of individual observation.

    a. Range

    b. Mean deviation or average deviation

    c. Standard deviation

    d. Quartile deviation (Semi-inter quartile range)

RANGE

Range is defined as 'difference between highest and lowest figures in a given sample plus one'. It is the simplest measure of dispersion. It is the unstable measure of dispersion, when compared to other three.

CALCULATION OF RANGE

Example:

1. Diastolic blood pressure of patients is given. Calculate range.

   86, 76, 80, 70, 90, 96, 94, 84, 98, 72

Firstly, we will arrange the data in ascending order as following-

70, 72, 76, 80, 84, 86, 90, 94, 96, 98

So, range is 98 to 70 or (98-70 =28)

2. If we have grouped data to calculate range the difference between mid-points of extreme groups minus mid points of low group.

For example: Table 15

Weight in kg	f
5-9	4
10-14	6
15-19	5
20-24	7

So, here the range is 7 kg (5-9) to 22 kg (20-24) or 15 kg.

Range is not of much practical importance because it indicates only the extreme values and nothing about the dispersion of values between these two extreme values.

Some other examples of Range:

Normal Range	
1. Systolic blood pressure	110-140 mm Hg
2. Diastolic blood pressure	80-90 mm Hg
3. Blood urea	15-40 mg/dL
4. Fasting blood sugar	80-120 mg/dL

MEAN DEVIATION OR AVERAGE DEVIATION

The average absolute deviation of a data set is the average of the absolute deviations from a central point. It is a summary statistic of statistical dispersion or variability. In this general form, the central point can be the mean, median, mode, or the result of another measure of central tendency.

It can be defined as 'the average of deviation from the arithmetic mean'. It is not a commonly used statistic. It was replaced by standard deviation, which is the commonly used one.

Formula = M.D. = $\sum$ (X- $\bar{X}$)

X = Raw Score

$\bar{X}$ = Mean

$\sum$ = Summation or add

N = Number of observations

Example: Calculate mean deviation of the following data.

10, 12, 8, 10, 6, 4, 8, 10,

Table 16

X	$\bar{X}$	X- $\bar{X}$
10	8.5	1.5
12	8.5	3.5
8	8.5	-0.5
10	8.5	1.5
6	8.5	-2.5
4	8.5	-4.5
8	8.5	-0.5
10	8.5	1.5
		$\sum(x - \bar{x} = 16)$

$$\bar{x} = \frac{68}{8} = 8.5$$

So, M.D. = $\frac{\sum(x-\bar{x})}{N}$ $= \frac{16}{8} = 2$

It should be noted that in any distribution, the sum of these deviations from the mean is equal to 'Zero' (0). So in calculation of mean deviation we should ignore the sign of deviation and add.

STANDARD DEVIATION (SD)

In statistics, the standard deviation (SD, also represented by the lower case Greek letter sigma σ or the Latin letter s) is a measure that is used to quantify the amount of variation or dispersion of a set of data values. A low standard deviation indicates that the data points tend to be close to the mean (also called the expected value) of the set, while a high standard deviation indicates that the data points are spread out over a wider range of values.

The standard deviation of a random variable, statistical population, data set, or probability distribution is the square root of its variance. It is algebraically simpler, though in practice less robust, than the average absolute deviation. A useful property of the standard deviation is that, unlike the variance, it is expressed in the same units as the data.

In addition to expressing the variability of a population, the standard deviation is commonly used to measure confidence in statistical conclusions. For example, the margin of error in polling data is determined by calculating the expected standard deviation in the results if the same poll were to be conducted multiple times. This derivation of a standard deviation is often called the "standard error" of the estimate or "standard error of the mean" when referring to a mean. It is computed as the standard deviation of all the means that would be computed from that population if an infinite number of samples were drawn and a mean for each sample were computed.

It is very important to note that the standard deviation of a population and the standard error of a statistic derived from that population (such as the mean) are quite different but related (related by the inverse of the square root of the number of observations). The reported margin of error of a poll is computed from the standard error of the mean (or alternatively from the product of the standard deviation of the population and the inverse of the square root of the sample size, which is the same thing) and is typically about twice the standard deviation—the half-width of a 95 percent confidence interval.

Of all the measures of dispersion the standard deviation is the most commonly used one. So, many other statistical operations need the calculation of standard deviation. Here we study how to calculate S.D for both ungrouped data and group data.

Calculation of SD for ungrouped data

Example: Incubation period of 10 measles cases is given below.

Calculate SD of following data as: 6, 7, 5, 4, 3, 4, 5, 6, 7, 8

Steps

1. Compute mean ($\bar{X}$).
2. Take the deviation of each value from mean (X- $\bar{X}$)
3. Then square each deviation (X- $\bar{X}$)^2
4. Add all these squared deviation $\sum$(X- $\bar{X}$)^2
5. Divide the result by number of observation $\frac{\sum(X-\bar{X})2}{N}$. if the sample size is less than 30, divide it by N- 1.
6. Then take the square root of it, which gives SD.

$$\frac{\sqrt{\sum (x-\bar{x})^2}}{N-1}$$

Table 17

X	$\bar{X}$	(X- $\bar{X}$)	(X- $\bar{X}$)^2
6	5.5	0.5	0.25
7	5.5	1.5	2.25
5	5.5	-0.5	0.25
4	5.5	-1.5	2.25
3	5.5	-2.5	6.25
4	5.5	-1.5	2.25
5	5.5	-0.5	0.25
6	5.5	0.5	0.25
7	5.5	1.5	2.25
8	5.5	2.5	6.25

$\sum$ = 55	$\sum$ (X-$\bar{X}$)^2 = 22.50

$$\bar{X} = \frac{55}{10} = 5.5$$

$$S.D. = \frac{\sqrt{22.5}}{10-1} = \sqrt{2.5} = 1.58$$

So, S.D = 1.58

Another method of calculating S.D by using Raw Score Formula:

Formula:

$$S.D. = \frac{\sqrt{\sum x^2 - \frac{(\sum x)^2}{N}}}{N-1}$$

So, Here we need to calculate X^2 (table 18)

Now we substitute these values into formula

X	X^2
6	36
7	49
5	25
4	16
3	9
4	16
5	25
6	36
7	49

$$= \frac{\sqrt{325 - \frac{(55)^2}{10}}}{10-1}$$

$$= \frac{\sqrt{325 - 302.5}}{9}$$

$$= \sqrt{2.5}$$

= 1.58

So, SD = 1.58

$\sum X = 55 \qquad \sum X^2 = 325$

CALCULATION OF STANDARD DEVIATION FROM GROUPED DATA

Here the beginning steps are the same as those in calculating the mean from grouped data.

Steps are:

1. Frequency distribution table is set up.
2. We will take the midpoint of the one of the intervals as the 'arbitrary reference piont'.
3. A second column is set up. This column is labeled as x' we should place zero (0), opposite to the interval, which we have taken as 'arbitrary reference point'.
   Give vallues like 1, 2, 3, 4, 5, from zero to upwards and -1, -2, -3, -4, -5 from zeom to downwards in the second column.
4. We get 3rd column by multiplying f with x' (fx').
5. We get 4rd column by multiplying f x' with x' which gives f x'^2
6. Now, we sum the various columns.
7. Calculate SD by using the formula given below.

Formula:

$$\frac{\sqrt{(\sum fx'^2 - \frac{[(\sum fx')^2]i^2}{N}}}{N}$$

Example: we take the same data used in **Table 8.**

Weight In kg	1 Frequency (f)	2 X'	3 f x'	4 f x'^2
65-69	6	3	18	54
60-64	5	2	10	20
55-59	10	1	10	10
50-54	8	0	0	0
45-49	9	-1	-9	9
40-44	8	-2	-16	32
35-39	7	-3	-21	63
	$\sum f = 53$	-8		188

	N		$\sum fx'$
$\sum fx'^2$			

188

```
                    5th column

                    f (x¹+1)²

                  6 x 16 = 96

                   5 x 9 = 45

                  10 x 4 = 40

                   8 x 1 = 8

                   9 x 0 = 0

                   8 x 1 = 8

                   7 x 4 = 28
         _____

                      225
         _____

                   ∑f (X' + 1)²
         _____
```

By substituting in the formula

$$= \frac{\sqrt{[(188 - \frac{(-8 \times -8)}{53}] 5^2}}{53}$$

$$= \frac{\sqrt{(188 - 1.2075)(25)}}{53}$$

$$= \frac{\sqrt{4669.81}}{53}$$

$$= \sqrt{88}$$

= SD = 9.39

PROBABILITY AND BINOMIAL DISTRIBUTION

To understand statistics, it is important to understand what is probability?, Laws of probability etc.

Probability can be defined as **"The relative frequency (or probable chances) of occurrence of an event"**

It denotes the odds with which an event is expected to occur. Probability enters into much of our daily living.

By using the principles of Probability we are forecasting weather, prognosis of a disease, chances of Recovery of a patient from a particular disease etc.

Probability values range from 0-1. Here the value of 1 stands for absolute certainty and zero indicates that there is no chance at all that the event can occur.

FOR EXAMPLE:

Example for absolute certainty is 'Death'. That is, everyone will die on some day or other. On the other hand, probability '0' is chance of survival after rabies.

In case of delivery, probability of having a male child is 0.5 and female child is 0.5 in every instance total probability will be one.

We use symbol p for the probability of an event occurring. Symbol 'q' for the event not occurring. The sum of p + q is always equal to one.

Example, if we toss a coin the chances of having head is 0.5(1/2). i.e. p and not having head (i.e., tail) is 0.5 = q. Here also the sum of p and q is one.

Like this, if we will take a dice (having 6 faces) and throw it into the air.Because it is having 6 faces, probability of any single side (6-spot) coming up is 1/6 or 0.167. There are five chances (5/6) not having 6-spot upper side. So, in this case:

$$p = \frac{1}{6} \text{ and } q = \frac{5}{6}$$

Again p + q = 1

LAWS OF PROBABILITY:

There are four laws of probability. They are:

1. Addition law of probability
2. Multiplication law of probability
3. Binomial law of probability
4. Probability from shape of normal curve

1st Law: The probability of occurrence of any two (or more) mutually exclusive events is equal to sum of their separate probabilities

Example: If we toss a coin, getting head excludes the possibility of getting tail. Same way birth of male child excludes birth of female child. We take a dice and throw it into the air, having any single side up (6-spot) will exclude the probability of having other five sides.

Thus, mutually exclusive events follow the addition law of probability.

2nd Law: The probability of the simultaneous or successive occurrence of two or more independent events is equal to the product of their separate probabilities.

Example:
Probability of having 3 male children successively is:

$$\frac{1}{2} \times \frac{1}{2} \times \frac{1}{2} = \frac{1}{8}$$

Probability of 6-spot coming up successively four times is:

$$\frac{1}{6} \times \frac{1}{6} \times \frac{1}{6} \times \frac{1}{6} = \frac{1}{1296}$$

So, here, multiplication law of probability is applied.

3rd Law: Binomial law of probability is applied to two mutually exclusive events. If we toss a coin twice successively we get four possible results. These are:

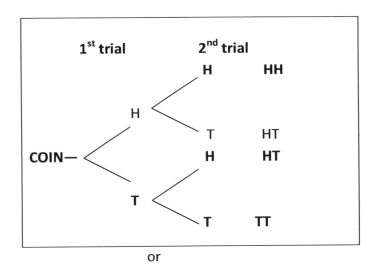

or

191

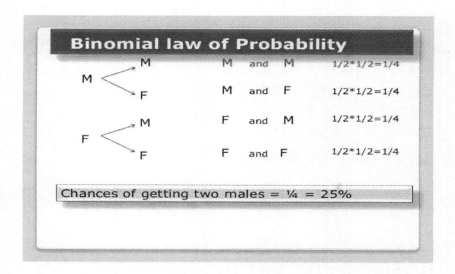

So, we have ¼ chances to get both heads and ¼ chances to get both tails. Probability of getting one tail and one head is ¼ + ¼ = ½

Here also, the sum of all these probabilities is one.

So, here binomial law is applied.

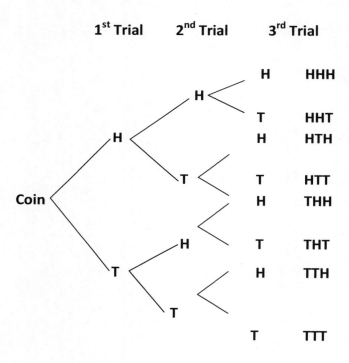

So, finally there are four possibilities. Possibility of having all heads is 1/8, all tails is 1/8, two heads and one tail is 3/8, two tails and one head is 3/8.

The sum of all these probabilities is again,

i.e., $\dfrac{1}{8} + \dfrac{3}{8} + \dfrac{3}{8} + \dfrac{1}{8} = 1$

The same can be applied to expectation of the sex of the child, who is going to be born.

So, the probability of getting 2 male children successively is ¼ and 2 female children successively is ¼ and getting one male child and one female child is ½ (1/4+1/4).

So, here also, the sum is one: $(\dfrac{1}{4} + \dfrac{1}{2} + \dfrac{1}{4} = 1)$

Similarly if we want to see for 3 successive issues:

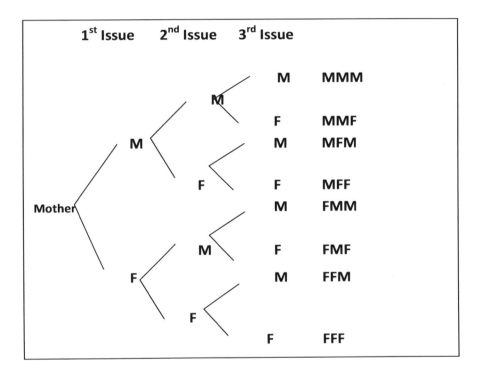

So, here there are four possibilities. Having all male children is 1/8, all female children is 1/8, one male and 2 female children is 3/8, one female and 2 male children is 3/8.

If number of issues increases (I want to have five children and want to know the possibilities) it is difficult to calculate. But, we can use binomial theorem for this purpose.

BINOMIAL THEORM

Pascal" s triangle is constructed depending on this binomial theorem

So, by using Pascal's triangle we can say that there are chances like this:

All male children (5) – 1/32

All female children (5) – 1/32

4 male children and one female child – 5/32

4 female children and one male child – 5/32

3 male children and 2 female children is 10/32

3 female children and 2 male children is 10/32

Again, the sum is one:

$$(\frac{1}{32} + \frac{5}{32} + \frac{10}{32} + \frac{10}{32} + \frac{5}{32} + \frac{1}{32} = 1)$$

PASCAL'S TRIANGLE

N	Binomial coefficient	Denominator of P

```
                          1
                      1       1
                  1       2       1
              1       3       3       1
          1       4       6       4       1
      1       5      10      10       5       1
  1       6      15      20      15       6       1
1     7      21      35      35      21       7       1
1   8    28     56     70     56     28     8     1
```

From the above triangle if we want to know the Binomial with 6 coins, we find that N = 6.

Column at the right gives denominator, i.e. 64.

The possibilities are given below:

All heads = $\frac{1}{64}$; All tails = $\frac{1}{64}$

5 heads and 1 tail = $\frac{6}{64}$; 5 tails and 1 head $\frac{6}{64}$

4 heads and 2 tail = $\frac{15}{64}$; 4 tail and 2 heads = $\frac{15}{64}$

194

3 heads and 3 tails = $\dfrac{20}{64}$

Now, we try to understand how Pascal's triangle is constructed. Here a triangle is drawn upon the table, where 5 and 10 at the top of small triangle are added and they produce 15, which is shown below.

The same we construct 6th row. Here, the first one is one. Second one is 1+5= 6, third one is 5+10 = 15; seventh one is 5+1 = 6. Last one is again 1.

It should be noted that the binomial distribution is symmetrical only when p = 0.5, and then it follows Pascal' triangle.

4th Principal: Probability from shape of normal curve.

BINOMIAL AND NORMAL DISTRIBUTION:

When p = 0.5 and N = 8 and we want to draw a histogram, there we see nine columns.   The height of each one is in proportion to its probability.

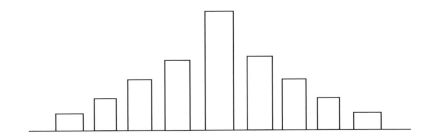

If we have very large number (say 100,000) the columns would be very narrow and this binomial distribution would then approximate the normal distribution. Actually, the Binomial distribution is always discontinuous. But, as the number of cases becomes large it gets closer to normal curve.

FORMULAS USED IN BINOMIAL DISTRIBUTION:

M = np

M = The mean of binomial distribution

P = probability of the event occurring

n = Number of objects involved.

Example:

195

n = 10 and p = 0.5; Calculation: Mean and S.D.

M = 10 (0.5) = 5

Formula for SD (σ) =$\sqrt{npq}$

So, SD = $\sqrt{10 X 0.5 X 0.5}$

= $\sqrt{2.5}$

=1.58

When the proportions are not 0.5 (i.e., 0.25 and 0.75) still we can apply this formula to find S.D. provided np or nq (whichever is smaller) is equal or greater than 5.

Example: N = 38, p = 0.25; q = 0.75 ; calculation S.D.

Here np = 38 x 0.25 = 9.5 (It is greater than 5, so we can calculate S.D.)

S.D = $\sqrt{npq}$

= $\sqrt{38 \ x \ 0.25 \ x \ 0.75}$

7.125

NULL HYPOTHESIS (H_O)

Null hypothesis means "There is no difference between the two samples". If any difference is observed this difference will be by "chance".

Application:

1. The null hypothesis is initially accepted and considered true for all analytical comparisons. So we start with the hypothesis that there is no difference between the two samples, the observed difference is due to chance. If the difference between the two samples is very high (i.e., significant difference) to disprove null hypothesis, we will accept alternate hypothesis (i.e., there is difference between two samples) (when no significant difference; that is accepting the null hypothesis does not necessarily mean the populations are identical).
2. The level of confidence for rejecting the Null Hypothesis is "arbitrary". One conventional cut-off for defining a significant difference is 5% (i.e., if the probability

that the difference is due to chance is 5%of less, then the null hypothesis is rejected).

3. Statistical testing using probability value evaluates only the Null Hypothesis and does not evaluate the accuracy of the proposed alternative hypothesis.

4. The probability value provides no information about the extent that two variables are associated or different.

5. Statistically significant differences may not be clinically important and clinically important differences may not be statistically significant.

6. Probability values are associated with sample size. If the study is large negligible, negligible differences may be associated with highly significant probability values, and if the study is small, strong associations may have insignificant probability values.

TESTING THE NULL HYPOTHESIS

To test Null hypothesis, we use either one-tailed test of two-tailed test (analytical test).

1. **ONE-TAILED TEST:**

   a) A one tailed test checks only one of the tails (the upper or lower tail) of the bell shaped normal distribution curve.

   b) A one-tailed test is used to test a Null Hypothesis for which the alternative hypothesis is assumed to be directional.

For example: In comparing the rates of cancer between a population exposed to a Known carcinogen and a control population, a one-tailed analytic test is useful. Here

   We know that exposure was not beneficial

2. **TWO- TAILED TEST:**

Two-tailed Test

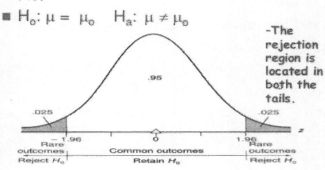

- The alternative hypothesis states that the population parameter may be either less than or greater than the value stated in Ho.

- $H_o: \mu = \mu_o$ $H_a: \mu \neq \mu_o$

-The rejection region is located in both the tails.

a) A two-tailed test checks both the upper and lower tails of the normal distribution Curve.

b) A two-tailed test is used to test a null hypothesis for which no as sumptions are mde concerning the lternative hypothesis .

c) Two-tailed tests are very useful in generating alternative hypothesis. So they are used most often than one-tailed test. Examples: In comparing the death rates of two neighbouring communities, a two-tailed analytical test to look for significant differences because no assumptions are made about the altermate hypothesis.

Calculation:

Null hypothesis (H_o) is $P_1 - P_2 = 0$

Alternative hypothesis (H_A) is $P_1 - P_0 \neq 0$

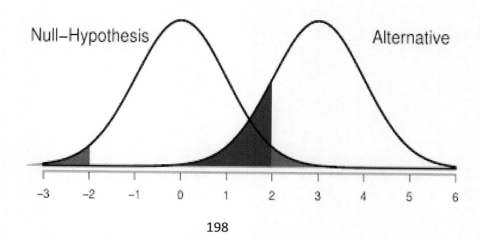

SAMPLING ERRORS:

Sampling errors are errors due to chance and concern incorrect rejection or acceptance of a null hypothesis.

The two types of sampling errors are:

Type I error or α error

Type II error or β error

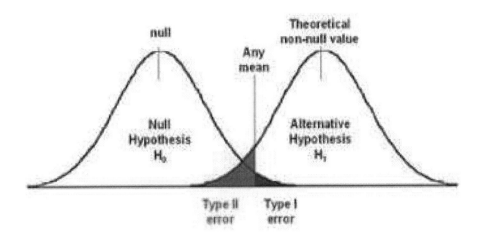

TYPE I ERROR:

DEFINITION: Type I error is also called an "error of the first kind" or α error. The rejection of null hypothesis that is actually true.

Applications and characteristics of type I error:

1. Statistical testing is based predominantly on error. In our studies of testing null hypothesis, we use an alpha error of 0.05 (5%) as the cut off for rejecting null hypothesis.
2. Sample size determination depends on the type I error and the type II error
   a) Prevalence of the problem under study
   b) Standard deviation
   c) The amount of difference to be detected
   d) The relative number of experimental to control subjects.
3. On studies designed to generate hypothesis, other values of the alpha error (α) may need to be considered.
4. Multiple comparison and repeated testing for significance increases the likelihood of a type I error.

a) When the null hypothesis is true, and n independent statistical tests are performed, the probability that at least one test will appear statistically significant is 1.0-(0.95)n. (when P <0.05)

b) In studies that test multiple hypotheses, more stringent (i.e., lower) values for α error or multi variate computerized methods can be used; but this assigns equal value to all alternative hypotheses. For example, in a study of Hb levels of students in different high schools, the error is defined as 5%. In this case, if the study is repeated 100 time the mean Hb level may appear significantly different for 5 (5% of 100) of the trials. For these trials the null hypothesis has been incorrectly rejected and type I error has been made.

TYPE II ERROR

DEFINITION: A type II error also called an "error of the second kind" or "ß error" is the acceptance of a null hypothesis as true when it actually is false. The type II error is inversely related to the type I error.

	Null hypothesis	
	False	**True**
Accept	Type II error or ß error	Correct decision
Reject	Correct decision	Type I error or α error

Our decision

	True difference	
	Present	**Absent**
Different	Correct decision	Type I error or α error
Not different	Type II or ß error	Correct decision

Our Conclusion

Applications and characteristics of type II error:

1. The type II error is used to determine the "power of a study".Which is equal to $1-\beta$.The power is the "probability that the study would reject a null hypothesis as false when it actually is false".

2. As the difference between a false null hypothesis and a true alternative hypothesis increase, the probability of accepting the null hypothesis (the β error) decreases and the power of the study increases.

3. As the sample size increases, the power of the study increases.

4. Power is most important when designing a study, in which the β error generally is at least double the α error. A power of 80% often is considered acceptable.

Example: In one study of school children the β error is defined as 20%. Therefore, the power of the study is 80%. If there is a difference between the Hb levels of the students, the probability of the study detecting the difference is 80% and of not detecting the difference is 20%

Chapter 14: INFERENTIAL STATISTICS

TESTS OF SIGNIFICANCE (Testing Hypothesis)

CHOOSING A SIGNIFICANT TEST:

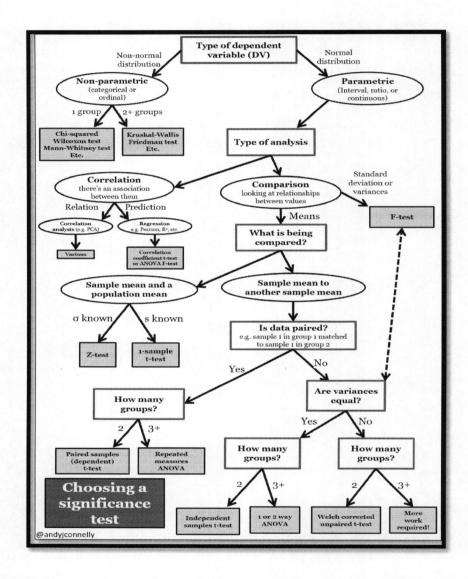

Hypothesis testing is an essential procedure in statistics. A hypothesis test evaluates two mutually exclusive statements about a population to determine which statement is best supported by the sample data. When we say that a finding is statistically significant, it's thanks to a hypothesis test.

In experiments and in statistical analysis we get some results, which are different from universe values. But we are in doubt whether the result occurred by chance or there is any significance of that result (i.e., Real difference).To find this, we will use some statistical tests. The tests used in testing our hypothesis are called 'tests of significance'. Here we use the hypothesis is called null hypothesis **(i.e., no difference between two samples).**

When we are taking about two samples from the same population, we would expect same results. This is called null hypothesis. If the difference appeared between these two samples, it may be due to chance or sampling error. It is allowed to certain extent; if the observed variation is more than chance variation our null hypothesis is proved wrong. Now we will accept the alternate hypothesis, i.e., there is difference between the two samples.

TESTS OF SIGNIFICANCE

There are two types of significance tests as:
1. Calculation of Standard error of mean (SE $\overline{X}$)
2. Standard error of difference between two means

Large sample (values more than 30)-Z test
Small sample (values less than 30)-t test

For application of these tests, the sample must meet the following criteria.
1. Samples should be selected randomly (Simple Random Sampling)
2. There should be homogeneity of variance in the two samples.

STANDARD ERROR OF MEAN (SE $\overline{X}$)

Suppose, there is a large population for study and we take samples from this population and study them. So we take large number of samples (say 6000), each sample having more than 30 individuals. Now, we calculate mean and standard deviation of each sample. So now we are having 6000 means and 6000 standard deviations. The distribution of these 6000 means is a good estimate of the parameter mean. The variability of this sampling distribution is measured by 'the standard error of mean'.
If the random samples are large enough and if there is large number of samples the mean of the samples means will equal the mean of the population and SD of these samples means will be equal to the SD of the population divided by square root N (number).

To calculation SE, find the mean (μ) of sample means (x) and then the difference of these individuals means from this grand mean (x - μ) is needed to be calculated

$(\overline{X}-\mu)$

Now, calculate SD of this series of mean

$$SD = \frac{\sqrt{(X-\mu)^2}}{N-1}$$

Because practically it is not possible to take large number of samples, we usually take one large sample and we calculate its S.D then we calculate S.E. of mean by using this formula:

$$SE\ \overline{X} = \frac{SD}{\sqrt{n}}$$

So, SE of mean is SD of the sample divided by the square root of the number of observations in the sample.

Sampling error or chance variation has to be minimized by taking large sample.

Application of SE:

To determine whether the sample is drawn from a known population or not, when its mean (μ) is known.

To work out the limits of desired confidence within which the population mean (μ) would lie.

For example: Diastolic blood pressures of 1200 doctors were taken. Mean diastolic Blood pressure was found to be 90 mm Hg and SD = 12 mm. Find 95% confidence limits of diastolic blood pressure of doctors (within which the doctors diastolic BP mean lies).

Here

$$SE = \frac{SD}{\sqrt{n}} = \frac{12}{\sqrt{1200}} = \frac{12}{34.64} = 0.35$$

So, mean diastolic BP + 2 SE = 90 + (2 X 0.35) = 90.70

Mean diastolic BP − 2 SE = 90 (2 X 0.35) = 89.30

Like this confidence limit of diastolic blood pressure of doctor population is 89.3 to 90.7 mm Hg. If mean diastolic BP of another doctor is 80 we can say he is not from the same group.

STANDARD ERROR OF DIFFERENCE BETWEEN MEANS OF LARGE SAMPLES (Z TEST)

If both the samples are taken from same population, their means will also be same. If there is a significant difference found, we may think some external factor is acting. So according to the null hypothesis, if the samples are drawn randomly and are of large size, their means should not differ from population mean or from means of each other.

If the observed difference between two means is greater than 2 times of standard error of difference (2 x standard error), it is significant at 5% level of significance. If the observed difference is greater than 3 standard error, it is real variability in more than 99.7% cases.Here ,it is due to chance in 0.3% cases only.

CALCULATIONS OF STANDARD ERROR OF DIFFERENCE BETWEEN TWO MEANS OF UN-CORRELATED DATA (Z test)

METHOD 1:

When population mean (μ) and population Standard Deviation (ó) are not known, but the samples are very large (I. e., more than 100),we can use this formula for calculation of **Standard Error of Difference**

$$SED = \frac{\sqrt{SD_1^2}}{N_1} + \frac{\sqrt{SD_2^2}}{N_2}$$

We will get SE of difference (SED)

Later Z = $\dfrac{\textbf{Obesrved differnce}}{\textbf{SED}}$

$$Z = \frac{\overline{x_1} - \overline{x_2}}{SED}$$

METHOD 2:

It is preferable to use this method if the sample size is between 30-100.

STEPS:

1.   First we calculate Standard deviation of each sample separately.

2.   Calculate standard Error of two samples separately by using this formula:

$$SE = \frac{SD}{\sqrt{N-1}}$$

3.   Next we calculate S.E. of difference (SED)

$$SE = \sqrt{SE_1^2 + SE_2^2}$$

4.   Next, we calculate Z value

$$Z = \frac{\textbf{Observed difference}}{\textbf{Standard error of difference}}$$

or $\dfrac{\overline{x_1} - \overline{x_2}}{SED}$

CALCULATION OF STANDARD ERROR OF DIFFERENCE BETWEEN MEANS ('t' Test):

Small Sample and Un–Corrected Data

CRITERIA FOR APPLYING 't' TEST:

1.   Random sample

2.   Quantitative data

3.   Variables are normally distributed

4.   Sample size is less than 30.

1st Method:

 STEPS INCLUDE:

1.   **FIRST CALCULATE COMBINED VARIANCE (OR S.D^2)**

$$SD^2 = \frac{\sum(x-\overline{x})^2 \ of \ group \ 1 + \sum(x-\overline{x})^2 \ of \ group \ 2}{N_1 + N_2 - 2}$$

because $(x-\overline{x})$ is equal to small x

$\sum(x - \overline{x})^2$, we can write as 'summation' of small x square, i.e.,$((\sum(x^2))$

So, above formula can be written as below.

$$SD^2 = \frac{\sum x_1^2 + \sum x_2^2}{N_1 + N_{2-2}} \quad SD = \frac{\sqrt{\sum x_1^2 + x_2^2}}{N_{1+} \ N_{2-2}}$$

2.   Second step is calculation of standard error of difference

$$SED = SD \frac{\sqrt{1}}{N_1} + \frac{\sqrt{1}}{N_2}$$

3.   Third step is calculation of t. The formula is:

$$\frac{\textbf{Observed difference}}{\textbf{SED}} = \frac{\overline{x}_1 - \overline{x}_2}{SED}$$

4. $Df = N_1 + N_2 - 2$

2nd Method or Direct Formula:

1st step is calculation of SED directly:

$$SED = \frac{\sqrt{\sum x_1^2 + \sum x_2^2}}{N_{1+N_{2-2}}} \left[\!\left[\frac{\sqrt{1}}{N_1} + \frac{\sqrt{1}}{N_2}\right]\!\right]$$

2nd step is calculation of 't'

$$t = \frac{\overline{x}_1 - \overline{x}_2}{SED}$$

STANDARD ERROR OF DIFFERENCE BETWEEN TWO MEANS:

Correlated Data (for this we can use both 't' test and 'z' test)

Example

Blood pressure Before Salt free diet	Blood Pressure after salt free diet	D	D^2
140	128	12	144
138	130	8	64
142	124	18	324
136	130	6	36
146	140	6	36
148	138	10	100
150	140	10	100
148	138	10	100
138	126	12	144
142	126	16	256
1428	1320	108	1301

STEPS:

1. Set up column No. 3 (Difference between values of column one and column two).Take one observation in column 2 and subtract it from the corresponding observation in column no 1. The same way all observations in column 2 are subtracted from corresponding observations of column 1 or we may subtract values of column 1 from column2. It makes no difference, which direction we subtract. But , once started, the direction should not change up to finishing.

2. Add the negative values and positive values separately. Then subtract the sum of negative values from the sum of positive values. Now, we get $\sum D$. Now, divide this sum by number of pairs' (10). So, now we get the mean difference (10.8).

3. Now square all the values in column 3 and enter these squares in column 4.

4. Now add all these squared difference in column 4. So Now we get $\sum D^2$ (1301).

5. We know that:

$$\sum x^2 = \sum X^2 - \frac{(\sum X)^2}{N}$$

The same way here also we get:

$$\sum d^2 = \sum D^2 - \frac{(\sum D)^2}{N}$$

$$= 1301 --- \frac{108 \times 108}{10} = 134.6$$

207

6. Next step is: To find SD of this difference.

We know that $SD = \dfrac{\sqrt{\sum X^2}}{N}$ and like this $SD = \dfrac{\sqrt{134.6}}{10} = 3.67$

7. Find S.E of difference. Formula is :

$$\dfrac{SD}{\sqrt{N-1}}$$

So, $\dfrac{3.67}{\sqrt{9}} = 1.22$

8. Find 't' value by following formula

$$t = \dfrac{\text{Observed Difference}}{SED}$$

$$= \dfrac{10.8}{1.22} = 8.85$$

9. Df = number of pairs – (minus)1 (one) = 10 – 1 = 9

It should be remembered that, we can use this same test for large samples also. Here we get Z values instead of 't' value.

For correlated data and large samples, we may use another formula, I .e.,

$$Z = \dfrac{\bar{X}_1 - \bar{X}_2}{\sqrt{SE_1^2 + SE_2^2 - 2(\gamma)(SE_1)(SE_2)}}$$

Here, (γ) = correlation coefficient of above two samples.

Examples:

You are given two samples. Mean weight of the sample 1 is 58.6 kg, N= 105 And SD = 8.3. Mean weight of sample 2 is 56 kg, N = 10 , SD is 6.2. Find whether the difference is statistically significant or not?

Now, we begin by stating null hypothesis, i.e., the observed difference between these two samples mean (58.6 – 56 = 2.6) is merely due to chance. Now , we examine whether this deviation is too large to disprove null hypothesis. Now, we use Z test to find if this difference is by chance or some other factor is acting for difference in their mean weights.

Calculation:

$\bar{X}_1$ = 58.6, N = 10 .5 ; SD = 8.3;

$\bar{X}_2$ = 56 N = 101; SD = 6.2.

$$SED = \dfrac{\sqrt{SD_1^2}}{N_1} + \dfrac{\sqrt{SD_2^2}}{N_2}$$

$$= \dfrac{\sqrt{8.3^2}}{105} + \dfrac{\sqrt{6.2^2}}{101}$$

$$= \sqrt{0.656 + 0.38}$$

SE = 1.018

$$Z = \frac{\bar{X_1} - \bar{X_2}}{SED} = \frac{2.6}{1.018} = 2.55$$

So, Z is 2.55

We do this problem with 2nd method:

$$SE = \frac{SD}{\sqrt{N-1}} = \frac{8.3}{\sqrt{105-1}} \ \& \ \frac{6.2}{\sqrt{101-1}}$$

$$= \frac{8.3}{10.198} = 0.814 \ \& \ \frac{6.2}{10} = 0.62$$

$$SED = \sqrt{SE_1^2 + SE_2^2} = \sqrt{0.814 + 0.62}$$

=1.197

$$Z = \frac{\bar{X_1} - \bar{X_2}}{SED} = \frac{2.6}{1.197} = 2.17$$

We will get this value in **z table**. So, Z value of 2.17 corresponds to 0.0150. So, the probability that we get this observation by chance is only 1%.

So, here p = < 0.005

We reject null hypothesis and accept alternate hypothesis, i.e., there is significant difference in these two samples and the observed difference is not by chance. It is true difference.

Example 2: 23 patients are taken for study. 12 members were fed on high fat diet and 11 members were given normal food. Their weight gain was recorded after 3 months. Find whether the weight gain was significant or not?

Table 26

Here, for weight gain group A = X_1, group B = X_2

X_1	X_1^2	X^2	X_2^2
10	100	2	4
9	81	1	1
6	36	5	25
8	64	3	9
5	25	4	16
10	100	7	49
12	144	3	9
4	16	5	25
13	169	6	36
10	100	4	16

9	81	8	64
8	64		
$\sum X_1 = 104$	$\sum X_1^2 = 980$	$\sum X_2 = 48$	$\sum X_2^2 = 254$

$\bar{X}_1 = 8.67$; $\bar{X}_2$ 4.36

Now we calculate X_1^2 and X_2^2

Formula:

$$\sum X^2 = \sum X^2 - \frac{(\sum X)^2}{N}$$

$$\sum X_1^2 = 980 - \frac{(104)^2}{12} = 78.67$$

So, $\sum X_2^2 = 254 - \frac{(48)^2}{11} = 44.5$

$$\text{SED} = \frac{\sqrt{\sum X_1^2} + \sqrt{\sum X_2^2}}{N_1 + N_2 - 2} \left[\sqrt{\frac{1}{N_1} + \frac{1}{N_1}} \right]$$

Here, N means number of

values

$$= \frac{\sqrt{78.67 + 44.5}}{25.2} \left(\sqrt{\frac{1}{12} + \frac{1}{11}} \right)$$

$$= \sqrt{5.36 \, (0.083 + 0.09)}$$

$$= \sqrt{0.93}$$

SED = 0.96

$$t = \frac{\bar{x}_1 - \bar{x}_2}{\text{SED}}$$

$$= \frac{8.67 - 4.36}{0.96}$$

210

$$= \frac{4.31}{0.96} \quad = 4.49$$

So, t = 4.49

Df = 23-2=21

Here, we do with another formula (or z test formula)

$$SED = \frac{\sqrt{SD_1^2}}{N_1} + \frac{\sqrt{SD_2^2}}{N_2}$$

$$t \quad = \frac{X_{1-} \ x_2}{SED}$$

Here SD_1 = 2.67 and SD_2 = 2.11

$$SED = \frac{\sqrt{(2.67)^2}}{12} + \frac{\sqrt{(2.11)^2}}{11}$$

$$= \sqrt{0.59 + 0.4}$$

$$= 0.99$$

$$t = \frac{4.31}{0.99} = 4.35$$

Example 3. 12 anemic patients were given green leafy vegetables for one month regularly. Their Hb % was recorded before and after treatment. Find whether the difference is statistically significant.

Before Hb% X	After Hb% Y	D Y-X	D^2 $(Y-X)^2$
8	9	1	1
10	12	2	4
7	8	1	1
6	8	2	4
9	11	2	4
10	10	0	0
8	10	2	4
7	9	2	4
11	11	0	0
9	10	1	1
12	13	1	1
8	11	3	9
105	122	17	33

$$\overline{X} = \frac{105}{12} = 8.75; \ \overline{Y} = \frac{122}{12} = 10.17$$

211

$$\sum d^2 = \sum D^2 -- \frac{(\sum D)^2}{N}$$

$$= 33 - \frac{(17)^2}{12} = 8.91 \qquad \sum d^2 = 8.91$$

Then SD $= \frac{\sqrt{\sum d^2}}{N_1 - 1} = \frac{8.91}{11} = 0.9$

$$SE = \frac{SD}{\sqrt{n-1}} = \frac{0.9}{\sqrt{11}} = \frac{0.9}{3.32} = 0.27$$

$$t = \frac{\bar{X} - \bar{Y}}{SE} = \frac{10.17 - 8.75}{0.27} = 5.26$$

Df = 12 − 1 = 11, df 't' value is 5.26
So, P<0.001

When we are doing tests of significance two conditions must be satisfied.

1. Two samples should be selected randomly by simple random sampling technique.

2. Homogeneity of variance, i.e., variance of two samples should be less.

 If the above two conditions are met, samples as small as five will also produce good result by rejecting null hypothesis at 5% level.

If the sample sizes are unequal and variances are basically the same, no problem is encountered. (Edward, in 1967, said that, if he 't' test is applied to independent random samples of size 25 or more, the 't' test is relatively unaffected by violation of homogeneity of variance).

Homogeneity of Variance is tested by using 'F' test:

$$F = \frac{SD_1^2}{SD_2^2}$$

SD_1^2 = It is the larger of the two sample variances.

SD_2^2 = It is the smaller of the two sample variances.

By using F test, we are evaluating the null hypothesis of no difference between two population variance. If F is not significant, the null hypothesis is proved. So, for these samples we can use this test of significance.

If F is significant, we use another procedure.

't' test when the variances differ:

't' is computed by usual formula; after computing 't' we use this formula.

$$t_{0.05} = \frac{SE_1^2\,(t_1) + (SE_2^2)\,(t_2)}{SE_1^2 + SE_2^2}$$

Here

t_1 = 5% value for 't' at N_1-1 df

t_2 = 5% value for 't' at N_2-1 df

So at N_1 - 1 df the 't' value in 0.05 column of 't' table is taken and this we should substitute in the above formula.

To understand this we take one example.

Example: We have a data of:

$\bar{X}_1 = 33$ $\quad\quad \bar{X}_2 = 40.4$

$SD_1^2 = 144$ $\quad SD_2^2 = 289$

$N_1 = 31$ $\quad\quad N_2 = 41$

To this data we compute F to find whether this sample is homogeneous or not.

$$F = \frac{289}{144} = 2.1$$

At 30, 40 df, 'F' value 2.01 is significant at 5% level (above 1.79 is a significant). So, here homogeneity is not present. We use above formula.

$$t_{0.05} = \frac{SE_1^2\,(t_1) + SE_2^2\,(t_2)}{SE_1^2 + SE_2^2}$$

Now, we know SD^2, so we calculate SE^2.

Formula for that

$$SE^2 = \frac{SD^2}{N+1}$$

So $SE_1^2 = \dfrac{144}{30} = 4.8$

$SE_2^2 \; \dfrac{289}{40} = 7.225$

t_1 and t_2 we can get from 't' table

't' at 30 df 0.05 significance is 2.042

't' at 40 df 0.05 significance is 2.021

Now, substituting these valuable into formula

$$t_{0.05} = \frac{SE_1^2\,(t_1) + SE_2^2\,(t_2)}{SE_1^2 + SE_2^2}$$

$$= \frac{(4.8)\,(2.042) + (7.225)\,(2.021)}{(4.8 + 7.225)}$$

$$= \frac{24.\,4033}{12.\,025} = \mathbf{2.03}$$

Now, we can say that if our computed 't' value is more than 2.03, **it is significant (even the samples are not homogeneous). Now we compute 't'**

$$t = \frac{40.4 - 33}{\sqrt{4.8 + 7.225}} = \mathbf{2.13}$$

So, here our computed 't' value (2.13) is more than 2.03. Like this we can say it is significant.

Testing Significance of Difference between Proportions (Larger Samples)

In previous chapter, we studied the test of significance (t test and z test) used for quantitative data. Now are studying the tests of significance used for qualitative data.

These are applicable mainly when the sample is divided into only two classes, as success and failures, vaccinated and unvaccinated, cured and not cured, dead and survived, obsess, and non-obese etc. It is said to have a bionomial classification (if the is divided into more than two classes it is called multinomial classification).

P + q = 1

Or 1 – p = q

If we express it in percentage

P + q = 100

Q = 100 - p

STANDARD ERROR OF PROPORTION (SEP)

DEFINITION: A unit which measures variation in proportions of a character from sample to sample.

Like as all sample means, they segregate around population mean around population mean: If we take large number of samples, than the groups in each sample will have proportion very close to that of population.

So, proportion if sample (p) have a central tendency , i. e., a large number of them concentrate around the population (p). This sample proportions are symmetrically very close to that of proportion (p).

Example; Death rate of tetanus is 40% which was found in Indian population. So of we take 100 sample, each one containing 30 individuals data in various places of India, the death rates of 100 samples will have a tendency to concentrate around (p = 40) and they will be symmetrically and normally distributed.

Here also:

68%if the sample proportions will lie within the limits of proportion ± 1 SE

1) 95% of the sample proportion will lie within the limit of population proportion ± 2 SEP

2) 99% of the sample proportion will lie within limits of population proportion ± 2.58 SEP

3) 99.73% of the sample proportions will lie within the limits of population proportion ± 3 SEP]

Calculation of Standard Error of proportion (SEP)

Formula for SEP is

$$\text{SEP} = \frac{\sqrt{p\,q}}{N}$$

Here

P= P= Percentage of +ve character

q = Percentage of negative character

N = Number

If, p = 40; q = 100-40 = 60; and N = 100

So, $\text{SED} = \frac{\sqrt{40 \times 60}}{100} = \sqrt{24} = 4.9$

To include 95% value it is 40 ± 9.8

Range = 30.2 to 49.8, so, 95% of sample lie in this range.

Uses of SEP:

1. By calculating sample proportion (p) we can find the confidence limits of population proportions (p)
2. To determine if the sample is drawn from the known population or not, when population proportions (p)
3. To find the standard error of difference beween two proportion.
4. To find the sample size when when we want to do survey

Standard Error of Difference between Two Proportions

SE $(P_1 - P_2)$

Like as in case of means, the proportions or percentages (i. e., difference in the pair if proportions) are also normally distributed.

Criteria for use of this test are:

1. N_1, N_2 are sufficiently large
2. Samples are selected randomly .

The significance of difference is found by Z test.

$$Z = \frac{\text{Observed difference}}{\text{SE of difference}} = \frac{P_1 - P_2}{SE\,(p_1 - p_2)}$$

CALCULATION OF SE $(P_1 - P_2)$

FORMULA 1:

$$SE(p_1 - p_2) = \frac{\sqrt{p_1 q_1}}{N_1} + \frac{\sqrt{p_2 q_2}}{N_2}$$

FORMULA 2:

$$SE(p_1 - p_2) = \sqrt{PQ}\ \frac{\sqrt{1}}{N_1} + \frac{\sqrt{1}}{N_2}$$

After doing this, Z is calculated by using the formula

$$Z = \frac{p_1 - p_2}{SE(p_1 - P_2}$$

Calculation of SE $(p_1 - p_2)$ in case of small sample

Here we should use the correction factor

i.e., $\frac{1}{2}\left(\frac{1}{N_1} + \frac{1}{N_2}\right)$

So, Z $= \dfrac{(p_1 - p_2) - \frac{1}{2}\left(\frac{1}{N_1} + \frac{1}{N_2}\right)}{\sqrt{PQ}\ \left(\frac{\sqrt{1}}{N} + \frac{\sqrt{1}}{N_2}\right)}$ Or

We may use the formulas given below

$$Z = \frac{(p_1 - P_2) - \frac{1}{2}\left(\frac{1}{N_1} + \frac{1}{N_2}\right)}{\sqrt{\left(\frac{p_1 q_1}{N_1} + \sqrt{\frac{p_2 q_2}{N_2}}\right)}}$$

Example 1: Deaths due to tetanus were 25 in 85 patients attended for treatment in IDH. Find the population proportion one would expect to die in another hospital of same area due to tetanus.

$P = \dfrac{25}{85}$ **x 100 = 29.41** Type equation here.

Q = 100 − p = 100 − 29.41 = 70.59

SEP $= \dfrac{\sqrt{p\ q}}{n} = \dfrac{\sqrt{29.41\ X\ 70.59}}{85} = \sqrt{24.42}$

SEP = 4-94

At 95 % confidence limits

Population proportion will lie in (that) IDH and other hospital in the same area will be between: **$29.41 \pm 2\ x\ 4.94$**

I.e.,   **29.41 +2 x 4.94 = 39.29** Type equation here.

       29.41 - 2 x 4.94 = 19.53

So, population proportion would lie between **19.53 to 39.29.**

CALCULATION OF SAMPLE SIZE

When we want to do some research or survey, the first doubt we get is, what is the sample size we need to get correct results. If we take small samples our study is not valid and if we take large it is laborious to do. So we need optimum size of sample which gives reliable results.

Precision depends upon the sample size. If the sample size increases precision also increases. Roughly, we can say that the minimum sample size advised is 30.

Precision is measured by the following formula:

Precision $= \dfrac{\sqrt{n}}{SD}$

So, precision is directly proportional to square root of sample size.

Sample Size for Qualitative Data:

Here, we deal with the calculation of sample size for qualitative data. Here we are dealing with proportions

To find suitable size of sample the allowable error should not exceed 10% or 20% of the positive character (p)

Formula of sample size is

N $= \dfrac{4\,p\,q}{L^2}$

N = sample size

P = positive character

Q = 1 – p

L = allowable error in p (10% or 20%)

Example: Death rate of measles in children is found to be 10% what should be the size of sample needed to find death rate of measles?

N $= \dfrac{4\,p\,q}{L^2}$

Here p = 10 %, q = 90% and L (allowable error) = 10% of p.

So, fist we calculate allowable error. Here it is 10% of p.

So, it is

L $= \dfrac{10 \times 10}{100} = 1$

So, sample size is

N $= \dfrac{4\,p\,q}{L^2} = \dfrac{4 \times 10 \times 90}{1 \times 1} = 3600$

Sample Size for quantitative Data:

If the SD of the population is known from the past experience, the size of the sample can be determined by the following formulae with desired allowable error (L) at 5% risk level.

Steps:

We should decide how large an error we would allow (due to sampling defects). So we should state about allowable error.

Next we should express the allowable error in terms of confidence limits. (L is the allowable error in sample mean, and we are willing to take 5% chance that error will exceed L). Here, 5% chance means 2 SD, So, $L = \dfrac{2\,SD}{\sqrt{n}}$

Or $\sqrt{n} = \dfrac{2\,SD}{L}$, $N = \dfrac{4\,SD^2}{L^2}$

If allowable error (L) = 1, SD = 5: SD^2 = 25

So, $N = \dfrac{4\,SD^2}{L^2} = \dfrac{4 \times 25}{1^2} = 100$

In a case in which S.D. is not known, pilot survey may be carried out to find the S.D. of character which we want to study.

Example: Mean pulse rate of a population is believed to be 72/minute with S.D. of 8. Calculate minimum sample size to verify this, if allowable error is 1 at 5% significance level

$N = \dfrac{4\,SD^2}{L^2}$

$= \dfrac{4 \times 8 \times 8}{1 \times 1} = 256$

More accurate formula for calculation of sample size in case of qualitativae data is given below.

$N = \dfrac{4\,p\,q}{L^2} \times \dfrac{f(1.1)}{m_h}$

Here:

N = required sample size

4 = Factor to achieve the 95% level of confidence

P = prevalence of indicator (positive character)

L = Margin of error to be tolerated (allowable error)

q = Prevalence of negative character

ƒ = Design effect

1.1 = Factor necessary to raise the sample sizes by 10% for non-response

Y = Proportion of our target population in the total population

n_h = Average household size

Example: In an area the report come to us is that 85% of children in age group of 12-23 months are covered with OPV. The average household size is 4.2. Children in that age group comprise 2% of total population. Design effect is 1.75.

Calculate sample size required

Here:

p = 85

y = Proportion of target population = 2% = 0.02

L = 5% = 1

n_h = average household size is 4.2

ƒ = (Design effect) 1.75

Now, we substitute these values into our formula:

$$N = \frac{4\,p\,q}{L^2} \; X \; \frac{f(1.1)}{m_h}$$

$$= \frac{4 \; X \; 85 \; X \; 15}{1 \; X \; 1} \; X \; \frac{1.75 \; X \; 1.1}{0.02 \; X \; 4.2}$$

$$= \frac{5100}{1} \; X \; \frac{1.75}{0.084}$$

= 5100 x 20.833

= 106,248.3

NON-PARAMETRIC STATISTICS

Significance test like **'z' test, 't' and 'F' test** are all based upon an assumption of a normal distribution in the population studied. Such statistics are called parametric statistics.

Here, we are discussing other type of statistics called 'distribution free statistics or non parametric statistics'. Here, the population studied is not needed to fulfill the assumption of normal distribution.

Advantages of distribution free statistics

1. Simplicity of derivation (her we use simple combinational formulae)
2. Ease of application (operation needed for this statistics are Ranking, Counting, adding, subtracting etc.)
3. Speed of application
4. Score of application (these statistics can be correctly applied to a much larger class of population)
5. Susceptibility to violation of assumption is less, even if violation happens, it is easy to detect.
6. Types of measurement required: Distribution free statistics usually require ordinal data and sometimes, nominal data, whereas parametric statistics usually need interval data and ratio scales.
7. Influence of sample size: When sample size are around 19, these statistics are easy, quick and give slightly less efficient results.

   When we want to use parametric statistic in small sample [10] slight violation of assumption give wrong result but this is not so in non parametric statistic so these are advised for simples less than 10; in large samples non – parametric statistic are less efficient and laborious
8. Statistical efficiency when assumption of the non- parametric tests are met and parametric test assumption are not met ,non parametric test give superior result

   If the assumption of both tests are met non-parametric tests are only slightly less efficient in very small sized sample . if sample size increases non parametric tests are less efficient

Disadvantages of Non – Parametric Tests

   i) Not useful in large samples
   ii) Lower statistical efficiency

TYPES OF NON- PARAMETRIC STATISTICS:

   A. NOMINAL DATA AND INDEPENDENT SAMPLES

1. Chi –square test

2. Binomial test

3. Fisher exact Test

B. NOMINAL DATA AND MATCHED SAMPLE

1. MC Nemar Chi- square test

C. ORDINAL DATA AND INDEPENDENT SAMPLES

1. Mann- whitney 'U' test

2. Median test

3. kruskal—wallis test

4. kolmogorov smirnov test

D. ORDINAL DATA AND MATCHED SAMPLES

1. Sign test

2. Wilcoxan test

CHI SQUARE TEST

Out of all these, the most commonly used non-parametric statistic test is chi- square test.
When the data are expressed in frequencies or proportions or percentages Chi square test is useful test Chi-square test is useful for discrete data. However any continuous data may be reduced to categorical data and chi- square test may be applied.

CALCULATION OF CHI-SQUARE VALUE:

STEPS:

1. Make the contingency (or 2 x 2) table. This is also called four-fold table

2. Note the frequencies observed (O) in 4 cells.

3. Calculate the expected (E) value in each cell on assumption of null hy-pothesis.

4. Find the difference between observed frequency and expected frequency in each cell (i.e., $O - E$)

5. Now calculate chi-square value by using the formula

$$X^2 = \frac{(O - E)^2}{E} \text{ in all cells}$$

6. Sum up chi- square values of all cell to get total chi square value

7. Calculation of Df. Df is (Colums-1) (Rows-1)

Example: 300 cases of Typhoid fever are admitted in a hospital in one year. 150 cases were given ciprofloxacin and another 150 cases were given chloramphenicol.Results are given in table (i.e., complete cure after 10 days of treatment).

Table 28:

Drug	Cured		Not Cured		Total	
Ciprofloxacin	143	a	7	b	150	a+b
Chloraphenicol	137	c	13	d	150	c+d
Total	**280**	a+c	**20**	b+d	**300**	a +b+c+d

Calculation:

Here we start the calculation with a hypothesis called 'Null Hypothesis'. Thus there is no difference between the effects of two drugs. If there is no difference between two drugs, cure rate will also be same. So, we are given same cure rate to both of the drugs in our expected frequencies.

So, out of 300, how many are cured by two drugs will be same. So, this total percentage of cure (280/300) rate will be our expected frequencies.

Now, first we pool the results of two drugs. Out of 300 complete cures occurred in 280. So, proportion of cured (all patients) is taken.

It is $\frac{280}{300} = 0.93$

Out of 300, not cured are 20. So, proportion of not cured was (all patients) taken.

It is $\frac{20}{300} = 0.07$

Not, to calculate expected values (E) we multiply values in cells with these proportions

1. 150 x 0.93 = 139.5
2. 150 x 0.93 = 139.5
3. 150 = 0. 07 = 10.5
4. 150 = 0.07 = 10.5

	Expected values	
	Cured	**Not cured**
Ciprofloxacin	139.5	10.5
Amoxicillin	139.5	10.5

Now we use the formula:

$$X^2 = \frac{(143-139.5)^2}{139.5} + \frac{(137-139.5)^2}{139.5} + \frac{(7-10.5)^2}{10.5} + \frac{(13-10.5)^2}{10.5}$$

= 0.08 + 0.0448 + 1.167 + 0.595

So chi-square value is 1.9 (1.895).

Now, we use another formula (Simple formula for chi-square)

$$X^2 = \frac{(ad - bc)^2 \, N}{(a + b)\,(c + d)\,(a + c)\,(b + d)} \quad , \quad \text{Here } N = a + b + c + d$$

$$X^2 = \frac{(143 \times 13 - 7 \times 137)^2}{150 \times 150 \times 280 \times 20} = \frac{810000 \times 300}{150 \times 150 \times 280 \times 20} = 1.928$$

At 95% confidence limits, x^2 value of 3.84 is significant; but our calculated Value is less than this. So ($p > 0.1$), it is not significant.

Another example: Table 29

Drug	Cured	Not cured	Total
Ciprofloxacin	A	B	a + b
	O = 190	O = 10	200
	E = 180	E = 20	
Amoxycilin	C	D	c+ d
	O = 350	O = 50	400
	E = 360	E = 40	
Total	a + c = 540	b + d = 60	600 (a + b + c + d)

CALCULATION:

1st step: It is the calculation of proportion:

$\frac{540}{600} = 0.9$: total proportion of cured

$\frac{60}{600} = 0.1$: total proportion of not cured

2^{n} step: Now, we calculate the expected values for the values in 4 cells.

200 x 0.9 = 180

400 x0.9 = 360

200 x 0.1 = 20

400 x 0.1 = 40

When we are calculating expected values, calculation of value in one cell is sufficient.

From this, we can get the values of rest of three cells.

Suppose the value in a = 180, so (a + c) – (a) gives values of c = (540 -180 = 360).

Same way (a + b) − (a) gives value in the b cell (200 − 180 = 20).Now, You know the value of b. So, (b + d) − (b) gives value of d (60-20 = 40). Now, We use formula;

$$X^2 = \frac{(190 - 180)^2}{180} + \frac{(10 - 20)^2}{20} + \frac{(350 - 360)^2}{360} + \frac{(50-40)^2}{40}$$

$$= 0.53 + 5 + 0.28 + 2.5 = 8.34$$

So, chi-square value is 8.34

With another formula

$$X^2 = \frac{(a\,d - b\,c)^2 \; N}{(a+b)\,(c+d)\,(a+c)\,(b+d)}$$

$$= \frac{(190 \times 50 - 40 \times 350)^2 \; 600}{200 \times 400 \times 540 \times 60}$$

$$= \frac{(9500 - 3500)^2 \; 600}{2592000000}$$

$$= \frac{36000000 \times 600}{25920000} = 8.33$$

So, $X^2 = 8.33$

Chi-square when frequencies are small and Df is one

If we to apply chi-square test in four-fold table, values in all four cells should be more than 5 and expected values in 4 cells must be more than 5. If the expected value in any cell is less than 5 using chi-square test gives overestimate. So, to prevent this problem "Yates correction" is needed. Some statisticians prefer using Yates correction if the expected value in any cell is less than 10.

Chi-square formula with Yates correction

$$X^2 = \sum \left[\frac{(\,(O-E) - 0.5\,)^2}{E} \right]$$

This formula should be applied to 4 cells and summation of that gives chi-square value.

We can apply Yates correction to direct formula also.

$$X^2 = \frac{N\left[(ad-bc) - N/2\right)^2\right]}{(a+b)\,(c+d)(a+c)\,(b+d)}$$

Example: Typhoid immunization was given to 50 children. 25 were given oral typhoid vaccine and another 25 were given injectable typhoid vaccine. After 2 years, typhoid epidemic has occurred in that area. Out of those who received oral vaccine, 2 got the disease and out of those received injectable vaccine, 4 got the disease. Find whether this difference is significant.

Vaccine	Protected	Not protected	Total
Oral typhoid Vaccine	a o = 23 E = 22	b O = 2 E = 3	25 (a +b)
Injectable typhoid vaccine	c o = 21 E = 22	d o = 4 E = 3	25 (c+d)
Total	**(a+c) 44**	**(b+d) 6**	**(a+b+c+d) 50**

$$=\sum \frac{[(23-22)-0.5)^2]}{22} + \frac{[(21-22)-0.5)^2]}{22} + \frac{[(2-3)-0.5)^2]}{3} + \frac{(4-3)-0.5)^2}{3}$$

=0.011+0.011+0.083+0.083

=0.188

So, chi-square value is 0.188

(if we have not used Yates correction, we get x^2 value 0.75)

Another formula

$$= \frac{N\left[(23 \times 4 - 2 \times 21) - \frac{50}{2}\right]^2}{25 \times 25 \times 44 \times 6}$$

$$= \frac{31250}{165000} = 0.189$$

Use of chi-square test in tables larger than 2 x 2

The contingency table given below shows the results obtained by using 4 toothpastes. Find whether the results are significant or not?

Table 31

Results	Brand A	Brand B	Brand C	Brand D	Total
No damage of teeth	9 a	13 b	17 c	11 d	50 m
Slight damage	63 e	70 f	85 g	82 h	300 n
More damage	28 i	37 j	48 k	37 l	150 o
Total	100 p	120 q	150 r	130 s	N = 500

Obtaining the expected frequencies:

	Brand A	Brand B	Brand C	Brand D	
Normal teeth	$\frac{PM}{T}$	$\frac{QM}{T}$	$\frac{RM}{T}$	$\frac{SM}{T}$	**M**
Slight Damage	$\frac{PN}{T}$	$\frac{QN}{T}$	$\frac{RN}{T}$	$\frac{SN}{T}$	**N**
More Damage	$\frac{PO}{T}$	$\frac{QO}{T}$	$\frac{RO}{T}$	$\frac{SO}{T}$	**O**
	P	**Q**	**R**	**S**	**T**

In the above table, we have shown how to get the expected frequencies in each cell. Here we designated each cell by a letter. The row and column are summed. Each row and each column after summation designated by a capital letter (MNO and PQ RS).Total number of frequencies are designated by T.

To obtain the expected value for the extreme upper left cell, we multiply p with M and divide this by total number of cases (i.e., (PM/T). The expected value for the cell below this is obtained by multiplying P with N and dividing this by T (PN/T). After finishing this column, we move to right. To obtain expected value of upper cell in second column, we multiply Q with M and divide this by T (QM/T). Next to obtain E Of upper cell in 3rd column we multiply R with M and divide it by T (RM/T). Like this we calculate expected values of all cells.

Table33

	Brand A	Brand B	Bran C	Brand D
No damage Of teeth	O = 9 E = 10	O=13 E=12	O=17 E=15	O=11 E=13
Slight Damage	O = 63 E = 60	O =70 E =72	O=85 E=90	O=82 E=78
More Damage	O = 28 E= 30	O = 37 E = 36	O=48 E=45	O=37 E=39

$$X^2 = \frac{(9-10)^2}{10} + \frac{(63-60)^2}{60} + \frac{(28-30)^2}{30} + \frac{(13-12)^2}{12} + \frac{(70-72)^2}{72} + \frac{(37-36)^2}{36} + \frac{(17-15)^2}{15} + \frac{(85-90)^2}{90} +$$

$$\frac{(48-45)^2}{45} + \frac{(11-13)^2}{13} + \frac{(82-78)^2}{78} + \frac{(37-39)^2}{39}$$

= 0.1 + 0.15 + 0.133 + 0.083 + 0.055 + 0.028 + 0.267 + 0.278 + 0.2 + 0.308 + 0.205 + 0.102

So x^2=1.92

Df = (3-1) (4-1)

= 2x3=6

So Df =6

At Df = 6, the chi-square value to become significant (i.e.,0.05) is 12.592. Our calculated value is 1.92 (that is less than needed). So we accept null hypothesis, i.e., then is no difference in results of 4 brands of toothpastes. What we observed is by chance.

To understand chi-square test further, it is better to understand chi-square probability curve.

Chapter 15: VITAL STATISTICS

The term "Vital Statistics" means the "data and analytical methods for describing vital events occurring in communities". Vital events are those pertaining to human life such as births, deaths, sickness, marriages, divorces, migration etc. So vital statistics means it covers various aspects of health, nutrition and demography.

We get raw data of vital statistics from population census, sample surveys, vital statistics registers etc.

MEASURES OF POPULATION:

For the measurements of population, Midyear population is taken and its socio-demographical composition is census which is carried out in every 10 years.

CALCULATION OF MIDYEAR POPULATION:

There are three methods for calculation of midyear population.

a. Natural increase method
b. Arithmetical progression method
c. Geometric progression method

Arithmetical progression method:

Out of the three, the most commonly used method is arithmetical progression method. Here, it is assumed that there is equal increase each year, and average increase per year is calculated in the intercensal period of 10 years (such as between 1971 and 1981).

Example: The population of Vijayawada in 1981 census was 510,000 and in 1991 census were 620,000. Calculate midyear population in 1997 and 2000.

Steps:

1. Here it is assumed that there is equal increase in each year. So increase in 10 year is 620000 − 51000 = 110000.

    Average increase per year $= \frac{110000}{10} = 11000$

2. Here we should remember two things.

    a. Census will be taken on 1st March of 1st Year of the decade (period of 10 yrs).

    b. Calculation of midyear population should be taken up to the 1st July of that year. So there is 4 months, i.e., from 1st March to 1st July.

3. Now we have to calculate midyear population of 1997 (i.e., 1997 − 1991 = 6 years), So, for 6 years and 4 months (i.e., from 1st March to 1st July.). The increase of

228

population is = 11000 x 6 1/3 = 69667. (Here we have converted 4 months into year, i.e., 1/3 yrs.)

4. This should be added to 1991 population which gives mid year population of 1997.

62000 + 69667 = 689667.

So, midyear population of 1997 is 689667.

The same way, we now calculate midyear population of 2000. So 2000 – 1991 = 9 years.

From 1st march of 2000 to 1st July of 2000 is 4 months, i.e., 9 years and 4 months or 9 1/3 years.

Rise in 10 Years = 620000 – 51000 = 110000

$$1 \text{ Year} = \frac{110000}{10} = \mathbf{11000}$$

So, 9 and 1/3 years is 11000 x 9 1/3 = 102667.

MYP of 2000 is 62000 + 102667 = 722667.

GEOMETRIC PROGRESSION METHOD:

In arithmetical progression method our assumption is the increase of the population is constant like simple interest, whereas in case of geometric progression method, it is calculated like compound interest. **For Example:** If the population of a town grew from one lack to two lacks in two years then in next two years it grows from two lakhs to 4 lakhs and in next two years it grows from four lakhs to 8 lakhs and so on.

Here, we are applying geometric law of growth. So we are calculating annual increase per person in intercensal years.

Formula: $P_1 = P_0 (1+Y)^t$

At the end of the year it becomes $P_0 (1+Y)$

At the end of 2 years it becomes $P_0 (1+Y) (1+Y)$ or $P_0 (1+Y)^2$

At the end of 10 years it becomes

$P_0 (1+Y) (1+Y)(1+Y) (1+Y)(1+Y) (1+Y)(1+Y) (1+Y)(1+Y) (1+Y)$ or $P_0 (1+Y)^{10}$

Here:

P_1 = Population at the required time

t = years after the last census

$ɤ$ = Annual increase rate

Example (geometric progression method):

Census population of Guntur city in 1981 was 322400 and in 1991 was 444400. Calculate midyear population in 1996.

Steps:

Population on first march, 1981 x $(1+ɤ)^{10}$ = population on 1st march 1991

Population on first march, 1991 = 444400 =322400 x $(1+ɤ)^{10}$

Taking logarithm:

Log 444400 = Log 322400 + 10 log (1+ɤ)

Log 4444 +2 log 10 = log 3224 + 2 log 10 + 10 log (1+ɤ)

Characteristic of log 4444 is 3 (here we are having 4 digits. So, 4-1=3)

Then we should see in logarithm table in 44 Row under column 4. Here the value is 64738 and we should take the value in 4th column of mean differences; this is 39. This we should add to 64738 (64738 + 39 = 64777).

The same way, characteristic of log 3224 is 3 (because here also we are having 4 digit number 4 – 1= 3). Then we should see in logarithm table in 32 row and under column 2. Here the value is 50786. Then we should take the value of 4th column of mean difference (this is 54). This we should add to 50786 (it is = 50840)

So, log 4444+2 log =10 log (1+ɤ) + log 3224+2 log

By applying values in logarithm it becomes

3. 64777 + 2 = 3.50840 + 2 +10 log (1+ɤ)

5. 64777 = 5.50840+10 log (1+ɤ)

So, 10 log (1+ɤ) = 5. 64777-5. 50840

10 log (1+ɤ) = 0.13937

Log (1+ɤ) = 0.13973 / 10 = 0.013973

So, midyear population of 1996 = 444400 (1+ɤ)

By substituting log value here

5.64777 + (0.013973 x 16/3)

= 5.64777 + 0.07433

= 5.7221

Now we should use anti logarithm in table to get original figures. In seeing anti logarithm table, we should see in 0. 72 row in 2nd column. It is 52723. Then we should take the value of first column in mean differences. It is 12. Both should be added (52723 + 12 = 52735).

So, by taking log, the value is 52735. Here the characteristic is five. So, our final value should be 6 digits. So, final value is 527350.

MYP = 527350

USING ARITHMETIC PROGRESSION METHOD

Increase of population in 10 years is 444400 - 322400 = 122000

In one year 122000/10 = 12200

(5 years and 4 months) i.e, 5.333 years is 12200 x 5.333 = 65067

So, population at MYP of 1996 is 444400 + 65067 = 509466

MEASURES OF VITAL STATISTICS:

It is easy to understand by converting the absolute number of vital events into rates and ratio and proportions.

Rate:

Rate is a proportion with a defined denominator (here it is population) and the numerator (here it is occurrence of an event in the same population) and multiplier (magnification agent), i.e. ., 100 or 1000 or 10000 or 100000 etc., as per magnification desired.

Example:

$$\textbf{Crude Birth rate} = \frac{\textbf{Numerator}}{\textbf{Denominator}} \textbf{ X multiplier}$$

or

$$= \frac{\textit{Total number of births in a year in a defined geographical area}}{\textit{Total midyear population}} \; x \; 1000$$

So, the rate is a measure of the speed at which new events are occurring in a community.

231

Rates in general are of two types:

a. Crude Rates

b. Specific Rates.

Specific rates means rate for specific groups (Age-sex groups, disease specific rates).

Commonly used rates are:

A. Mortality rates
1. Crude death rate
2. Standardized death rates (direct method and indirect method)
3. **Specific death rates:** includes-
    a. Age specific death rates & sex specific death rates
    b. Infant Mortality rate (IMR)
    c. Neonatal mortality rate
    d. Perinatal mortality rate
    e. Maternal mortality rate
    f. Proportional mortality rate
    g. Case fatality rate

B. Morbidity Rates
1. Incidence rates
2. Prevalence rates
3. Notification rates

C. Fertility related rates (or statistics)
1. Birth rate (crude birth rate)
2. GFR (General fertility rate)
3. General marital fertility rate
4. Age specific fertility rate
5. Age specific marital fertility rate
6. TFR (Total fertility rate)
7. Total marital fertility rate
8. GRR (Gross reproduction rate)
9. NRR (Net reproduction rate)
10. Pregnancy rate
11. Abortion rate

12. Marriage rate (Crude marriage rate and General marriage rate)

13. Couple protection rate (CPR)

Fertility related ratios are as following
    a. Child Woman Ratio
    b. Abortion Ratio

STANDARDIZED RATES (OR ADJUSTED RATES)

When we want to compare death rates of two populations with a different age group composition, the crude death rate is not the correct yardstick. The correct one is age-adjusted or age-standardized death rate, which removes the confounding effect of different age structures. This yields a single standardized death rate.

This adjustment can be made not only for age but also for sex, race, parity etc.

Standardization is carried out by two methods:
a. Direct Standardization
b. Indirect Standardization
In both methods we use standard population.

Direct Standardization Method

A standard million population is taken (a city or country as a whole). To this population age and sex-wise death rates of various groups (which we want to study) is applied, which gives the standardized death rate of that group. So now we can compare death rates of any two places.

Standard Population:

Standard population is defined as "one for which the numbers in age and sex groups are known".

Steps in direct standardization:

Following steps are taken in direct standardization as:
a. From the given table, age-specific death rates (per 1000 population) are calculated.
b. The application of these age-specific death rates to the standard population gives expected deaths.

Example: Calculate standardized death rates of given population,

Population:

Age	Mid-year population	Deaths in the year
0-1	4000	60
1-4	4500	20
5-14	4000	12
15-19	5000	15
20-24	4000	16
25-34	8000	25
35-44	9000	48
45-54	8000	100
55-64	7000	150
Total	**53500**	**446**

Standard Population

Age	Population
0-1	1653500
1-4	3163800
5-14	4095000
15-19	3641900
20-24	3484200
25-34	2731700
35-44	2589700
45-54	1989600
55-64	1143100
Total	**24492500**

Calculation

Age	MYP	Death in the year	Age-specific death rate
0-1	4000	60	15.0
1-4	4500	20	4.4
5-14	4000	12	3.0
15-24	5000	15	3.0
25-34	4000	16	4.0
35-44	8000	25	3.1

45-54	9000	48	5.3
55-64	8000	100	12.5
65 & above	7000	150	21.4
Total	**53500**	**446**	

Crude death rate = $\dfrac{446}{53500}$ **x 1000** = **8.3**

So, above we have calculated age-specific death rate (per 1000). Now we are applying this age specific rates to standard population

Age	Standard population	Age-specific Death rates/1000	Calculated Expected deaths
0-1	1653500	15.0	24802.5
1-4	3163800	4.4	13920.7
5-14	4095000	3.0	12285.0
15-24	3641900	3.0	10925.7
25-34	3484200	4.0	13936.8
35-44	2731700	3.1	8468.3
45-54	2589700	5.3	13725.4
55-64	1989600	12.5	24870.0
65 & above	1143100	21.4	24642.3
Total	**24492500**		**147396.74**

Standardized Death Rate = $\dfrac{147396.74 \times 1000}{24492500}$ = $\dfrac{6.02}{1000}$ **population**

Indirect method

In indirect standardization of death rate, we choose the "age-specific death rates" of country as a whole. These rates are applied to the group to whom it is needed. It gives "index death rate". Crude death rate of the standardized population divided by index death rate gives "standardizing factor". Then multiplying the crude death rate of the place by this standardizing factor gives standardized death rate.

Example:

Age	Estimated population	Standard Death rates/1000	Expected deaths at standard rates
0-4	461000		
5-14	998400	2.55	1176

15-24	1011600	0.12	120
25-34	1030700	0.40	405
35-44	845500	0.88	907
45-54	727900	1.67	1412
55-64	590900	5.01	3647
65-74	431100	15.47	9437
70 +	108700	41.22	17028
		110.18	11977
Total	**6187800**		**46109**

CDR = 11.45

Steps

a. Selecting a series of standard death rates at ages.

b. These rates are applied to the population we are studying. By this we get expected rates.

c. These are then totalled.

d. Dividing the expected deaths by total populations, we get "Index Death Rates".

e. Crude death rate of the standardized population divided by index death rate gives "standardizing factor".

f. Then multiplying the crude death rate of the place by the standardizing facto gives "standardized death rate".

$$\textbf{Index death rate} = \frac{46109 \; x \; 1000}{6187800} = \textbf{7.45}$$

$$\textbf{Standardizing factor} = \frac{11.45}{7.45} = \textbf{1.54}$$

So, now for which area we want to calculate the standardizing death rate, that area's crude death rate multiplied by standardizing factor, we get the "Standardized death rate".

Standardized Mortality Ratio (SMR)

It is also indirect method. It is useful in certain circumstances. Here also we use age and sex specific morality rates. We first calculate the number of deaths that would have occurred at these rates (expected deaths).

SMR is a "ratio of the total number of deaths that occurred in the study group, to the number of deaths that would have been expected to occur, if the study group has experienced the death rates of the standard population".

The particular index is useful in the study of occupational mortality. So, we take mortality rates of all male population and we compare these rates with the mortality rates of occupational groups.

$$\text{SMR} = \frac{\text{Observed deaths}}{\text{Expected deaths}} \times 100$$

Age Group	Annual death rate of all males/1000 (1970-72)	Population of Social Class-I	Expected deaths	Observed Deaths from 1970-72
15-24	0.92	95190	263	193
25-34	1.00	214680	644	431
35-44	2.32	171060	1185	854
45-54	7.20	137080	2961	2079
55-64	20.54	100000	6162	5029
Total			11215	8586

We need to calculate deaths of 3 years. So 3 x annual death rates x population of social class-I gives expected deaths.

$$\text{SMR} = \frac{8586}{11215} \times 100 = 77\%$$

So, social 'class I' is enjoying 23 % less mortality than general population.

Another Example:

Calculation of SMR for Coal Workers

Age	Standard Death Rate of all males/1000	Coal Workers Population	Observed Deaths	Expected Deaths
20-29	3.5	2500	10.0	8.75
30-39	5.0	4000	25.2	20.0

40-49	6.2	5000	38.2	31.0
50-59	7.2	3000	26.0	21.6
60 +	25.1	2000	58.0	50.2
Total			**157.4**	**131.55**

$$SMR = \frac{157.4}{131.55} \times 100 = 119.65\%$$

So, coal worker are facing 19.65% extra risk or extra mortality than standard population.

SOME IMPORTANT DEFINITIONS

1. **Birth Rate (Crude birth rate) CBR =**

$$\frac{\text{Number of live births during the year in a defind geographical area}}{\text{Estimated mid year population}} \times 1000$$

$$\textbf{Simplified Formula} = \frac{\text{Number of births}}{\text{MYP}} \times 1000$$

2. **Crude death rate**

$$CDR = \frac{\text{Number of deaths during the year in a defined geographical area}}{\text{Estimated mid−year population}} \times 1000$$

$$\textbf{Simplified Formula} = \frac{Number\ of\ deaths}{MYP} \times 1000$$

3. **Specific death rates:**

   A. **IMR (Infant Mortality Rate)**

$$IMR = \frac{\text{Number of infant deaths during one year}}{\text{Total live births in one year}} \times 1000$$

Here, infant means "Children below one year of age".

238

B. **Maternal Mortality rate (MMR)**

$$MMR = \frac{\text{Number of death in females due to peurperal causes}}{\text{Total number of live births}} \times 1000$$

Here also, we will calculate for one year in a defined geographical area.

C. **Neonatal Mortality Rate (NMR):**

$$NMR = \frac{\text{Number of deaths up to 28 days of lie of infant}}{\text{Total number of live births}} \times 1000$$

D. **Early Neonatal Mortality Rate (ENMR)**

$$ENMR = \frac{\text{Number of deaths up to 1st 7 days of life of infant}}{\text{Total number live births}} \times 1000$$

E. **Late Neonatal Mortality Rate (LNMR)**

$$LNMR = \frac{\text{Number of death from 7th day to 28 th days after birth}}{\text{Total live births}} \times 1000$$

F. **Post Neonatal Mortality rate (or Late Infant Mortality Rate)**

$$PNMR = \frac{\text{Deaths of infants after 28 days of life to 1 year}}{\text{Total number of live births}} \times 1000$$

or

$$PNMR = \frac{\text{Infant deaths} - \text{Neonatal deaths}}{\text{Number of live births}} \times 1000$$

G. **Perinatal Mortality Rate (PMR)**

$$PMR = \frac{\textit{Late foetal deaths (Foetal deaths after 28 wks or more)} + \textit{Early neonatal deaths (deaths under 1 wk)}}{\textit{Total births (Live births+Still births)}} \times 1000$$

4. Proportional Mortality Rate or Ratio:

Here in this condition, death rates due to different causes are expressed in percentages of crude death rates. For example-

A. Proportional Mortality from specific disease (TB, AIDS, Diarrhoea)

$$P M R = \frac{\text{Number of deaths from specific disease in 1 year}}{\text{Total deasths in that year}} \times 100$$

So here, in place of "Specific disease" if you want to calculate PMR of TB you should place "TB" there.

B. Under-5 Proportional Mortality Rate

$$\text{PMR (<5 year)} = \frac{\text{Number of deaths in under 5-years of age group children in one year}}{\text{Total deaths in that year}} \times 100$$

C. Proportional Mortality Rate for age 50 and above

$$PMR = \frac{\text{Number of deaths of persons aged 50 yrs \& above}}{\text{Total deaths in that year}} \times 100$$

5. Cases Fatality Rate or Ratio

$$= \frac{\text{Total number of deaths due to particular disease}}{\text{Total number of cases of same disese}} \times 100$$

6. Specific Death Rates (Age-specific, Sex-specific, Disease-specific, Period-specific etc). For example-

A. Specific Death Rate due to TB

$$= \frac{\text{Number of deaths from TB in a year}}{\text{Mid} - \text{year population}} \times 1000$$

B. Specific Death Rate for Males

240

$$= \frac{\text{Number of deaths among males in a year}}{\text{Mid−year population of males}} \text{ x } 1000$$

C. Specific Death Rate in age group 15-20 yrs:

$$= \frac{\substack{\text{Number of deaths of persons} \\ \text{aged 15−20 yrs during the year}}}{\text{Mid−year population of persons aged 15−20 yrs}} \text{ x } 1000$$

D. Death Rate per January:

$$= \frac{\text{Deaths in January x 12}}{\text{Mid Year Population}} \text{ x } 1000$$

E. Weekly Death Rate

$$= \frac{\text{Deaths in the week x 52}}{\text{Mid Year Population}} \text{ x } 1000$$

EXERCISES

1. **Midyear population of a town was 210000. The following events occurred during the year 2000**

Total live births	5000
Total deaths	2000
Total maternal deaths	22
Infant deaths	300

   Calculate CBR, CDR, IMR, MMR

Answer:

a. CBR $= \frac{Total\ births}{MYP} \ x\ 1000$

$$= \frac{5000}{210000} \; x \; 1000 \; = 23.81 \; per \; 1000 \; population$$

b. CDR $= \dfrac{Total\ deaths}{MYP} \; x \; 1000$

$$= \frac{2000}{210000} \; x \; 1000 = \; 9.52 \; per \; 1000 \; population$$

c. IMR $= \dfrac{Infant\ deaths}{Total\ live\ births} \; x \; 1000$

$$= \frac{300}{5000} \; x \; 1000 \; = \; 60 \; per \; 1000 \; live \; births$$

d. MMR $= \dfrac{Maternal\ deaths}{Total\ live\ births} \; x \; 1000$

$$= \frac{22}{5000} \; x \; 1000 \; = \; 4.4 \; per \; 1000 \; live \; births$$

2. Census population of a city in 1991 was 600000. The following events occurred in 1991.

- Total live births   15000
- Total deaths   6000
- Maternal deaths due to puerperal causes   60
- Deaths of children within 1 year after birth   800
  (infant deaths)
- Deaths of children with 28 days after birth   720
  (Neonatal deaths)
- Still births in 1991   140
- Deaths within one week after birth   480

Calculate CBR, CDR, IMR, MMR, Neonatal mortality rate, Early neonates mortality rate, Late neonatal mortality rate, Post neonatal mortality rate, Perinatal mortality rate.

Answer:

$$\text{CBR} = \frac{15000}{600000} \times 1000 = 25 \text{ per 1000 population}$$

$$\text{CDR} = \frac{6000}{600000} \times 1000 = 10 \text{ per 1000 population}$$

$$\text{IMR} = \frac{800}{15000} \times 1000 = 53.3 \text{ per 1000 population}$$

$$\text{MMR} = \frac{60}{15000} \times 1000 = 4 \text{ per 1000 live births}$$

National Mortality rate $= \dfrac{\text{Infant death with in 28 days after births}}{\text{Total live births}} \times 1000$

$$= \frac{720}{15000} \times 1000 = 48 \text{ per 1000 live births}$$

Post Neonatal Mortality rate $= \dfrac{\text{Infant deaths} - \text{neonatal deaths}}{\text{Total live births}} \times 1000$

$$= \frac{800 - 720}{15000} \times 1000 = 5.3 \text{ per 1000 live births}$$

Early neonatal Mortality rate

$$= \frac{\text{Early neonatal deaths}}{\text{Total live births}} \times 1000$$

$$= \frac{480}{15000} \times 1000 = 32 \text{ per1 1000 live births}$$

Late neonatal Mortality rate

$$= \frac{\text{Neonatal deaths} - \text{Early neonatal deaths}}{\text{Total live births}} \times 1000$$

$$= \frac{720 - 480}{15000} \times 1000 = 16 \text{ per 1000 live births}$$

Perinatal Mortality rate

$$= \frac{\text{Still births} + \text{Early neonatal deaths}}{\text{Total births (i.e., both live and alive)}} \times 10000$$

243

$$= \frac{140+480}{15000+140} = 40.95 \; per \; 1000 \; births$$

3. **Census population of a village in 2001 was 6000. Males are 3400 and females are 2600. Following events occurred in 2001.**

• Total live births	220
• Total deaths	100
• Out of 100 deaths, males	60
• Deaths in age group under 5 yrs	30
• Deaths in December month	16
• Out of 16 deaths, 4 deaths were in 1st week of dec.	
• Infant deaths	25
• Number of TB case present	120
• Deaths due to TB are	8

Calculate relevant indices.

Answer:

- **CBR** = $\frac{220}{6000}$ x **1000** = **36.67 per 1000 population**

- **CDR** = $\frac{100}{6000}$ x **1000** = **16.67 per 1000 population**

- **IMR** = $\frac{25}{220}$ x **1000** = **113.67 per 1000 live births**

- **Specific death Rate** = $\frac{No. of \; deaths \; among \; males}{Mid \; year \; population \; of \; males}$ x **1000**

  = $\frac{60}{3400}$ x **1000** = **17.65 per 1000 males**

- **Specific death Rate** = $\frac{No. of \; deaths \; among \; females}{Mid \; year \; population \; of \; females}$ x **1000**

  = $\frac{40}{2600}$ x **1000** = **15.38 per 1000 females**

- **Specific death Rate due to TB**

$$= \frac{\text{No. of deaths from TB}}{\text{Mid year population}} \times 1000$$

$$= \frac{8}{6000} \times 1000 = \quad 1.33 \text{ per 1000 population}$$

- **Proportional Mortality rate due to TB**

$$= \frac{\text{No. of deaths from TB}}{\text{Total deaths}} \times 100$$

$$= \frac{8}{100} \times 100 = 8\% \text{ or 8 per 100 deaths}$$

- **Case fatality Rate**

$$= \frac{\text{No. of deaths due to TB}}{\text{Total number of TB cases}} \times 100$$

$$= \frac{8}{120} \times 100 = 6.67\% \text{ or 6.67 per 100 cases}$$

- **Under 5 yrs Mortality rate**

$$= \frac{\text{Deaths in children below 5 yrs of age}}{\text{Total live births}} \times 1000$$

$$= \frac{30}{220} \times 1000 \quad = 136.36 \text{ per 1000 live births}$$

- **Under 5 yrs Proportional Mortality rate**

$$= \frac{\text{Deaths in children below 5 yrs of age}}{\text{Total deaths}} \times 100$$

$$= \frac{30}{100} \times 100 \quad = 30\% \text{ or 30 per 100 deaths}$$

- **Death rate for December**

$$= \frac{\text{Deaths in December} \times 12}{\text{Mid year population}} \times 1000$$

245

$$= \frac{16 \times 12}{6000} \times 1000 \quad = 32 \text{ per 1000 population}$$

- **Weekly Death Rate**

$$= \frac{\text{Deaths in the week} \times 52}{\text{Mid year population}} \times 1000$$

$$= \frac{4 \times 52}{6000} \times 1000 \quad = 34.67 \text{ per 1000 population}$$

STATISTICS RELATED TO EPIDEMIOLOGY

STATISTICAL EPIDEMIOLOGY: It is an emerging branch of the disciplines of epidemiology and biostatistics that aims to:

- Bring more statistical rigour to bear in the field of epidemiology
- Recognize the importance of applied statistics, especially with respect to the context in which statistical methods are appropriate and inappropriate
- Aid and improve interpretation of our observations

By statistical epidemiology we can find risk of disease, incidence, and prevalence of a disease accurately.

Risk means the probability of some unwanted event or The chance or likelihood that an undesirable event or effect will occur, as a result of use or n onuse,incidence, or influence of a chemical, physical, or biologic agent, especially during a st ated period; the probability ofdeveloping a given disease over a specified time period

Risk factor: "Factor which is associated with an increased risk of acquiring a disease".

Uses of risk:

1. **Prediction:** By calculating the risk, we can predict about the future of an incidence of a disease
2. **Diagnosis:** The presence of risk factor increases the probability of a disease and more often it may give clue to rule out a disease (absence of risk factor).
3. **Prevention:** A risk factor is also a cause of disease and its removal can prevent it.

Here, we consider how "estimates of risk" are obtained by observing the relationship between exposure to risk factor and subsequent acquiring a disease.

CALCULATION OF RISKS

Basic expression of risk is "incidence".

DEFINITIONS:

1. **Incidence:** Number of new cases of a disease arising in defined period of time in a defined population
   a. Incidence among exposed

     b. Incidence among not exposed

     c. Incidence in general population

2. **Attributable risk:** (risk difference, additional risk)

   Definition:

   Incidence of disease attributable to exposure of risk factor

   It is (IE – IO) incidence among exposed – Incidence among not exposed

3. **Relative risk (risk ratio)**

   $$RR = \frac{IE}{IO}$$

   Definition:

How many times more likely exposed people will get disease in relation to non-exposed. It is also called "Ratio of incidence in exposed to incidence in non-exposed.

4. **Population attributable risk (PAR):** It is IP – IO (incidence in general population – incidence in not exposed)

   Definition:

   It is the incidence of disease in a population which is associated with risk factor.

5. **Population attributable risk proportion (PARP):** The fraction (or proportion) of disease in a population is attributable to risk factor.

$$\frac{IP - IO}{IP} \times 100 = \frac{\text{Population attributable risk}}{\text{Incidence of disease in population}} \times 100$$

6. **Attributable fraction (exposed)**

$$= \frac{IE - IO}{IE} \times 100 \quad \text{also called etiologoical fraction}$$

The fraction of disease in exposed (smoking) is attributable to risk factor (exposure)

Example: Lung cancer

	Present	Absent	Total
Smokers	100	99900	100000
Non smokers	8	99992	100000

Total	108	199892	200000

Calculations

1. Incidence of disease in population (IP) $= \dfrac{108}{200000} = 0.54/1000 \ population$

2. Incidence of disease in exposed (IE) $= \dfrac{100}{100000} = 1/1000 \ population$

3. Incidence of disease in non exposed (IO) $= \dfrac{8}{100000} = 0.08/1000 \ population$

4. Attributable risk (AR) $= IE - IO = 1 - 0.08 = 0.92/1000 \ population$

5. Relative risk $= \dfrac{IE}{IO} = \dfrac{1}{0.08} = 1.25$

6. Population attributable risk (PAR) $= IP - IQ$

$$PAR = 0.54 - 0.08 = 0.46 \text{ per } 1000$$

7. PARP (AR$_3$) $= \dfrac{IP - IO}{IP} \times 100$

$$= \dfrac{0.54 - 0.08}{0.54} \times 100 = 0.85 \text{ (or) } 85.18\%$$

8. Attributable fraction (exposed) (AR$_1$) $= \dfrac{IE - IO}{IE} \times 100$

(AFE) $\dfrac{1 - 0.08}{1} \times 100 = 92\%$

9. AR$_2$ = Smoking rate in cancer patients x AR$_1$

Derivation of formulae

	Cases	Non Cases	Total
Exposed	A 900	B 400	A + B =1300
Non exposed	C 100	D 600	C + D =700
Total	1000 A + C	1000 B + D	2000 A + B + C + D

Calculations

1. **Attributable risk:** Incidence among exposed minus Incidence among non exposed

Here exposed is A + B. In them incidence is A (cases). So, incidence among exposed is

$$\frac{A}{A+B}$$

Non exposed is C + D. In them incidence is C (cases). Here incidence among non-exposed is $\frac{C}{C+D}$

So AR $= \frac{A}{A+B} - \frac{C}{C+D}$

2. **Relative risk:** It is ratio of incidence in exposed to incidence in non-exposed

$$\text{So, AR} = \frac{IE.}{IO} = \frac{\frac{A}{A+B}}{\frac{C}{C+D}}$$

DEVIATION OF FORMULA FOR ODDS RATIO

It is also called cross product ratio.

Definition: $\dfrac{\text{Odds that cases is exposed by}}{\text{Odds that control is exposed by}}$

Next steps

Calculation of odds exposed by cases $= \dfrac{\text{Number of exposed in cases}}{\text{Number of not exposed in cases}}$

Calculation of odds exposed by Control (i.e. non cases) $= \dfrac{\text{Number of exposed in cases}}{\text{Number of not exposed in cases}}$

So, final formula for Odds ratio is:

$$\frac{\text{Exposed people in cases}}{\text{Not exposed people in cases}} + \frac{\text{Exposed people in non-cases}}{\text{Not exposed people in non-cases}}$$

$$\frac{\frac{A}{A+C}}{\frac{C}{A+C}} \div \frac{\frac{B}{B+D}}{\frac{D}{B+D}} \qquad \textbf{Now we do cancellation}$$

250

$$\frac{\frac{A}{A+C}}{\frac{C}{A+C}} \div \frac{\frac{B}{B+D}}{\frac{D}{B+D}}$$

$$= \frac{C}{A} \div \frac{D}{B} \qquad \text{Simplified}$$

$$= \frac{A\,D}{B\,C}$$

Calculation

OR $= \dfrac{900 \times 600}{400 \times 100} = \dfrac{540000}{40000} = 13.5$

SCREENING TESTS:

Screening is defined as: "Presumptive identification of unrecognized disease by application of rapidly applied tests".

If we want to use a test as screening test the test should have high sensitivity, high specificity, high predictive values.

Definition:

1. **Sensitivity:** Proportion of true positive correctly identified as positive
2. **Specificity:** Proportion of true negatives correctly identified as negatives
3. **Positive predictive value:** Probability of disease in persons who have positive test result
4. **Negative predictive value:** Probability of not having the disease in persons who have negative test result.

		Disease		
		Present	**Absent**	
Test	Positive	True positive **(a)**	False positive **(b)**	**a + b**
	Negative	False negative **(c)**	True negative **(d)**	**c + d**
		a + c	**b + d**	

1. **Sensitivity** $= \dfrac{a}{a+c} \times 100$

2. Specificity $= \dfrac{d}{b+d} \times 100$

3. Positive predictive value $= \dfrac{a}{a+b} \times 100$

4. Negative predictive value $= \dfrac{d}{c+d} \times 100$

5. Percentage of false negatives $= \dfrac{c}{a+c} \times 100$

6. Percentage of false positives $= \dfrac{b}{b+d} \times 100$

Example: AIDS

WESTERN BLOT TEST

		Disease		
		Present	**Absent**	
	Positive	85 a	50 b	105 a + b
	Negative	25 c	80 d	105 c + d
Tridot Test	Total	110 a + c	100 b + d	

1. **Sensitivity:** $\dfrac{a}{a+c} \times 100 = \dfrac{85}{110} \times 100 = 77.27\%$

2. **Specificity:** $\dfrac{d}{b+d} \times 100 = \dfrac{80}{100} \times 100 = 80\%$

3. **Positive predictive Value:** $\dfrac{a}{a+b} \times 100 = \dfrac{85}{105} \times 100 = 81\%$

4. **Negative predictive Value:** $\dfrac{d}{c+d} \times 100 = \dfrac{80}{105} \times 100 = 76\%$

5. **Percentage of false** $\dfrac{c}{a+c} \times 100 = \dfrac{25}{110} \times 100 = 22.73\%$

Negative:

6. **Percentage of false** $\dfrac{b}{b+d}$ **x 100** $= \dfrac{20}{100}$ **x 100 = 20%**

   Positives:

EPIDEMIOLOGICAL EXERCISES

EXERCISE NO 1.

In a district with a population of 3,000,000, the following data was recorded under NTCP in the year 1999.

Cases as on	1.1.1999	= 3000
New cases detected during	1999	= 700
Cases died during	1999	= 180
Cases discharged as cured		= 650

Calculate the prevalence of TB as on 1.1.99 and 31.12.99, incidence rate and case fatality rate.

Answer:

a. **Prevalence of TB as on 1.1.99 is :**

$$\dfrac{\text{Total No. of TB cases as on 1.1.1999}}{\text{Estimated population}} \text{ x } 1000$$

So, $\dfrac{3000}{3000000} \, x \, 1000 = 1 \, per \, 1000$ population

b. **Prevalence of TB as on 31.12.99.**

   Total tuberculosis cases as on 31.12.99 are: (3000 + 7000) − (650 + 180) = 2870. So point prevalence as on 31.12.99 is:

$$\dfrac{2870}{3000000} \text{ x } 1000 = \dfrac{287}{30000300000} = 0.93 \text{ per } 1000$$

c. **Incidence rate =** $\dfrac{700}{3000000} \, x \, 1000 = \dfrac{7}{30} = 0.23$ **per 1000 population**

d. **Case fatality =** $\dfrac{\text{Total No. of deaths due to TB}}{\text{Total number of cases of TB}} \, x \, 100$

   $= \dfrac{180}{3000} \, x \, 100 = 6\%$

e. **Specific death rate due to TB =**

$$\frac{\text{Number of deaths due to TB during one year}}{\text{Mid year population}} \times 1000$$

$$= \frac{180}{3000000} \times 1000 = 0.06/1000 \text{ population}$$

Exercise no 2: Malarial indices

In a PHC covering a population of 45,000, the following data was recorded under NMEP.

Total slides examined	= 3700
Slides positive for MP (malaria parasite)	= 150
Of these 150, positive for falciparum	= 60

Calculate API, ABER, annual falciparum incidence (AFI), slide positivity rate, slide falciparum rate.

Answer:

a) API (Annual Parasite Incidence)

$$= \frac{\textit{Confirmed caes during one year}}{\textit{Population under surveillance}} \; x \; 1000$$

$$= \frac{150}{45000} \; x \; 1000 = \frac{3.333}{1000} \; \text{population}$$

b) ABER (Annual Blood Examination Rate)

$$= \frac{\text{Number of slides examined}}{\text{Total Population}} \; x \; 100$$

c) Annual Falciparum Incidence (AFI)

$$= \frac{\text{Confirmed falciparum cases during one year}}{\text{Total population under surveillance}} \; x \; 1000$$

$$= \frac{60}{45000} \; x \; 1000 = \frac{4}{3} = 1.33 \; \textit{per} \; \textbf{1000}$$

d) Slide Positivity Rate (SPR)

$$= \frac{\text{Number of slides positive for MP}}{\text{Total slides examined}} \times 100$$

$$= \frac{150}{3700} \times 100 = 4.05 \text{ per 100 slides} = 4.05\%$$

e) Slide Falciparum Rate (SFR):

$$\frac{\text{Number of slides positive for falciparum}}{\text{Total slides examined}} \times 100$$

$$= \frac{60}{3700} \times 100 = 1.62 \text{ per 100 slides}$$

f) Falciparum rate :

$$= \frac{\textit{Number of falciparum positive}}{\textit{Total malaria positive}} \times 100 = \frac{60}{150} \times 100 = 40\%$$

Exercise No 3:

In a district with a population of 20,00,000, the following data was received under NLEP.

Cases as on 1.1.1999	=	3000
New cases detected during the year	=	450
Cases discharged as cured	=	900
Cases left the area	=	100
Out of 3000 leprosy cases lepromatous leprosy case	=	1000
Cases with deformities	=	900

Calculate point prevalence of leprosy as on 1.1.1999 and 31.12.1999, incidence of the leprosy for the year 1999, lepromatous leprosy rate and deformity rate.

Answer:

a. **Point prevalence of leprosy as on 1.1.1999**

$$\frac{\textit{No. of all current cases of leprosy (old + new)}}{\textit{Estimated population at the same point of time}} \times 100$$

$$\frac{3000}{2000000} \times 1000 = \frac{3}{2} = 1.5 \text{ per } 1000$$

255

b. Point prevalence of leprosy as on 31.12.1999.

Added cases during that one year are 450, discharged cases and cases left area are 900 + 100 = 1000. So, total cases as on 31.12.99 are (1000 − 450 = 550) = 3000 − 550 = 2450

So, point prevalence as on 31.12.99 is:

$$\frac{2450}{2000000} \; x \; 1000 = \frac{245}{200} = 1.2 \; per \; 1000$$

c. Incidence of leprosy for the year 1999 is:

$$\frac{No.\,of\ new\ cases\ of\ leprosy\ during\ one\ year}{Population\ at\ risk} \; x \; 1000$$

$$\frac{450}{2000000} \; x \; 1000 = \frac{45}{200} = 0.225 \; per \; 1000$$

d. Lepromatous leprosy rate

$$\frac{Total\ lepromatous\ leprosy\ cases}{Total\ leprosy\ cases} \; x \; 100$$

$$\frac{1000}{3000} \; x \; 100 = 33.33\%$$

e. Deformity Rate

$$\frac{No.\,of\ cases\ of\ deformity\ due\ to\ leprosy}{Total\ leprosy\ cases} \; x \; 100$$

$$\frac{900}{3000} \; x \; 100 = 30\%$$

Exercise no 4:

In a PHC with a population of 40000, filarial survey was carried out. Following are the findings:

Population examined – 10000.

Positive for MF alone (without symptoms) = 300

Patient with only clinical symptoms (without MF positivity) = 400

Patients with both MF positivity and symptoms = 100

Calculate filarial disease rate, filarial endemicity rate, MF rate

Answers:

a. Filarial disease rate

$$= \frac{Patients\ with\ symptoms + patients\ with\ both\ symptoms\ \&\ MF\ +ve}{Population\ examined} \; x \; 1000$$

$$\frac{400 + 100}{10000} \times 1000 = \textbf{50 per 1000}$$

c. **MF rate**

$$= \frac{Patients\ with\ both + Patients\ with\ MF\ positive}{Population\ examined} \times \textbf{1000}$$

$$= \frac{300 + 100}{10000} \times 1000 = \textbf{40 per 1000 or 4\%}$$

d. **Filarial endemicity rate =**

$$\frac{Patients\ with\ both,\ with\ symptoms\ and\ MF\ positive}{Population\ examined} \times 1000$$

So, patients with both symptoms and MF + ve are

= 300 + 400 + 100 = 800

$$= \frac{800}{10000} \times 1000 = \textbf{80 per 1000}$$

Exercise no 5:

A circular well with a diameter of 1 meter and with a depth of water column is 3.6 meter, to be chlorinated. On doing Harrock test, blue colour was developed in the 4 [th] cup. **Calculate the amount of bleaching powder required.**

Calculation

Depth of water column = 3.6 m (h)

Diameter of well = 1 m (d)

Formula for calculation of water in liters:

$$= \frac{\prod d^2 h}{4}$$

$$= \frac{3.14\ x\ 1^2 x\ 3.6}{4} = \textbf{2.826 cubic meters}$$

Here, 2.826 cubic meters is equal to 2826 liters.

455 liters is equal to 1 gallon water.

For each gallon water (455 liters) we need bleaching powder as show below:

Colour changed in 1st cup 2 grams/gallon water (455 litres)

Colour change in 2nd cup 4 grams/gallon water (455 litres)

Colour change in 3rd cup 6 grams/gallon water (455 litres)

Colour change in 4th cup 8 gramps/gallon water (455 litres)

Here, colour change is in 4th cup. So we add bleaching powder 8 grams/455 litres of water (gallon water)

So,

$$\frac{2826}{455} \; x \; 8 = 49.687 \; g \; m \; bleaching \; power$$

 like this, 6.21 gallons x 8 = 49.687 gm bleaching powder

So, the amount of bleaching powder required is 49.687 gm

Absolute risk: Same as risk. Contrast it with relative risk.

Absolute risk reduction: Risk difference between the control group and the intervention group.

Addition rule (of probability): The probability of occurrence of either of two or more mutually exclusive events is the sum of the probabilities of their individual occurrence.

Additive: A model stating that combined effect of two or more factors is the sun total of their **individual effects:** valid when there is no interaction.

Adjusted correlation: Same as partial correlation.

Adjusted odds ratio: The odds ratio obtained after eliminating the effect of other concomitant variables that might affecting the OR. This is generally obtained by including these concomitants in the logistic regression.

Etiological factSor: The characteristic that contributes to the occurrence of disease or a health condition. It may or may not be causal factor.

Alpha error: Same as type I error.

Alpha error rate: The probability of Type I error.

Alpha level: Same as significance level.

Alternative hypothesis: A plausible hypothesis that is accepted when the null hypothesis is rejected.

Analysis: The process of going into the deep of a phenomenon, data-set, thought, etc., and looking at its various components.

Analysis bias (for data): Gearing data analysis to support a particular hypothesis and ignoring aspects that contradict the hypothesis, e.g., using an inflated P-value for some statistical tests, using proportions when mean is appropriate, etc.

Analysis of variance: Breaking variance into its components such as within groups and between groups. Thimethod is used in regression analysis and in various other situations but more commonly for comparing their or more means.

Analytical study: A Study with the objective to identify the determinants or correlates of an outcome, such as a etiological factors, or to delineate their specific contribution to the outcome. See observational study, experiment.

Attributable risk: The additional risk that can be attributed to the presence of a risk factor. If risk of diabetes in those with both parents diabetics is 0.30 and in those with one parent diabetic is 0.25 (no other difference) then risk attributable to the diabetes in the second parent is 0.30 − 0.25 = 0.05.

Beta erro: Same as Type II error.

Bias: A systematic error that can falsify or distort the results of a study. Contrast it with random error. Bias can arise due to a variety of sources:

(i)   errors form faulty logic or incorrect of premises;

(ii)   nonrandom sample such as volunteers;

(iii)   small sample that fails to represent the entire spectrum of subjects;
(iv)   concomitant medication or concurrent disease that might seem unrelated;
(v)   lack of matching in case and control groups;
(vi)   unaccounted confounders;
(vii)   wrong or blurred definitions that give room to assessor to use subjective interpretations;

Bibliography: A list of citations of the relate literature. This is different from the list of references because references are restricted to the literature actually cited in the text. Bibliography includes references to the other literature as well that are not cited but are related.

Blinding: Keeping the experimental subject or observer or both ignorant about which subject is in the case group and which in the control group in a trial.

Case: A person or unit of interest possessing a specified characteristic, such as a person with the disease or a family living in the conditions of interest.

Case-contol stude: Investigation of the antecedents in a group of cases and equivalent controls without introducing any intervention. The groups are defined on the basis of presence or absence of disease or any other outcome of interest. The logic of the design leads from effect to the cause. All case-control studies are inherently retrospective.

Census: Survey of the entire population.

Control (group): Used in two senses:

1. The group of subjects that do not receive the test regimen. They may receive placebo, or the existing standard regimen, or any other regimen that is appropriate for comparison.

2. The group without disease or without any other outcome of interest. A defined series of steps to reduce or eliminate a disease.

Control (statistical): The statistical process of adjusting for any extraneous influence on the results.

Control (subject): A person or unit of interest but not possessing the specified characteristic, such as person not having the disease of interest, or a person being treated by regimen other than under test.

Controlled trial: A trial that compares intervention group to a control group: when not further qualified this generally indicates a trial with nonrandom or quasi-random allocation of subjects to the test and the control group.

Data: A set of observations, generally in numerical format but can be in text format also (plural of datum).

False negative: A person with disease classified as without disease. In place disease, false negativity can be for any other attribute.

False positive: A person without disease classified as with disease. In place of disease, false positivity can be for any other attribute.

Field trial: An experiment on human subjects in a community, such as vitamin A supplementation to children less than 3 years for examining improvement in their nutrition status.

International Classification of Diseases (ICD)

Index: A composite of two or more indicators, such as body mass index (BMI) for obesity that combines height and weight, and Indrayan's smoking index for a combination of age at initiation, duration, quantity an type of smoking, and the time elapsed since quitting by exsmokers.

Index case: An affected person who might affect others also. In the case of infection, the infected person is an index case who can spread the disease. When a new person is infected, he can be an index case for other susceptible.

Indicator: A single measurement that indicates the existence or magnitude of a condition. Signs-symptoms are indicators of a disease, smoking an indicator of lung cancer risk, and infant mortality rate (IMR) is an indicator of mortality. Contrast it with an index, which is obtained by combining two or more indicators.

Keywords: The set of words that describes the essential features of a study. These words are used for indexing purposes so that the article is quickly retrieved for that category.

Mean: The average.

Measurement bias: Systematic error in measurement. This could be either due to faulty instrument, or due to carelessness of the observer.

Measures of association: The parameters that quantify the degree of association between two or more qualitative factors. Chi-square based measures are (i) phi coefficient, (ii) Cramer's V, and (iii) contingency coefficient. More useful measures are (i) proportional reduction in error, and (ii) relative risk or odds ratio. For data on ordinal scale, these are Kendall is tau, Somer's d and Goodman-Kruskal gamma.

Median: The most middle value obtained after arranging values in increasing or decreasing order. Median seeks to divide the group in two equal halves, each with n/2 individuals. Sometimes in practice exactly equal halves are not possible, and they are divided into nearly equal halves.

Medical ethics: The discipline that considers individual patient's welfare above very thing else—thus puts restrictions on how research involving human subjects should be done. Sometimes animal experimentation is also included in its domain. See Helsinki Declaration.

Research design: Same as design.

Sample: A part of the target population. which is actually studied.

Survey: A descriptive study done generally on scientifically selected subjects. Another descriptive study methodology is case series.

Glossary of Some other important Terminologies

Accuracy: Truthfulness or correctness of particular value of a measurement to the reality. Age recorded as 7 years 4 months and 14 days is more accurate than recorded only as 7 years, although this additional accuracy may be redundant. Also BMI is more accurate measurement of overall obesity then ecto-, meso-, and endomorphy categories.

Adaptive design: A research design that builts flexibility into itself at the time of designing. This flexibility could be adding or deleting a group, changing the outcome of interest, but most often, changing the sample size in each group when interim results indicate the need for doing so.

Addition rule (of probability)— The probability of occurrence of either of two or more mutually exclusive events is the sum of the probabilities of their individual occurrence.

Additive —A model stating that combined effect of two or more factors is the sum total of their individual effects, valid when there is no interaction.

Adjusted odds ratio-The odds ratio obtained after eliminating the effect of other concomitant variables that might affecting the OR. This is generally obtained by including these concomitants in the logistic regression.

Adjusted rate— The net rate obtained after eliminating the effect of other concomitants that might be affecting the rate. This Adjustment increases the comparability between rates in different segments of population.

Adjustment- A procedure by which the effect of structural differences in the two or more groups is minimized, thus improving the comparability. Common methods of adjustment are regression and standardization.

Etiological diagram- A diagram that depicts the inter-relationship of various a etiological factors leading to the disease.

Aetiological factor— The characteristic that contributes to the occurrence of disease or a health condition. It may or may not be causal factor.

Age-adjusted death rate— See age standardization.

Age-standardization— A procedure of adjustment to remove the effect of differences in age composition of the groups to increase comparability. This adjustment is required when, for example, one group has older subject than in the other and the outcome of interest is death. For deaths, this is called age-adjusted death rate. This could be done by direct standardization or indirect standardization.

Agreement— When two procedures, Two observers, or two sites, etc., tend to give same result in each subject, they are said to be in agreement with one another. For qualitative data the extent of agreement is statistically measured by Cohen's kappa and for qualitative data by limits of disagreement.

Aleatory uncertainties— Uncertainties arising from variation in the factors internal to the system such as biological, psychological and environmental. Contrast it with epistemic uncertainties.

Allocation — The systematic error in results arising from specific allocation of subjects to the test and contrsol group, such group, such as due to nonrandom allocation.

Alpha error— Same as type I error.

Alpha error rate— The probability of Type I error.

Alpha level— Same as significance level.

Alternative hypothesis— A plausible hypothesis that is accepted when the null hypothesis is rejected.

Analysis— The process of going into the deep of a phenomenon, data-set, thought, etc., and looking at its various components.

Analysis bias (for data)— Gearing data analysis to support a particular hypothesis and ignoring aspects that contradict the hypothesis, e.g., using an inflated P-value for some statistical tests, using proportions when mean is appropriate, etc.

Analysis of variance— Breaking variance into its components such as within groups and between groups. This method is used in regression analysis and in various other situations but more commonly for comparing their or more means.

Analytical study— A Study with the objective to identify the determinants or correlates of an outcome, such as aetiological factors, or to delineate their specific contribution to the outcome. See observational study, experiment.

Anecdotal evidence— Incidental observation that lacks scientific scrutiny.

ANCOVA— Acronym for ANalysis Of COVAriance a statistical procedure used when the dependent (or outcome) variable is quantitative, and the independent (or antecedents) variables are a mixture of quantitative and qualitative variables.

ANCOVA— Acronym for ANalysis VAriance: A method for analysis of quantitative out-come when it is dependent on qualitative characteristics, particularly the groups of subjects.

Antagonism— The situation where combination of two or more factors depresses the intensity of outcome compared to the sum of their individual effects: a negative interaction effect.

Antecedent— A characteristic that precedes the outcome. In may or may not be (fully or partially) responsible for the outcome.

APACHE score— **Acronym for Acute Physiology and Chronic Health Evaluation:** A scoring system that helps to assess the prognosis in case of critical condition of a patient. This is based on state of consciousness, reflexes, eye movements, blood pressure, etc.

Apgar score— Sum total of (0 to 2) scores assigned to each of heart rate, respiration, muscle tone, skin colour, and response to stimulation in a newborn. A low score such as less than 4 out of possible 10 is an indication of poor prognosis.

Area sampling— The method of sampling the uses geographical area as the unit. When the sampling frame of the study units is not available, area sampling can be used in a community-based study to select some areas by using a map, and then all the subjects in those selected areas can be included.

Area under the curve— The area from the ROC curve to the base: Used as an indicator of the efficacy of a test tin terms of sensitivity ans specificity – can be used to compare performance of various medical tests. The area under the concentration curve is used to assess the efficacy of a regimen and to compare performance of two or more regimens.

Arithmetic mean— Same as mean.

Arm of a trial— The case (or test or intervention) group is one arm of trial and the control group is the other arm. The test arm may have more than one regimen.

Ascertainment (or assessment) bias— Bias due to paying more attention to cases than controls in assessment, or giving more attention to specific outcomes of interest. Also when more accurate history is given by diseased then nondiseased, or when they are more cooperative than the others. Also when outcome of interest is morbidity but there are early deaths that no longer can contribute to morbidity. Assessment bias also occurs when the observer is able to establish more rapport with some respondents than others, e.g., due to cultural similarities. Diabetes and gallstone may appear to be associated because diabetics are regularly checked for gall stone and nondiabetics are not checked. The property of change in one qualitative factor being accompanied by the change in the othe. This change can be causal, incidental, or due to a third intervening factor. The association can be full or partial of various degrees, and can be negative or positive.

Attack rate— New spells during a specified time interval (such as the period of an epidemic) as percentage of the total population at risk in the same interval. See secondary attack rate.

Attributable fraction (of risk)— The proportion of risk that can be validly assigned to a particular exposure.

Attributable risk- The additional risk that can be attributed to the presence of a risk factor. If risk of diabetes in those with both parents diabetics is 0.30 and in those with one parent diabetic is 0.25 (no other difference) then risk attributable to the diabetes in the second parent is $0.30 - 0.25 = 0.05$.

Attribute— A qualitative characteristic.

Attrition— Loss of subjects during the course of the study. This can happen due to temporary unavailability, migration, refusal to participate, severe injury, or unrelated death.

Attrition bias— Systematic difference between the groups in the pattern of attrition of the subjects.

Bar diagram— A diagram appropriate for disjoint categories to show th number of subjects or mean or rates by bars of corresponding height.

Baseline date— The data that show the status of the subjects at the initial stage, generally at the time of beginning of the study. The baseline is used for evaluating whether any subsequent change is either due to intervention or some other factor.

Bayes' rule— The rule that converts probability of A given B to the inverse probability of B given A. Most common use of this in medicine is obtaining the probability of disease given signs/symptoms by first obtaining the probability of sings/symptoms given disease, and in obtaining predictivities on the basis of sensitivity and specificity. Both require some additional information.

Before-after study— Assessing subjects before and intervention, and after the intervention to find changes — thus assessing the utility of the intervention without using a control group; also called a non-controlled trial. Part of the effect found in this study could be due to psychological factors.

Bell-shaped distribution— Same as Gaussian distribution.

Berkson's bias— Occurs when the study is based on hospital cases but the exposure is such that increases the chance of admission. Thus hospital cases will have more exposure than hospital controls such as fracture in motor vehicle injury cases.

Beta error— Same as Type II error.

Beta error rate— The probability of Type II error.

Bias— A systematic error that can falsify or distort the results of a study. Contrast it with random error. Bias can arise due to a variety of sources:

    (i)   errors form faulty logic or incorrect of premises;

    (ii)   nonrandom sample such as volunteers;

    (iii)   small sample that fails to represent the entire spectrum of subjects;

    (iv)   concomitant medication or concurrent disease that might seem unrelated;

    (v)   lack of matching in case and control groups;

    (vi)   unaccounted confounders;

    (vii)   wrong or blurred definitions that give room to assessor to use subjective interpretations;

Bibliography— A list of citations of the relate literature. This is different from the list of references because references are restricted to the literature actually cited in the text. Bibliography includes references to the other literature as well that are not cited but are related.

Binary variable— A characteristics that is assessed only in two categories such as ascites present or absent (or yes/no), or gender as male or female. A qualitative variable is mostly binary (in some cases could be polytomous/and/or ordinal) but a quantitative variable can also be made binary by dividing into two categories such systolic blood pressure < 140 and->140 mmHg.

Bioequivalence— Similar course of the disease process in the two regimens under comparison: also evaluated in terms of comparable bioavailability of drug products, say, within 80% to 125% with respect to area under the curve and Cmax Also see equivalence and therapeutic equivalence.

Biological plausibility— Consistency with the present biological knowledge, which can be explained.

Biosis— The UK-based citation service that processes articles from a large number of journals, books, monographs, conference proceedings, etc, on all topics of biological sciences.

Biostatistics— The science dealing with medical uncertainties in a group of subjects — their identification, measurement, and control—leading to decision with less error.

Bivariate analysis— A statistical analysis of data by considering two variables together, such as maternal hemoglobin level and birth-weight category, or alcohol intake and occurrence of liver cirrhosis. One or both variables can be either quantitative or qualitative.

Black box approach— Using computer to solve problems without understanding the implications of the underlying procedure.

Blinding— Keeping the experimental subject or observer or both ignorant about which subject is in the case group and which in the control group in a trial.

Body mass index (BMI)— Weight in kg divided by square of height in meters: a measure of obesity in adults. A BMI <20.0 kg/m2 is considered lean, 20.0-25.9 is considered 'normal', 25.0-29.9 overweight, and >3-0.0 obese.

Bonferroni procedure— When two or more comparisons or other statistical tests of hypothesis are done on the same set of data, the total probability of alpha error can increase much beyond the prefixed level such as 5%. In order to keep the error probability within the specified level a, the Bonferroni procedure is to do individual comparisons at a/k level of significance where k is the total number of comparisons. If k = 4 and a = 0.05, each comparison is done at 0.05/4 = 0.0125 level. This is a conservative procedure in the sense that the total level of significance is actually less than a.

Bootstrapping— A computer based data resembling method that helps in estimating the sampling variance and other features — usually used when the features of the parent population are obscure or complex.

Box-and-whiskers plot— same as box plot.

Box plot— A diagram that shows the median, the first and the third quartile (The difference between them giving an idea of dispersion, and the distance from median on either side, of skewers), and the lowest and highest value after excluding outliers: a very effective method to present so many features of data in one diagram.

Burden of disease— A composite measure of premature mortality from a disease and morbidity equated to mortality through a weighting system based on age, discounted duration and severity of disease. Premature mortality is assessed in comparison to the mortality in the population with highest life expectancy.

Case - A person or unit of interest possessing a specified characteristic, such as a person with the disease or a family living in the conditions of interest.

Case-control study— Investigation of the antecedents in a group of cases and equivalent controls without introducing any intervention. The groups are defined on the basis of presence or absence of disease or any other outcome of interest. The logic of the design leads from effect to the cause. All case-control studies are inherently retrospective.

Case-fatality rate— The number of cases who die out those who are suffering from a particular disease. This measures the virulence of the disease. Case-fatality in typhoid is low and high in tetanus. For chronic diseases such as cancers, the case-fatality may be 100% but measures such as 5-year death rate may be better indicators of the 'virulence' of disease.

Case group— The group of subjects that already has the disease or the condition under study.

Case- referent study—same as case-control study but comparison is with some other disease and not placebo-

Case series— A specific group of patients with the disease of interest; generally consecutive cases reporting in a clinic, or observed in a community. There is no control group in this setup. Case series is one method of a descriptive study.

Case study—Study of one individual, particularly with regard to the antecedent and outcome factors as observed in that person.

Categorical data— All qualitative data are categorical. In addition, quantitative data are also summarized into categories. For example, for smoking index of 300 individuals, the table may have categories such as 0, 0.4-4.9, 5.0-9.9 and 10.0+. Some times such categories are used for analysis and inference purposes also.

Cause-effect relationship— Statistically significant dependence of an outcome on an antecedent so that any change in antecedent makes corresponding changes in the outcome when all confounders are absent. The relationship should also meet other criteria such as temporality, consistency and biological plausibility. See necessary cause and sufficient. cause.

Cause-specific rate— The rete obtained when numerator is restricted to a particular cause (e.g., of morbidity or fo mortality). Cause-specific death rate is the number of deaths due to a cause per thousand population. Sum of cause-specific death rates for all causes in the same as crude death rate.

Census— Survey of the entire population.

Centiles— Same as percentiles. See also deciles, quartiles, tertiles,

Central tendency— Among variations, there is still a tendency for a set of values of gather around a central value. Mean, Median and mode are measures of central tendency.

Chi-square test— A versatile statistical procedure that is used to test different types of hypothesis on proportions, such as equality, trend and relationship.

Citation— Identification data of a document containing the authors' name, title, publication name, volume, publication data, page numbers, etc.

Classification— Placing a unit to one of the two or more known classes or categories. Units within each category share some similarity among them, and units in different classes are dissimilar.

Clinical agreement— See agreement.

Clinical epidemiology— Application of principle of epidemiology to individual subjects, particularly to the patients.

Clinical equipoise— Genuine uncertainty among the experts about the relative merits of the regimens under trial: thus no research group is particularly disadvantaged.

Clinical significance— A situation where a result is capable of modifying the management of a patient.

Clinical thresholds (of normal range)— A range of values of a quantitative medical measurement in healthy subjects that has least overlap with the values found in diseased subjects so that chance of misclassification is minimum. But the chance of error remains. for example, for blood pressure that is 140/90 mmHg.

268

Clinical trial— A medical experiment on human subjects, particularly in a clinic setup, such as to find efficacy and safety of a new therapeutic or diagnostic regimen.

Clinimetrics— Assigning scores to clinical entities for diagnostic or rating purposes — thus qualities are converted to quantities.

Close-ended question— A question for which list of possible answers is already provided.

Cluster— A group of subjects with some commonality — generally available in close proximity of time or space.

Cluster random samping—Dividing the largest population into cluslers of specified size and selecting a few clusters by random method.

Cochrane Callaboration — An international organisation of producers and consumers of medical research that helps to clarify the research achievements, particularly health care interventions such as drugs, diet alteration and behaviour change. The focus is mostly on systematic reviews or correct meta-analysis of the relevant studies.

Cochrane Review— A review of trials, mostly based on meta-analysis, following specific guidelines of Cochrane Collaboration.

Coding— Assigning a numeric to a qualitative characteristic, such as code 1 for hypertension, code 2 for diabetes, code 3 for cancer, etc. Codes are not quantities, and care should be exercised that they are not used as quantities at the time of analysis. These are used only for convenience in data entry.

Coefficient of determination— The percentage of total variation in a variable explained by one or more of the others. In a simple linear regression setup, this is square of the correlation coefficient. In a multiple linear regression setup, this is square of the multiple correlation coefficient.

Coefficient of variation— Standard deviation divided by mean. This unit-free measure is used to compare dispersion of one variable with the other, such as dispersion of cholesterol level with dispersion of body temperature in a group of cases.

Cohen's kappa— for qualitative data, a measure of agreement in excess of chance between two or more observes, methods, sites, etc.

Cohort— A clearly defined person or a group of persons with some common feature, who are followed for an outcome in a specific period beginning from a defined common baseline: not necessarily beginning at the same time. A cohort of women taking contraceptive pill may start from the day of first intake but it may include women staring in any chronological month of the year. See also inception cohort.

Cohort study— A prospective study of a cohort for a specified period, generally to observe the occurrence of an outcome of interest, and thereby determine the incidence and risk.

Collation of data— The process of rearranging the data into intelligible form so that either the conclusions can be drawn or analysis can be done.

muComnity trial— Same as field trial.

Compliance bias — Either higher noncompliance by treatment group relative to the control because of discomfort or poor intake of the drug, or better compliance by them because they are improving.

Concealment of allocation— The process of allocation of subjects to groups that is impervious to any influence of the person making the allocation. Among methods of such concealment are centralised randomisation without participation of the observer, coded and identically looking packing of the placebo and drug, and sequentially numbered opaque envelopes.

Concentration curve— Plot of quantitative response versus time such as of concentration of drug in body at different points of time after intake.

Conceptual bias— errors arising from faulty logic or incorrect premises.

Concomitant variable — Same as confounder.

Concordance— Agreement or similarity between two individuals in a paired setup.

Concurrent validity— Consistency of response to two or more questions in the sense that they reflect the same pattern. For example, high calorie intake and low exercise together should correspond to greater obesity. Response to these three items should be consistent with one another.

Conditional probability— The probability to occurrence of an event such as disease when some a-priori information such as sign symptoms are known: denoted by P(A/B) where after slash (/) sign is what is known a-priori.

Confidence interval— The interval within which results of other similar studies is expected to lie with a certain confidence level.

Confidence level— The degree of assurance that other studies of similar type will have the same results as obtained by the participants in the current study.

Conflict of interest— Personal, financial, or other interest of any investigator that could influence the finding or the interpretation.

Confidence limits— The upper and lower boundaries of confidence interval.

Confounder— An extraneous factor that could be a full or partial explanation of the outcome of interest in addition to the factor under study so that its effect can not be differentiated from the other: such as dietary factors when examining relationship between smoking and cervical cancer. Presence of unaccounted confounders decreases the validity of a study.

Confounder bias— Bias due to presence of one or more unaccounted confounders.

Consecutive sample— The sample of subjects enrolled on the basis of the sequence of their arrival, and none is excluded if eligible till the desired number is reached.

Consistency— Same as reliability.

CONSORT— Acronym for CONsolidated Standards of Reporting of Trials: This provides guidelines on how a trial results should be reported.

Construct validity— The ability of a set of items or questions to assess a given theoretical concept. Suppose positive health is defined as the ability to withstand physical stress. and the intention is to measure it by excess in hemoglobin level, forced vital capacity, and pain bearing capacity.

The ability to withstand stress is also separately measured by items such as lack of restriction in daily activity by injury or fever. The correspondence between these two assessments will indicate construct validity of the measurements. It is the agreement between the theoretical concept and the specific device used to measure that concept.

Content validity— Sufficiency or adequacy of the items or questions to measure a phenomenon. For example, spinal placatory test may not have good content validity to identify spinal neuromusculoskeletal dysfunction. Content validity is judged by a panel of experts.

Contingency table— A table containing the number of subjects with different characteristics, which should be mutually exclusive and exhaustive, such as number of subjects with and without disease, and each with a positive or negative test. A contingency table is used to test if one characteristic is associated with the other.

Continuous variable— A variable that can theoretically have infinite number of possible values within a short range. Age is continuous since within 8 and 12, it can be 8.17, 10.874, 9.756 years, etc. Age can be measured in terms of days, hours and minutes, although practically there is no need to do this. Blood pressure is a continuous variable but measured in integers for convenience. Parity is not a continuous variable because there is no possibility of it being 2.75 or 1.6.

Control group - Used in two senses:

1. The group of subjects that do not receive the test regimen. They may receive placebo, or the existing standard regimen, or any other regimen that is appropriate for comparison.

2. The group without disease or without any other outcome of interest.

Control (programme)— A defined series of steps to reduce or eliminate a disease.

Control (statistical)— The statistical process of adjusting for any extraneous influence on the results.

Control (subject)— A person or unit of interest but not possessing the specified characteristic, such as person not having the disease of interest, or a person being treated by regimen other than under test.

Controlled trial— A trial that compares intervention group to a control group: when not further qualified this generally indicates a trial with nonrandom or quasi-random allocation of subjects to the test and the control group.

Convenience sample— The group of subjects that are selected primarily because they were available at a convenient time or place. This is one of the several ways that a purposive sample can be drawn.

Correlates— Factors that are related in someway to an outcome of interest. They may or may not be contributors to the outcome.

Correlation— The degree or strength of relationship between two quantitative variables. Loosely used for qualitative variables also. For linear relationships, it is measured by Pearsonian correlation coefficient that ranges from −1 to + 1. A negative correlation means that increase in the value of one variable is accompanied by linear decrease in the other, and vice-versa. A positive correlation means that the two move together in the same direction. A correlation close to zero means that increase or decrease in on does not linearly affect the other. Correlation coefficient can be close to zero when a strong relationship is present but the nonlinear.

Correlation coefficient— See Pearsonian correlation coefficient. The other types of correlation are Spearman's, multiple, partial, etc.

Cost-benefit analysis— The assessment of benefit per unit of cost, when both are measured in monetary units.

Cost-effectiveness analysis— The assessment of effectiveness (life saved, disability restricted, year of life gained, etc.) per unit of cost.

272

Covariance— A measure of how the product of two quantitative variables behave — used in calculatiny correlation coefficient.

Covariate— Same as confounder: generally used in a restrictive sense for quantitative variables only.

Cox regression— A type of regression that models logarithm of hazard ratio on the covariates that affect this ratio. Also see proportional hazards model.

Criterion standard— Same as gold standard, but a preferred term.

Criterion validity— Ability of a device to provide a measure that correlates or agrees with the criterion known to correctly measure the characteristic of interest.

Critical value (in the hypothesis testing)— The threshold value of the statistical test criterion such as X^2, t and F, beyond which it is considered statisticall significant.

Cross-voer design— A design that stipulates that same subjects will get the test and the control regimen after a washout period, but the sequence is randomised. Half the subjects get regimen A followed by B, and the other half B followed by A. Using same subjects for both the regimens reduces variability and thus also the level of uncertainty in the results.

Cross-product ratio— Same as odds ratio.

Cross-sectional study— An analytical study with a format that elicits information on the antecedents and the outcomes at the same time. Such a format is poor to investigate cause-effect type of relationship but is good to generate hypothesis.

Cross-tabulation— The process of obtaining the number of subjects of various types when divided by two characteristics simultaneously such as distribution of myocardial infarction cases by their lipoprotein (a) and homocysteine levels. In most cross-tabulations, these levels would be in categories such as 10.0-14.9, 15.0-19.9, etc.

c-statistic— A statistic that measures the area under an ROC curve.

Crude death rate— Total deaths in one year in a population divided by mid-year population.

Current contents— The electronic database of table of contents and bibliographic citations from current issues of more than 7500 research journals in sciences, social sciences, arts, and humanities.

Curve— Opposed to straight line, the curve depicts relationship that varies at different values of two variables. For example, one variable may increase for lower values of the other and then decrease for the higher values of the other. Another example is the relationship between glomerular filtration rate (GFR) in chronic renal failure cases and plasma creatinine level. As creatinine level rises, GFR declines steeply in the beginning and then declines slowly.

Curvilinear relationship— A relationship that is depicted by a curve opposed to a line, but can be converted to a line through some mathematical transformation.

Data— A set of observations, generally in numerical format but can be in text format also (plural of datum).

Database— A collection of items of data arranged in a predefined format, usually held on a computer.

Data cleaning— The process of correcting and deleting the incomplete or apparently wrong observations from the data set. Sometimes this may suggest a relook at the original source for finding the correct value.

Data dredging— Initially used for excessive analysis of data in search of new hypotheses, but now used for re-analysing data after deleting some inconvenient values so as to fit them into supporting a particular hypothesis — a very unfair practice that has now become so easy because of wide availability of computers.

Data editing— Same as Data cleaning.

Data Safety and Monitoring Board (DSMB) — An independent body of reputable persons who agree to monitor a research project regarding the integrity of data and adherance to protocol.

Death spectrum— Variety of causes of death: some people meet death slowly such as by cancer, and some sudden such as by myocardial infarction.

Deciles— Nine cut-points of values of a variable that divide the total number of subjects in ten equal parts: obtained after arranging the values in ascending order.

Decision analysis— The process of reaching to a decision after considering probabilities of various outcomes and value judgments regarding the utility of those outcomes.

Decision analysis is considered a very effective method to take a valid decision under conditions of uncertainties.

Deduction method— The method of reaching to a conclusion for a particular individual on the basis of a known genera alised result-from general to particular.

Degrees of freedom— The number of observations in a dataset that can freely very once the parameters have been estimated. This concept is used in chi-square, Student's t and other statistical procedures since their distribution depends on degrees of freedom. .

Definition bias— The bias due to

1. wrong or substandard definition such as of impotence on the basis of erectile dysfunction alone; or

2. blurred definition that gives room to assessor to use subjective interpretation such as blood pressure-> 140/190 for hypertension without specifying what to do is systolic level is higher and diastolic is lower. Errors in diagnostic or screening criteria also come under this category.

Delphi method— A less scientific but a quick method t arrive at a consensus among experts. In this method, the responses from a panel of experts are iteratively obtained that are progressively refined by reducing the options in successive rounds depending on what options are preferred in the previous rounds.

Dependent variable— A variable that is sought to be explained by one or more of the other variables. The dependent variable is generally the outcome of interest whereas independent variables are the antecedents.

Descriptive study— A study with the objective to delineate the distribution of disease or a health condition in a defined population, or to describe clinical features of specific kind of subjects. It also includes estimation of parameters such as mean and percentiles.

This does not examine causality or aetiology.

A descriptive study could be a census, a sample survey or a case series.

Design (of research)— The format of collective, compilation and analysis of observations. See descriptive study, analytical study. Also see sampling design.

Design bias— A design of a study were the selection of subjects is not random, control group is not adequately matched, definitions of subjects of characteristics to be studied are loose, confounders are not properly accounted, etc.

Design effect— The effect on the variance of an estimate, and thus on efficiency of a study, due to the design of the study, such as of cluster random sampling relative to the simple random sampling.

Determinant— A factor that is responsible, fully or partially, for an outcome.

Diagnostic score— A numerical score used as an aid in establishing diagnosis, such as thyroid scoring system to distinguish hypo-, eu- and hyperthyroidism on the basis of clinical assessment.

Diagnostic test— A criterion used for confirming the presence of disease or a condition. This should have high positive productivity. The criterion could be a laboratory test, a radiological test, or a clinical observation.

Dichotomous variable — Same as binary variable.

Digit preference— Preference for certain digits such as 0 and 5. Then they become predominant in reporting and recording. This can affect the result.

Direct standardisation— A procedure of adjustment to bring the differential structure of two or more groups to a common (standard) base to increase their comparability: most commonly done for differential age structure that can easily affect mortality. In direct standardisation the observed subgroup specific rates are used on the standard group structure.

Disability-adjusted life expectancy— Life expectancy adjusted for equivalent life lost due to disability of varying degrees during the life time.

Disability-adjusted life years (DALYs) lost— The loss of years of life due to premature mortality compared to the most healthy population, plus loss of equivalent years of life due to various disabilities of different severity and duration from morbidities or otherwise. This measures the burden of disease in a population. The disability arises from sickness from time to time.

Discrete variable— A variable that can take only finite, practically small, number of possible values. Parity for a woman is a discrete variable.

Deaths in an area with population 200,000 is theoretically discrete but can be considered continuous for statistical purposes it can take a large number of possible values.

Disease spectrum— Among many types of disease spectra, the one of special epidemiological interest is the proportion of population that is susceptible, proportion that has infection (apparent + inapparent), proportion that has disease, the proportion that has serious from of disease, and the proportion that die. Note that the proportion is nested in the subsequent preceding proportion. Disease spectrum helps to plan the research accordingly, and to take measures to control the disease.

Disease thresholds (of normal range)— The range of values of a quantitative measurement beyond which there is a considerable risk of presence of disease or occurrence of disease. The chance of misclassification remains in this threshold also as in any other such threshold.

Dispersion— The degree of variability or scatteredness of the values of a variable when measured for different subjects or at different times.

Dissertation— A detailed discourse or treaties on a particular topic providing it a new perspective generally the written work submitted by a candidate for the award of a doctoral (PhD) degree.

Distal measures of health— The background characteristics that indirectly affect the health condition under consideration. Socioeconomic factors such as education, income and occupation make an impact on diet, hygiene and exercise that in turn affect the pathophysiological parameters, on the basis of which a condition is assessed. Thus socioeconomic are distal and pathophysiological parameters are proximal measures.

Distribution (statistical)— The pattern of values when obtained for a large number of subjects. For incubation period of AIDS, the distribution would tell us how many or what percentage of cases have incubation period between 5 and 6 years, what percentage between 6 and 7, 7 and 8, etc. Thus, the distribution tell what has been the dispersion and where has been the concentration of values. See Gaussian distribution, skewed distribution.

Dose-ranging trial— A clinical trial in which two or more doses of an agent are tested against each other to determine their relative efficacy and safety.

Dose-response relationship— Any kind of relationship between quantity of does and the degree of response but generally indicating that higher the does, higher the response, such as between smoking and lung cancer.

Double-blind trial— A trial in which neither the experimental subject nor the assessor knows that the subject has received the test regimen or the control regimen. This removes the possible bias in response and ascertainment.

Dropout— A subject who is initially enrolled for a study but whose subsequent measurements as required under the study protocol could not be obtained.

DSMB— short for Data Safety and Monitoring Board.

Dunnett's test— A statistical test used to compare means in two or more test groups with mean in the control group.

Ecological study— A study in which broad, between-population differences in patterns of exposure to a particular factor are compared with the incidence rates of the disease of interest in those population.

Effectiveness— The extent to which a regimen is effective in meeting its objectives in actual field conditions or routine circumstances generally measured in percentage. Pragmatic trials, field trials or post-marketing surveillance is used to evaluate effectiveness of drugs.

Effect size— Magnitude of effect of a factor on an outcome. This could be proportion, difference, odds ratio, measure of association, etc. This could also be standardized mean difference between the test and control group obtained as the mean difference divided by its standard error.

Efficacy— The extent to which a regimen is effective in meeting its objectives in ideal conditions — generally measured in percentage. Generally RCTs are used to evaluate efficacy of a regimen.

Efficiency— The frequency of desired outcome per unit of resource inputs such as time, money and manpower. For example, coronary angiography using 4 French catheters may be more efficient procedure than 6 french catheters because of early ambulation without sacrificing the quality of images. Case-control studies are considered more efficient, particularly for rare outcomes, than prospective studies because of lower cost. Campaign against smoking may be more efficient for reducing deaths or for increasing life-years than treatment of lung cancer patients.

Electronic resources— Resources available in electronic format such as on compact disk (CD), diskette, and particularly the World Wide Web (www). For literature, these include books, journals, other documents, citation databases (e.g., PubMed), etc.

Empiricism— The system based on observations and evidence, opposed to theories.

Endpoint— The outcome that a study is designed to assess. The examples are recovery. pain relief, duration of hospital stay, side-effects, disease progression, and death.

Epidemiology The study of factors that affect distribution and determinants of disease or a health condition in a human population.

Epidemiologic consistency— The correspondence among the incidence, prevalence, duration of disease, mortality, etc., so that their underlying relationship is properly reflected.

Epistemic uncertainties— Uncertainties arising form limitation knowledge and biases. Contrast it with aleatory uncertainties.

Equipoise (subject)— Subjects are such that the outcome of test or control regimen is uncertain, i.e., the subjects are not chosen in a manner that they favour one regimen or the other — an ideal situation for conducting RCTs because either of the two regimens can be used without raising ethical issues, and the results would be more valid. Also see clinical equipoise.

Equipoise (clinical)— See clinical equipoise.

Equivalence— Difference between two or more groups or regimens by not more than a prespecified clinically irrelevant amount. Two regimens are considered therapeutically equivalent if their efficacy does not differ by more than a prespecified small amount. They are considered bioequivalent if the course of the disease or recovery in the two regimens is nearly the same. Therapeutic equivalence considers only the outcome whereas bioequivalence considers the entire course.

Equivalence trial— A clinical trial with the objective to examine the equivalence of two regimens.

ERMed— Short for Electronic Resources in Medicine: A database of literature (more than 1200 medical journals) being promoted by National Medical Library (India) for medical researchers in the country.

Error— See bias, false positive, false negative, random error, Type I and Type II error.

Error in research (honest, negligent and deliberate)— Honest error is absolutely unintentional that arises from limitation of knowledge, such as not taking care of unforeseen bias. Negligent error is gearing up investigations of findings to support a particular view neglecting the other evidence. Deliberate error is misconduct of plagiarism, reporting inflated sample size, cooking up the results, etc.

Ethics— See medical ethics.

Evidence-based— Using evidence as available in literature, in records, or in newly generated data, for managing patients after proper accounting of risks and benefits.

Exclusion criteria— The set of conditions presence of which will exclude and otherwise eligible subject from the study. Generally these conditions are indicative or severe from of disease or complications that render a subject unsuitable for that research. Exclusion criteria are part of the case definition that delineates the target population. The other part is inclusion criteria.

Expectation of life— Same as life expectancy.

Experiment— A study of effect intentionally introduced intervention or alteration of a factor, under controlled conditions. In medicine, the term is generally used for laboratory experiments. See trial.

Experimental design— The structure of an experiment in terms of inclusion and exclusion criteria for subjects, method of allocation of subjects to intervention or other groups, and number of subjects in various groups. Sometimes this also includes details of assessments, reliability and validity of tools and of measurements, etc.

Expert system (medical)— An intelligent computer aid to diagnosis, treatment and prognosis. It is capable of storing all the information, and more importantly to slectively retrieve the relevant information as an aid to the physician, and is capable of suggesting a spectrum of diagnosis for the given set of complaints, examination results, laboratory findings, etc., and also suggests a possible line of treatment and the prognostic implications.

Explanatory trial — A trial done under near ideal conditions with practically no deviation. Contrast it with pragmatic trial.

Explanatory variable – Same as independent variable.

Exploratory analysis— A method for examining the patterns and features of a dataset– generally based on graphical display.

Exploratory study— A small-scale study of relatively short duration, which is carried out to gain baseline knowledge about a problem for which little is known.

Exposure factors— The conditions to which a group is a suspected to have been exposed, which may alter the risk of outcome of interest.

Face Validity— The property of a measurement or an instrument to apparently look right or reasonable.

Factor— A characteristic that can, or suspected to, cause alteration in an outcome.

Factorial design— A design that includes all possible combinations of the antecedent factors under study. If there are three antecedent factors for visual acuity in adults—age in years as <40, 40-49 or 50+, gender as male or female, and hemoglobin level in g/ dl as <10.0, 10.0-12.9, 13.0-14.9 or 15.0+ then a total of 3×2×4 = 24 combinations are required to be studied in a factorial experiment, and each combination must be tried on at least some subjects by design.

False negative— A person with disease classified as without disease. In place disease, false negativity can be for any other attribute.

False positive— A person without disease classified as with disease. In place of disease, false positivity can be for any other attribute.

Field trial— An experiment on human subjects in a community, such as vitamin A supplementation to children less than 3 years for examining improvement in their nutrition status..

Fisher's exact test— A statistical test used for 2×2 contingency table to find statistically significant difference when the number of subjects is small. When the number is large, this is approximated by chi-square.

Fixed effects model— A statistical model that stipulates that the levels of factors under study are the ones of interest. Contrast it with random effects model.

Follow-up study—Same as prospective study.

Food-frequency questionnaire— A form which includes as list of 100-150 commonly consumed foods and provides space to fill-in how often each food is eaten. It may also include information on serving-size, variation by season, etc.

Four-fold table— A contingency table with tow rows and two columns so that the total number of cells is four (excluding the totals).

Frequency— Used in two senses:

1. Frequency of occurrence per unit of time (per month, per year, etc.).

2. Number of subject with a particular characteristic or with values in a particular interval, such as how many have homocysteine level between 10 and 14 mull/l.

Frequency curve— A graphical representation of a frequency distribution by a smooth curve.

Frequency distribution— A statistical distribution of subject that displays the number of subjects with different levels of measurement, e.g., how many have diastolic blood pressure <70 mmHg, how many between 70-74, 75-79, etc.

Frequency matching— Same as group matching.

Frequency polygon— A graphical representation of the frequency distribution by a polygon. shape.

Friedman test— A nonparametric test for comparing central tendency in more than two groups in a two-way design.

F-test— A statistical procedure for test of hypothesis on equality of three or more means, and for other setups such as regression.

Garbage-in, garbage-ot syndrome— The tendency of getting poor output or poor outcome when the inputs of efforts are poor.

Gaussian distribution— Distribution of values of a quantitative variable such that they are symmetric with respect to a middle value with same mean, median and mode, and the frequencies taper-off rapidly in a particular manner on both sides—a bell-shaped distribution.

General linear model— A model that describes a dependent variable as a linear combination of a set of independent variables with two important features –

1. the variables could be qualitative or quantitative or mixture, and

2. the variable could be square, cube, logarithm, or any such function of the original variable.

ANOVA, ANCOVA and regression are special cases of general linear model.

g-index— A measure of quality of a researcher based on the papers cited by other. A g-index = 15 means that top cited 15 papers of a researcher have been cited at least $15^2 = 225$ times. Also see h-index.

Gantt chart— A chart that shows time-line of project: the duration and dates of beginning and ending its various phases.

Gold standard— In medical assessment, a method, procedure or a measurement with almost 100% sensitivity/specificity or 100% productivity: an extremely difficult proposition to achieve. As a compromise, the best available is considered "gold", against which the newer tests are compared. Thus the better term is criterion standard. This need not be a single or simple procedure but could include follow-up of subjects.

Goodness of fit— How well the actual observations fit into a specified pattern. The goodness of fit is statistically tested mostly by chi-square method.

Group matching— See matching.

Group's sequential design— A research design under which pre-decided number of cases are sequentially added in groups when so required to get convincing evidence of efficacy of the regimen or of its futility.

Grouped data— Quantitative values in categories such as age into 0-4, 5-9, 10-14, etc. Half-life-The duration at which time-dependent outcome or response is 50%. Half life of a drug could be few hours when it's availability in the body is one-half of what was injested.

Haphazard sampling— A mixture of convenience, volunteer, snowball sampling, etc. that does not follow any specific procedure.

Hawthorne effect— The tendency of subjects changing their response when they know that they are being observed. This can happen with the test group as well as the control group.

Hazard rate— The force of occurrence of events at a (instantaneous) point of time, such as force of mortality or of morbidity when measured per unit of time. This could exceed one.

Healthy life expectancy— The remaining portion of life at any age that would be spent without any morbidity. Life expectancy at age 40 may be 36 years but healthy life expectancy would be only 30 years if 6 years on average are spent in nonhealthy states as per the current pattern of morbidities.

Helsinki Declaration— set of ethical rules of plan, conduct and report a study on human subjects.

Herd immunity— When a large percentage of susceptible such as more than 90% is immunized, the infection feels strangulated, as it is not able to find susceptible in its proximity. Thus the infection fails to spread.

H-index— A measure of quality of research of a person based on the citations of his work. An h-index = 12 means that his 12 papers have received at least 12 citations each. Also see, g-index.

Histogram— A diagram showing the number or percentage of subjects with values in different intervals by means of contiguous bars: used only for quantitative variables.

Historical cohort— A cohort whose common baseline is in the past, and mostly outcomes too have already occurred. But the format of investigation still is from antecedent to outcome. The past is reconstructed mostly on the basis of records or recall.

Historical control— A control group or a subject for which information was collected earlier than the group being currently st udied. This information can be biased because of changes over time in risk pattern, techniques, concepts, etc.

Homogeneity— Similarity among measurements, subjects, specimen, results, estimates, etc. Contrast is with heterogeneity.

Hypothesis— A statement of belief that is made before the investigation regarding the status of parameters under study, including those that measure relationship. See null hypothesis, alternative hypothesis.

ICD— Short for International Classification of Diseases.

Iceberg phenomena— on When there are a large number of undetected cases for each detected case, such as in the case of HIV infection. Also when one clinical case means many infected but in apparent cases such as for AIDS.

Impact factor (of a journal)— The average number of times articles from a journal are cited by others in preceding two years — a service of the Institute for Scientific Information for journals covered by Citation Index.

Imputation— The process of filing in of plausible values for missing data.

IMRaD format— A format for writing research articles—Introduction, Material and Methods, Results, and Discussion.

Inception cohort— A cohort assembled at the beginning phase of disease of condition that is followed up to examine its course.

Incidence— The number of cases newly occurring or arising over a defined period of time.

Incidence density— Same as incidence but now number of new spells are counted instead of persons newly affected. One person can have more than one spell of diseases such as diarrhea and angina in a defined period.

Incidence rate— Incidence per unit of time and per unit of population. If incidence of benign prostatic hyperplasia in a population of 1,00,000 adults in six months is 16 cases, the incidence rate is 0.32 per 1000 adults per year. This can also be calculated per person-year or per 100 person-years, etc.

Incident cases— Same as incidence.

Inclusion criteria— The set of characteristics such as age, disease and severity, which are necessary in a subject to be considered eligible for inclusion in the study. Some of these subjects may become ineligible when exclusion criteria are imposed. The inclusion and exclusion criteria together define the study subject and the target population.

Independence— If occurrence of one event does not affect the occurrence of the other, they are called independent. Body temperature is generally independent of blood pressure levels but not of heart rate. Occurrence of typhoid is independent of colour blindness— none affects the other. Although, weight does not affect height in adults but they are not independent since height affects weight. Independence is both ways.

variable—A Independent variable that is used as an explanation of another variable. Independent variables are mostly the antecedent factors that affect or suspected to affect the (dependent) outcome. Some of these variables can be manipulated by the researcher to alter the outcome.

Index— **A** composite of two or more indicators, such as body mass index (BMI) for obesity that combines height and weight, and Indrayan's smoking index for a combination of age at initiation, duration, quantity an type of smoking, and the time elapsed since quitting by exsmokers.

Index case— An affected person who might affect others also. In the case of infection, the infected person is an index case who can spread the disease. When a new person is infected, he can be an index case for other susceptibles.

Indicator— A single measurement that indicates the existence or magnitude of a condition. Signs-symptoms are indicators of a disease, smoking an indicator of lung cancer risk, and infant mortality rate (IMR) is an indicator of mortality. Contrast it with an index, which is obtained by combining two or more indicators.

Indirect standardization - Removing the effect of differential structure of the group by using standard subgroup specific rates on two or more groups.

Indirectly standardized death rate— For age, same age-specific death rates are used on the observed age-structure of two or more groups to recalculate the death rate. These (called, standard) age-specific death rates are chosen by the researcher. Age is the most frequent factor for standardization is used when observed specific rates are unreliable due to small numbers, or are not available.

Induction— The method of reaching to a generalized conclusion after compiling the individual cases—from particular to general.

Infectiousness— The property of a disease to be able to infect susceptibles on exposure: but generally used to measure how many can be infected. Measles is a highly infectious disease since an exposed susceptible is very likely to catch the infection.

Infectivity— The proportion a actually got infected out of those exposed.

Information bias— Suppression of some information by some subjects because of stigma or any other reason. Also loosely used for any type of bias in the data.

Informed consent— Agreement by a subject to participate in a research or some such endeavour after he is fully explained the favourable and adverse implications of participation.

Instruction bias— Use of varying individual discretion to resolve doubtful and unforeseen situations when the instructions are not complete, or not properly understood.

Instrument bias— A systematic error in an instrument to consistently give either lower or higher values than actual. Presence of air bubble in mercury column of a sphygmomanometer makes the instrument biased. Improper use of an instrument can also cause this bias.

Intention-to-treat analysis— Analysis that includes dropouts or other subjects with incomplete data or those who had to be changed from one therapy to the other due to developing a medical complication assuming worst or average scenario for them: all subjects continue to be considered in the group to which they were originally assigned.

Interaction— Simultaneous presence of two or more antecedent factors affecting the outcome either negatively or positively so that the net effect is not the same as the sum of their individual effects .It is called antagonism when the interaction effect is negative and called synergism when this is positive. But there could be other interactions that are not classifiable into any of these two categories.

Internal consistency— Mostly, consistency within the set of actual observations. One observation should be consistent with the other, or one variable should be consistent with the other. If systolic blood pressure of a person is 110 mmHg and the diastolic blood pressure is 95 mmHg then they are inconsistent unless there are specific reasons for such disparate readings. At the group level, HIV prevalence should be higher for among those practicing multi partner sex, If the prevalence in this group is lower Than those with single partner then this is inconsistent, and raises doubts about internal validity of data. If a study shows lower morbidity after exposure to a risk factor but lower mortality without the risk then this also may be internally inconsistent.

Internal validity (of a study)— When the biases are sufficiently under control so that the difference in the outcomes among group can be legitimately ascribed to the hypothesized factor under investigation. Thus the results hold true at least for the subjects included in the study. An internally valid study may or may not be externally valid. There are situations when a sample provides excellent results for itself but fails when used on another sample form the same target population.

International Classification of Diseases (ICD) — A system of classification of diseases, injuries and causes of death into relevant groups, and assigning code to each condition, so as to promote uniformity and comparability across health care establishments in various countries. The ICD is revised every 10 years by the World Health Organization to incorporate new diseases and new understandings.

Interpretation bias— Incorrect interpretation of results, either knowingly to support a particular hypothesis, or unknowingly.

Interval estimation— The process of assigning a range of values to a parameter within which it is expected to lie in respected studies of that type.

Intervention study— A study of the impact of an intentionally introduced intervention on a predefined outcome. Experiments and trials are intervention studies.

Interviewer bias— Greater attention paid by interviewers to certain type of subjects or certain responses, relative to the other—thus introducing bias in the recorded responses.

Inter-observer variability— The variation between observers that occurs when the measurement on the same subject it taken by different observers. A high inter-observer variability indicates poor reliability of the measurement.

Intra-class correlation— The correlation among same quantitative measurements within the same subjects or such other units at different times, by different observers, by different methods, etc.

Intra-observer variability— The variation that occurs when a measurement is taken repeatedly by the same observer. This indicates poor reliability of that observer.

Inter-rater reliability— The extent of agreement between the measurements obtained by different raters when they use the same measuring device on the same group of subjects.

Kaplan-Meir method— The method of survival analysis that is used when the exact survival duration is assessed—thus these durations are not fixed time intervals.

kappa— A measure of agreement in excess of chance in qualitative data; used for assessing inter-rater reliability and for other such agreements.

Keywords— The set of words that describes the essential features of a study. These words are used for indexing purposes so that the article is quickly retrieved for that category.

Lead-time bias— Can occur when some subjects under study are enrolled in early phase of the disease and some in late phase of the disease. This may apparently show that early detected cases have higher duration of survival without any real prolongation of life.

Left-skewed distribution— See skewed distribution.

Length bias— The bias due to inclusion of disproportionately more case with longer survival time one group than the other: Thus cases that show rapid progression of disease are not well represented.

Level of significance— The maximum tolerable probability of Type I error that is fixed in advance, such as 5% denoted by a. In statistical terms, this is the agreed tolerated threshold of probability of rejecting a true null hypothesis.

Life expectancy— The average number of years a person is expected to live in a given community on the basis of current pattern of mortality. It can be calculated' at birth' or at any other age. A life expectancy of 36 years at age 40 means that the average life span after the age 40 years is 36 years in that community. In this population, life expectancy at birth could be only 71 years. Life expectancy is a mortality indicator measured in terms of survival duration.

Life table— A summary of the death and survival pattern of a group of people—generally for the entire population of an area, but can be used for patients of a particular disease also.

Life table method— The method of survival analysis that is used when the survival is assessed at fixed time intervals, such as weeks, months or years. The time intervals are fixed in advance.

Likelihood ratio— Relative odds of the result of interest (such as occurrence of a complication) in patients against the controls. Positive likelihood ratio measures the increase in odds of disease when the test result is positive, and negative likelihood ratio measures the decrease in odds of disease when the test result is negative.

Limits of disagreement— A procedure for measuring extent of disagreement between two quantitative measurements obtained by two methods, two laboratories, two sites, etc., on the same subjects. These limits are obtained as (mean of differences) " 2(SD of differences). If these limits are far too wide that can change. clinical assessment, the disagreement is considered beyond clinical to tolerance.

Line diagram— A diagram showing the trend by lines.

Linear regression— See linear relationship.

Linear relationship— A relationship that moves in a line with either positive or negative slope. The essential feature of a linear relationship is that one variable changes exactly by same amount when the other changes by one unit. If systolic blood pressure rises by 1/2mmHg per year of age over the entire adult age from 20 to 59 years, the relationship is linear in this age-interval. Linearity can also include many variables-See multiple linear regression, also curvilinear relationship. curvilinear relationship.

Logistic regression— The regression where the dependent variable is the probability of an event. The independent variables may be qualitative or quantitative. This regression is based on a specific mathematical form, called logistic model.

Longitudinal study— A study where the same set of individuals is periodically assessed for one or more defined outcomes.

Mann-Whitney test— A nonparametric test for comparing central tendency in two groups: analogous to t-test for Gaussian data. Gives exactly same result as Wilcoxon test.

Mantel-Hansel procedure— A statistical procedure for stratified analysis of qualitative data that combines evidence form two or more inter-related contingency tables.

Masking— Whereas the term blinding is used for the subjects and investigators, masking is for the regimen and the procedures. They are packaged or administered in a manner that they look similar.

Master chart— An arrangement of the prepares one record for each subject: thus data available in several pages of questionnaire/ schedule are converted to one line in, say, Excel software. This helps to get full view of the data in one shot.

Matching— Deliberate selection of control subjects that have the same characteristics as the cases except for the disease or the condition under study so as to increase the comparability. In practice only a few characteristics can be matched. Mostly it is one-to-one matching, which is called pari-matching, but sometimes can be group matching also. In the former, each control is matching with one case, and in the latter one group is matched with the other on average or for the pattern on the whole.

McNemar test— A chi-square test used for paired qualitative data, e.g., same subjects tested by histology and polymerase chain reaction (PCR) for extra pulmonary tuberculosis. Mc Nemar test will reveal whether histology and PCR significantly disagree or not.

Mean— The average.

Measurement bias— Systematic error in measurement. This could be either due to faulty instrument, or due to carelessness of the observer.

Measures of association— The parameters that quantify the degree of association between two or more qualitative factors. Chi-square based measures are (i) phi coefficient, (ii) Cramer's V, and (iii) contingency coefficient. More useful measures are (i) proportional reduction in error, and (ii) relative risk or odds ratio. For data on ordinal scale, these are Kendall is tau, Somer's d and Goodman-Kruskal gamma.

Median— The most middle value obtained after arranging values in increasing or decreasing order. Median seeks to divide the group in two equal halves, each with n/2 individuals. Sometimes in practice exactly equal halves are not possible, and they are divided into nearly equal halves.

Medical decision process— The process of taking decisions regarding diagnosis, treating or not treating a patient, what treatment to prescribe, when to stop, etc. after considering the chances of success of various alternatives and their respective utility in terms of likely outcome.

Medical ethics— The discipline that considers individual patient's welfare above very thing else—thus puts restrictions on how research involving human subjects should be done. Sometimes animal experimentation is also included in its domain. See Helsinki Declaration.

Medically significant— A result that is capable of modifying the management of any aspect of health or disease.

Memory lapse— See recall bias.

MeSH— Medical Subject Heading: an important resource to search articles in MedLine. This reduces problems arising from, e.g., British and American spellings, and has a tree structure that branches off into a series of progressively narrower terms.

Meta-analysis— A procedure of combining evidence in different reports on the same aspect. If different trials on the same regimen report varying efficacy, they can be combined to come to a unified conclusion, which may command substantially more confidence than result of any one of the individual trials.

Metic scale— Measurement in terms of numerics such as blood glucose and cholesterol level. Contrast it with measurement in terms of attributes such as gender and signs-symptoms. Metric scale give rise to quantitative data.

Mid-course bias— During the course of the study period, some patients who develop conditions unrelated to the one under investigation, such as injury, and thus have to be excluded. Some may have to be excluded because of related but serious condition requiring special care. In a field trial, this bias can occur when a new health facility or a new health problem starts in the study area that was not visualised earlier, and has potential to affect the results.

Misclassification— Classifying diseased as healthy (or nondiseased) or nondiseased as diseased. The first could be called missed diagnosis and the second as misdiagnosis. In place of healthy/diseased this could be any other categorization.

Misdiagnosis— Diagnosing a person as suffering from a particular disease when he does not have that disease (the person can have any other disease).

Missed diagnosis— Not being able to detect a particular disease in a person when it is present.

Mode— The most commonly occurring value, i.e., a value seen in highest number of subjects.

Model— A simplified version of a complex process. A model could be mathematical, graphical, structural, etc.

Morbidity— Any aberration in health — can be measured in a person by frequency. severity and duration of illness, and in a community by incidence, prevalence, severity pattern, and duration distribution.

Multicentric study— A study conducted at different locations with a common protocol

Multicolinearity— Existence of high correlation between two or more independent variables in a regression analysis setup.

Multifactorial aetiology— Occurrence of disease depending on multiple factors: hypertension is a univariate disease because the diagnosis depends entirely on blood pressure level, but it has multi factorial etiology since its occurrence depends on heredity factors, life stress, diet, obesity, etc. Malaria has one-factor etiology.

Multiple comparisons— several comparisons based on the same data. If each comparison is statistically done with 0.05 level of significance, the total probability of Type I error can be enormously large. To keep this within the specified level, statistical procedures such as Tukey, Bonferroni and Dennett are used for companion of groups means.

Multiple controls— More than one control subject for each case. In a case-control setup, sometimes it is easier to enroll controls than cases. The reliability of the results can be increased in this situation by enrolling 2 or 3 or even 4 controls per case.

Multiple correlation coefficient— The degree of linear relationship of one quantitative variable with two or more simultaneously considered quantitative variables.

Multiple regression— A regression in which a dependent variable is sought to be explained by linear combination of more than one independent variables: such as regression of systolic blood pressure on age, obesity, and socio-economic status. For one dependent and one independent variable, see simple linear regression.

Multiple responses— More than one response to one question or one item, such as two or more complaints of a patient at the same time, or listing of two or more sources of infection when asked about HIV.

Multiplication rule (of probability)— The probability of joint occurrence of two or more independent events is the multiplication of their individual probabilities.

Multistage random sampling— The process of sampling where a subset is chosen at random from units at different stages. First stage units can be cities, second stage hospitals (within chosen cities), third stage wards (within chosen hospital) and fourth stage patients (within chosen wards).

Multivariate analysis— A set of statistical procedures that considers several variables together for drawing a conclusion. If variables are inter-related, as they would in most situations, the results of multivariate analysis could be very different from separate univariate analyses.

Multivariate diagnosis— The diagnosis that depends on a multitude of measurements. The diagnosis of liver cirrhosis depends on oedema, ascites, spider naevi on the chest, esophageal varices, gastric ulcers, etc., whereas the diagnosis mellitus depends only on blood glucose level.
The former is a multivariate diagnosis and the latter is univariate.

Multivariate setup— A situation where several variable are considered simultaneously.

Mutually exclusive events— The set of events wherein only one can occur at a point of time. Blood group of a patient would either be O, or A, or B or AB. These are mutually exclusive. Sings-symptoms such as pain, diarrhoea and vomiting are mutually exclusive–they can occur together in a patient.

Necessary cause— A cause that must be present to change the outcome. Exposure to an infection is necessary for it to produce that particular disease but is it is not sufficient since in some cases infection can remain subclinical and may not produce the disease. Hypertension is not a necessary cause of stroke (neither it is sufficient). See sufficient cause.

Negative association— Presence of one factor associated with absence of the other, and vice-versa, in more subjects than expected by chance.

Negative correlation— Higher values of one variable generally accompanied by lower values of the other, and vice-versa, i.e., the two variables tend to move in quantitatively reverse direction.

Negative predictivity— Short for 'predictive value of a negative test'. This is the probability that a person with negative test really turns out to be free the disease. Since a test is used only on suspected cases, the predictivity should be evaluated on the basis of suspected cases only.

Negative trial— A trial that reports that difference between the test ant control regimens is not statistically significant, i.e., the test regimen is not found effective.

Nested case-control study— A case-control study where cases are identified through a prospective study. Controls may or may not be from the prospective study.

N-of-1 trial— A trial on one patient t who undergoes repeated pairs of treatment periods such that he gets experimental treatment one period and the control therapy the other period. The sequence can be randomised. The patient and the physician can be blinded regarding the sequence. Treatment periods are replicated until a result one way or the other is obtained.

Nominal scale — Assessment of a characteristic in terms of names only. Blood group is on a nominal scale since O, A, B and AB are just name with no order or no grading among them. The other type of scale for qualitative is ordinal where grading is present such as hypertensive, normotensive, porbably hypertensive and definitely hypertensive.

Nonparametric test— A statistical test of hypothesis that does not focus on a parameter such as mean. This does not require Gaussian or any other specific form of distribution of the variable. The usual tests such as t and F require Gaussianity but chi-square is nonparametric. Other popular nonparametric tests are Mann-Whitney (or Wilcoxon), Krusal-Wallis, and Friedman.

Nonrandom sample— Same as purposive sample. Can include volunteers, referred cases, case series, convenience sample, etc.

Nonrandomised control trial— A trial in which the subjects are assigned to the case group and the control group as per the convenience. Contrast it with RCT.

Nonresponse— Not being to able to collect full or partial information on subjects once they are included in a study. This can happen due to unrelated death, injury, moving out of the area, left against medical advice, refusal to cooperate, etc.

Nonsampling errors— Opposed to sampling errors, these arise mostly due to lack of planning or due to lack of knowledge. The examples are presence of confounde Bared to the absolute difference, this deviate give a more realistic assessment of how far the value is from mean. Generally, same as z-score.

Normal distribution— Same as Gussian distribution.

Normalisation (of variables)— Standardisation of variable values to (0,1) scale.

Normal level— A level generally seen in healthy individuals. This is not necessarily ideal or optimal. Normal level may be different for children than of adults, or different for males than for females, etc.

Normal range— The range of values (of a quantitative medical measurement), which is generally seen in healthy individuals in a population or its specified segment.

Nuisance variable— A variable not of interest but interfering and spoiling the picture.

Null hypothesis— A hypothesis that says that there is no difference, or that asserts the existing knowledge, and is tested for refutation by the study.

Number needed to treat (NNT)— The average number of subjects that must be treated to get one favourable outcome or to prevent one adverse outcome.

If improved blood Pressure control of 15 Subjects is required for 10 years to prevent one death one death from myocardial infarction, then NNT for this outcome is 15 subjects for 10 years. Mathematically, this is reciprocal fo absolute risk reduction.-

Observational study— A study based on observation of the natural occurrences (no intervention). See case-control study, cross-sectional study, prospective study,

Observer bias— Observer being more careful or attentive to specific type of patients or particular responses.

Odds— The chance or frequency of occurrence or presence of a characteristic relative to its nonoccurrence or absence. If the chance of occurrence is 75% the odds are 3: 1. Generally calculated for presence of antecedent factors.

Odds ratio— The ratio of odds in one group to the other (generally the control group).

One-sided alternative— A directional alternative hypothesis in the sense of asserting that the value can be only either more or less than the null value. Contrast it with the two-side alternative.

One-tailed test— While testing equality of two groups, it is sometimes not known before hand that which group could be better (or worse). For example, this happens when a test regimen is being compared with the existing regimen. This requires a two-tailed test. However, while comparing a test regimen with placebo, if there is an assurance that test regimen can not be worse than placebo, one-tailed test is used.

One-to-one matching— See matching.

One-way classification— The division of subjects of interest by only one characteristic, such as dividing cases of bronchial asthma by their smoking status only.

One-way design— A study that is planned to investigate the effect of levels of only one factor. The levels could be two such as presence and absence, or more than two such as none, mild, moderate, and serious.

Open-ended question— A question whose answer is allowed to be recorded in verbatim as given by the respondent. Contrast it with a close-ended question that provides a list of possible answers.

Open trial— Nonblind trial.

Ordinal association — Association between two ordinal characteristics such as severity of disease and socio-economic status. This is measured by Kendall's tau, Somer's d or Goodman-Kruskal gamma.

Ordinal scale— A scale that measures a polytomous characteristic in a defined order, such as severity of disease into mild, moderate, serious and critical. The 'distance' between mild and moderate is undefined. Division of blood group into O, A, B, and AB is polytomous but not ordinal since these blood groups do not have and order—none is better or worse than the other.

Outcome— A disease or a health condition of interest including any change in health status that may occur after exposure to antecedents or interventions. It may or may not be a result of the antecedents.

Outlier— A value that is far away from the other values. If duration of hospital stay after a cholecystectomy is 2, 3 or 4 days for most patients but happens to be 14 days for one patient because of complication, this value 14 days is an outlier.

Outlier bias— Differential management of different outliers: e.g., considering some extreme value as outlier and not others, or not ignoring outliers if they support a particular hypothesis.

Pair-matching— See matching.

Paradigm— A system, a pattern of thought, or a model regarding a phenomenon.

294

Parallel control group— Opposed to treatment group that receives regimen under test, parallel control group is another group of subjects that receive either placebo or an existing regimen. Contrast if with before-after study where there is no separate (parallel) control group.

Parameter— A summary measure for any characteristic in the target population, such as percentage of cirrhosis patients with high aspartate aminotransferase, or rate of increase of systolic blood pressure in healthy subject per year of age. The parameter pertains to the entire population of interest and not to the sample.

Parsimonious model— A model containing small number of factors yet providing adequate explanation.

Partial correlation— The correlation between two quantitative measurements when third or other measurements affecting them are considered fixed, and thus their effect is eliminated. Generally considers only the linear relationship.

Pathogenicity— The ability to produce the clinical manifestation of disease in an infected person. Measles is not only infectious but also highly pathogenic—the disease appears in most susceptible when infected. Generally measured by the percentage of infected who develop the disease. Tuberculosis is not a highly pathogenic disease.

Pearsonian correlation coefficient— A measure of the degree of linear relationship between two quantitative variables. This ranges from -1 to $+1$ with zero in between indicating no linear relationship. A negative correlation means that increase in one is accompanied by decrease in the other or vice-versa, whereas a positive correlation means that both increase or decrease or decrease together at least to some extent.

Peer review— A refereeing process of a research proposal, article, thesis, etc, by expert colleagues for technical merit.

Percentiles— Ninety nine cut-points of a variable that divide a group of subjects into one hundred segments after arranging in ascending order such that each segment has the same number (n/100) of subjects.

Person-years— The sum total of years observed for different individuals. If one person is followed-up for 3 years, second for1 ½ years and third for 2 years, then the person-years of follow-up is 3 + 1 ½ + 2 = ⅓3 years. Similarly there could be person-weeks or person-months.

Phases of a trial— IN phase I, the maximum tolerated dose and pharmacological properties including toxicity and safety are determined by a trial on a group of volunteers. usually without controls. The objective of phase II are to investigate clinical efficacy, incidence of side-effects, identify a does schedule, and to collect further pharmacological data. Most phase II trials have a control group. Phases III is an RCT that is done after achieving success in the first two phases to firmly establish efficacy and safety. Post-marketing surveillance is sometimes called phase IV.

Pie diagram— A diagram showing the proportions of subjects in different groups or with different mutually exclusive characteristics by means of segments of a circular pie.

Pilot study— A small-scale forerunner study to learn about the situation and the variables.

Placebo— An inert substance or procedure that is neither harmful nor beneficial. The objective of placebo is that the subject gets the perception that he is receiving treatment—thus removing perception bias in trials.

Placebo-controlled trial— Study of efficacy and safety of a regimen in comparison to a group that receives placebo. Contrast it with trials in which the comparison group receives existing (active) regimen.

Placebo effect— The psychological effect on a patient of the perception that he is receiving a treatment although the treatment is dummy. This is the main reason for conducting placebo-controlled trials. Also see Hawthorne effect.

Plagiarism— Unauthorized use of some one else's language and thoughts and projecting them as your own.

Point estimation— The process of identifying a single value of a parameter as an estimate based on the study group.

Polytomous variable— A characteristic divided into three or more exclusive categories, such as severity of disease into mild, moderate, serious and critical, or liver disease as cirrhosis, hepatitis, and malignancy. A quantitative measurement such as cholesterol level can be made polytomous when divided into small number of categories such as -99, 100-179, 180-249 and 250+ mg/dl.

Population— The totality of individuals or units of interest. There could be a 'population' of blood samples collected in a year. If the interest is restricted to only suspected cases of liver diseases, the population comprises blood samples of such cases only. If the interest is further restricted to the cases attending OPD in a group of hospitals, the population is also accordingly restricted.

Population attributable risk — The risk in the total population minus the risk in unexposed subjects. In the population, some are unexposed. This measures the impact on the population, of eliminating that exposure.

Positive association— Presence of one factor associated with presence of the other, and absence with absence, in more subject than expected by chance.

Positive correlation— Higher values of one variable generally accompanied by higher values of the other and lower values with lower, i.e., they tend to move in the same direction.

Positive predictivity— Short for 'predictive value of a positive test'. This is the probability that a person with positive test really turns out to be suffering from the disease. Depends heavily on the prevalence of the disease. Since a test is used only on suspected. cases, the predictivity should be evaluated on the basis of suspected cases only.

Posterior probability— See prior probability.

Posthoc comparison— The comparison of groups with regard to their initial equivalence after collection fo data.

Post-marketing surveillance— Keeping a tab on outcome and side-effects of a formulation after it is introduced into the market: sometimes called phase IV of a clinical trial.

Post-test probability— probability— The probability of occurrence or presence of an event such as disease after the test results are available. See prior probability.

Power— The probability that a study or a trial will be able to detect a specified difference. This is calculated as 1 − Probability of Type II error—i.e., the probability of correctly concluding that a difference exists when it is indeed present. This measures the ability to demonstrate an association when one really exists, and depends primarily on the number of subjects in a study.

Power Point— A software of Microsoft Corporation that helps to make slides, which can be directly projected from the electronic format. This software has several features regarding designing the slide. The presentation of research to an audience can be very effective with the help of PowerPoint slides.

Pragmatic trial— A trial done under standard clinical practice so that accepted variation such as during drug intake are allowed. Contrast it with explanatory trial done under near-ideal conditions with practically no deviation.

Precision— Same as reliability but measured statistically as inverse of the variance.

Prediction error— The difference between an observed value and a predicted value based on models or based on other considerations.

Predictive validity (of a test)— The average of the positive predictivity and negative predictivity of a test. This can be used as a combined measure of the two types of predictivities when both are equally important for the outcome of interest..

Predictivity (of a test)— See positive predictivity and negative predictivity.

Prevention trial— A human experiment for a preventive strategy such as exercise and diet changes or a regimen involving vitamins, to prevent occurrence or recurrence of a disease, or any other adverbs condition.

Pretest probability— The probability of occurrence or presence of an event such as disease before the test results are available: generally the same as prevalence rate in the specified group. Contrast it with post-test probability. See also prior probability.

Pretesting— Checking the workability, adequacy, reliability, etc., of a tool before using it for actual study. The tool could be an instrument, a laboratory procedure, a questionnaire, or any other.

Prevalence— The number of cases of interest present or existing at any specific time, usually at the time of the survey.

Prevalence rate— Prevalence per unit of population or per unit of susceptible, such as percent, per thousand and per million. Note that prevalence rate is not a 'rate' as it does not signify

frequency of occurrence per unit of time—it is only a proportion. Conventionally, but wrongly, it is called a rate.

Prevalence ratio— Ratio of prevalence rate in one group to the other.

Prevalent cases— Same as prevalence.

Primary data— Data that are directly collected from the respondents. Contrast it with secondary data that already exist in databases, records, reports, articles, etc.

Primordial factors— Factors that work behind the scene, are precursors, or are those that give rise to risk factors. Life style is a primordial factor that can give rise to risk factors such as obesity and smoking.

Prior probability— The chance of occurrence or presence of an event such as disease or death in a patient when nothing is known about the condition of the patient. Once something such as signs-symptoms-measurements are known, the diagnosis becomes substantially more focuses and the probability changes. The latter is called the posterior probability. When further information becomes available, this posterior becomes prior probability and the new probability based on the fresh information becomes posterior.

PRISMA— Acronym of Preferred Reporting Items for Systematic Reviews and Meta Analyses: A checklist of 27 items and a flow diagram of how the studies for reviews were selected and processed for joint conclusion.

Probability— A measure of belief in occurrence of an event or presence of a characteristic. This can be obtained either on the basis of theoretical considerations such as 1/6 for each of the 6 faces of a dice, on the basis of experience, or on the basis of frequency of occurrence when total occurrence are very large. Probability is the degree of certainty of occurrence of an event on a 0 to 1 scale. Probability of death is 1 for all individuals but the probability of death of a pancreatic cancer case within 5 years of detection could be 0.6.

Pro Cite— The software that manages bibliographic citations; can be used in conjunction with Med Line.

Performa— A prototype or a sample of a format on which the observation are to be recorded.

Prognostic factor— A characteristic that can help in prediction of the eventual development of an outcome such as recovery, complication, and death. This does not necessarily imply a cause-effect relationship.

Prognostic stratification— A stratification done after examining the pattern of observations, such as categorizing patients as mild, moderate, serious on the basis of new criteria developed after the patients are seen. In the usual stratification, the criteria are decided before seeing the patients.

Prophylactic trial— An experiment on a prophylactic measure such as amnioinfusion for meconium-stained amniotic fluid at the time of child-birth, or in the community such as iron supplementation of adolescent girls.

Proportion— The measure of how big is the part of a whole. The whole is considered as one. If 20% of a population have blood group A, the proportion is 020 or 1/5.

Proportional hazards model— A model the works when ratio of logarithm of hazard in test group to control group remains same all through the period of observation. This is an important prerequisite for the validity of Cox model.

Proportional reduction in error— The reduction in error in prediction of the outcome when a particular antecedent is used for prediction relative to when it is not used.

Prospective study— A study that investigates outcomes for known antecedents. The follow-up of subjects is inherent in this kind of study since the occurrence of outcome can take time.

Protocol— A comprehensive statement regarding steps to be taken–the plan of a study. See research protocol.

Proximal measures— Measurements directly on outcome, contrasted with distal measures. For example, Impact to vitamin A supplementation to the children below three years can be measured proximally by rise in retinol level. In contrast, distally, the impact can be measured by growth pattern. Research results many times depend on appropriate choice of proximal measures for the outcome of interest.

PubMed— An extension of Med Line database of articles published in selected journals.

Publication bias— Publication of one type of articles more often than the other types, such as more frequent publication of positive results than negative results.

Purposive sampling— Nonrandom sampling to include subjects that serve the specific purpose, such as volunteers in phase I of clinical trials. See convenience sampling, haphazard sampling. snowball sampling, volunteer studies.

P-value— The probability of Type I error, i.e., The chance that a difference or association is concluded when actually there is none: the chance that the result could have been produced by random sampling fluctuations rather than being actual.

Qualitative data— A set of observations on qualitative characteristics of individuals such as signs and symptoms. These can be nominal or ordinal. The only real summary measure for qualitative data is proportion of subject with a specified characteristic, although for some ordinal data, scores can be assigned that can be treated as numeric.

Qualitative variable— A characteristic that is assessed in terms of attributes such as gender and degree of severity of disease: a variable that yields qualitative data.

Quality of life— Comfort and functionality of person, generally as perceived by the person himself.

Quality of life trial— A trial for a regimen that could improve quality of life of people in ill-health, particularly those with chronic diseases or degenerative conditions.

Quantitative data— Collection of observations on characteristics that could be numerically expressed for an individual such as hemoglobin level, blood pressure, and blood glucose level. Most common summary measures for quantitative data are mean and standard deviation (SD).

Quantitative variable— A characteristic that is measured in terms of numerics, such as creatinine level and parity of a woman: a variable that yields quantitative data. See also continuous variable, discrete variable.

Quartiles— Three cut-points of values of a variable that divide a group in four equal parts with regard to number of subjects, after the values are arranged in ascending order.

Quasi-random allocation— Allocation of subjects to test and control group by following apparently random method such as alternation and based on birth data that are not strictly random.

Questionnaire— A survey instrument that contains a predetermined series of questions that are supposed to be put in verbatim to the respondent or can be self-administered. It contains space for recording responses also.

Quota sampling— Purposive selection of pres-pecified number (quota) of subjects from each segment of population without using random method.

Random— Unpredictable, like lottery.

Random allocation— Same as randomisation.

Random effects model— A statistical model that stipulates that the levels of factors under study are random random samples of the possible levels. Contrast it with fixed effects model.

Random error— An error that h — Aas no bias, and which is natural to occur in observations because fo biological or other variation beyond control. These errors are small, and some are positive some negative so that the long-term average is close to zero.

Random sampling— Sampling in a manner that the selection can not be predicted. The chance of selection of various unites can be equal or unequal. The popular methods of random sampling are simple, systematic, stratified, cluster, and multistage.

Randomization— Allocation of subjects to different groups in a random manner with equal chance. The objective is that unaccounted factors are almost equally distributed among groups, and there is no bias on this count. Randomization could be open os that the participants or the observes know which subject is in which group, or it could be concealed.

Randomized clinical trial— An experiment on human beings where the subjects are randomly allocated to various arms of a trial. Theses arms may be various dosage groups. When one arm is the control group, this becomes randomized controlled trial.

Randomized controlled trial— A trial where there is a control group in (in addition to the test groups). and the allocation of subjects to the control and test groups is by random method. This is considered to be the ideal methodology to evaluate efficacy of a new regimen (preventive, therapeutic or diagnostic) particularly when it is double-blind.

Rate— The frequency with which events occur per unit of time, such as deaths per year or new cases per month. Time is a necessary ingredient of a rate. Generally measured per unit of population such as percent, per thousand and per million.

Ratio- Strength or magnitude or number of one quantity relative to the other, such as male-female ratio and albumin-globulin ratio.

RCT— Short for randomized controlled trial.

Recall bias— Not being able to recall events occurring far away in the past with the same frequency as those occurring recently. This introduces bias in favour of recent occurrences. Also occurs when diseased cases are able to recall because of their suffering but controls fail to recall as much. Also when serious episodes are easily recalled and mild episodes tend to be neglected.

receiving operating characteristic curve — Same as ROC curve.

Record linkage—The process of linking different records of one person to make one comprehensive record.

Reference values: Same as normal levels.

Reference sample— A group of subjects that are referred for specialised handling. A study can be carried out on a referred sample although the results would be biased.

Regression analysis— The statistical procedure to find a regression equation.

Regression equation— The nature of relationship of one variable with one or more of others, generally expressed as a mathematical equation that best fits the data. Also called regression model.

Regression coefficient— The quantity that delineates the change in dependent variable for one unite change in independent variable. If regression coefficient of birth weight (in gm) on maternal hemoglobin level is +60, it means that birth weight increases on average by 60 gm for each 1g/ dl increase in maternal hemoglobin level.

Regression line— Graphical presentation of linear regression.

Regression model— Same as regression equation.

Repressor— Same as independent variable in a regression equation.

Relationship— The property of change in one variable when the other changes. This change can be causal, incidental, or due to a third intervening variable.

Relative risk— Risk of occurrence of an outcome in the presence of one factor (exposure) relative to the risk in the presence of another (generally control) factor.

Relative risk reduction— Reduction in absolute risk after an intervention as percentage of the risk in exposed group before intervention.

Reliability— Ability to repeat the performance. The performance could be poor but same performance very time means good reliability. Statistically, this means smaller variance in repeated measurements.

Repeatability— Same as reproducibility.

Repeated measures— When the same subject is observed repeatedly after specified time gaps, such as monitoring blood pressure and heart rate at 1, 5, 10, 15 and 30 minutes after a administering anaesthesia.

Replication— Trying the same regimen on more than one equivalent group so as to get an idea of the repeatability. Replications, when yielding similar results, increase the reliability of the results.

Reporting bias— Highlighting findings in a report that support a particular view at the cost of the other.

Reproducibility— The ability to give similar result when conducted in identical conditions.

Reproductive rate (of infection) — The rate at which an index case infects others in the entire transmission phase.

If the reproductive rate is one or more, the infection sustains itself and spreads in the population, like HIV is doing in some countries. If the reproductive rate is less than one, the infection will die down or will stabilize at a low level.

Research design— Same as design.

Research protocol— Statement on planned steps of research, including background information and rationale, objectives and hypotheses, review of literature, methodology, ethics, statistical and references.

Response bias:

(i) Not giving proper history due to stigma such as in STDs or for any other reason, and

(ii) Selective nonresponsive, i.e., persons who are not seriously ill do not fully cooperate.

Retrospective cohort— Same as historical cohort.

Retrospective follow-up study— A study based on a historical cohort.

Retrospective study— A study that investigates antecedents for known outcomes. The recruitment of cases can be prospective spanning a duration such as all cases reporting in one year period. But the logic is from effect to the cause.

Right-skewed distribution— See skewed distribution.

Risk— The chance of occurrence of an outcome of interest, generally calculated per year of exposure. It is not necessary that the outcome is adverse to health. See attributable risk, population attributable risk, and relative risk.

Risk difference— The difference in risk of occurrence of a condition in two setups, such as risk of glaucoma in vegetarians vs. risk in non vegetarians same as attributable risk.

Risk factor— A characteristic that is suspected to affect the outcome, such as obesity for hypertension. Risk factor could be an aspect of personal behaviour or life-style, an environmental exposure, an inherited or in-born characteristic, or any other.

Risk ratio— Same as relative risk.

Robust method— A method that is not much affected by minor variation in its applicability conditions.

ROC curve— A curve that depicts the relationship between sensitivity of a test for different thresholds and the corresponding (1–specificity), such as for different T4 values for diagnosis of hyperthyroidism.

This curve help to evaluate the applicabilities of a test and helps to compare performance of one test with the other, such as of T4 with T3 or T4 with TSH.

Sample— A part of the target population. which is actually studied.

Sample size— The number of subjects or units in a sample.

Sampling— Choosing a part from the whole, such as choosing 300 child births out of 5000 in a hospital in one year for studying the intrauterine growth retardation. See random sampling, purposive sampling.

Sampling bias— The bias due to (i) nonrandom sample such as volunteers that do not represent the Target population, and (ii) small sample that fails to represent the entire spectrum of subjects.

Sampling design— The method of selection of sample out of the population of subjects.

Sampling error— The tendency of one sample giving a different result than the other sample, and neither possibly giving exactly same result as in the population. This is not an error in conventional sense but is natural fluctuation.

Sampling fluctuation— The tendency of different samples giving different results, even if drawn from the same target population. This happens because different samples contain individuals who are different from those in other samples.

Sampling fraction— The extent of sampling such as one out of eight, or one out of twenty.

Sampling frame— A list of units in the target population from which sample is drawn.

Sampling method— The procedure to choose or select a fraction out of the target population.

Sampling unit— The unit used for sampling. In a multistage sampling, there is a separate sampling unit for each stage.

Sampling variation— Same as sampling fluctuation.

Scales of measurement— the system of differentiating one type of observation from the other. When names are used (opposed to grades) for differentiation, the scale is called nominal. Signs and symptoms are generally measured on nominal scale. Textual grades such as mild, moderate, serious, are measurements on ordinal scale. Numeric measurements such as body mass index are on metric scale.

Scatter diagram— A diagram displaying values of one quantitative variable for different values of the other variables by plotting points. This is also called the (x, y) plot.

Schedule— A form that contains a set of items on which information is to be obtained. It contains space also to record the responses.

Sci Search— The software of the Institute for Scientific Information for searching citations in Science Citation Index and Current Contents.

Score— Quantification of a set of (mostly) qualitative measurements, such as APACHE score. Scores in medicine are used either to grade severity of a condition, as an aid to reach to a diagnosis, or to assess prognosis.

Screening test— A criterion used to locate possible positives that can be later confirmed by stricter criterion, A screening criterion should have high negative predictivity. The criterion could be a laboratory test, a radiological test, or clinical observation.

Screening trial— A trial for evaluating efficacy and safety of a procedure that can detect the disease or can detect risk factors.

SD— Short for standard deviation.

Secondary attack rate— The number of people who get sick within the incubation period after exposure to an infective person. This infective person is called the index case.

Secondary data— The data that are already lying somewhere as in records or literature. Contrast it with primary data.

Selection bias— The bias occurring due to selection of nonrepresentative group of subjects—thus affecting the generalisability of the findings. This can occur either because the selection is done with a purpose, such as of volunteers, or unwittingly due to selection of surviving subjects (if the disease under study is rapidly fatal), due to selection of younger subjects who have survived (many of the older ones may have died), etc. Lack of matching in case and control groups can also be called selection bias. All these can affect the validity of results.

Sensitivity— Ability to identify known positives as positives. If CPK >120 IU is present in 60% known cases of myocardial infarction then sensitivity of this cut-off is 60% Sensitivity is not a valid indicator of diagnostic value of the test. It only measures the intrinsic ability of a test to detect a disease when it is already known to be present.

Sensitivity analysis— The analysis to assess the impact of changes in assumptions on the outcome. Because of limitation of knowledge, various assumptions are made in a study.

For example, it is generally assumed that cure rate depends linearly on treatment regimen, host characteristics. and compliance Two kinds of epistemic uncertainties arise–one what happens if the dependence is not linear but is quadratic or any other type, and second, what happens if this is assumed to depend also on physical strength and mental toughness of the patients. Answers to such questions are obtained by sensitivity analysis.

Sequential sampling— Serial sampling of subjects, one by one, to be stopped when scientifically acceptable result either way is available.

Severity score— A score used to grade severity of a condition such as Apgar score and APACHE score.

Sign test— A nonparametric test based on sign (negative or positive) of differences between two sets of observations. This test is used to compare two groups for their central tendency.

Significance— See statistical significance and medial significance.

Significance level— Same as level of significance.

Simple linear regression— A regression in which a dependent variable is sought to be explained linearly by only one independent variable, such as regression of systolic blood pressure on age. Other correlates are ignored in this setup, and the relationship format is limited to linear.

Simple random sampling— Sampling in a manner that all individuals have same chance of being selected.

Simple regression— Relationship between one independent and one dependent variable. It could be linear or nonlinear.

Simpson's paradox— In some case the tendency of aggregated data showing a result very different from the results from disaggregated (stratified) data. This can happen due to interaction effect of stratifying variable.

Simulation— Generation of data based on certain model.

Single blind— No subject is informed that he is receiving test regimen or the control regimen in a trial. But the investigator is aware of the allocation.

Skewed distribution— Opposed to symmetric such as Gaussian, generally a distribution is considered skewed when values on one side of mode vary much more than on the other side. It is right-skewed when values more than mode have more variation, and left-skewed when values less than mode have more variation.

Smoking index— A measure of life-long burden of smoking with weight age for age at initiation, quantity of smoking, duration of smoking, type of somking (filter/nonfilter/bidi/cigar), and duration elapsed since quitting by ex smokers.

Snowball sampling— One eligible person, such as a client of sex-worker, is asked to list others known to him and eligible that can be included in the sample, and those in turn are asked to identify others, so on.

Spearman's correlation— A measure of strength of relationship between two quantitative variables when they are converted to ranks.

Specificity— Ability to identify known negative as negatives. If AFB is negative in 95% of the healthy subjects, its specificity is 95%. In practice, a test is rarely used on healthy subjects. It is used on suspected cases. In them, the specificity may be very different.

Spectrum of disease— The distribution of subjects by affected and not affected, and among affected by severity of affliction.

spurious association— A false association that could arise due to presence of confounders, bias, or merely a chance.

Spurious correlation— A false correlation that could arise due to presence of confounders, bias, or merely a chance.

Spurious association— A false association that could arise due to presence of confounders, bias, or merely a chance.

Standard deviation (SD)— Most common and generally most appropriate measure of dispersion obtained as positive square root of variance.

Standard error (SE)— The measure for sample-to-sample variability in a summary measure such as mean and median. Just as the measurements such as hemoglobin level differ from person to person, so do the sample summaries from sample to sample. Mean hemoglobin level in one sample would be different from another sample even when both are drawn from the same target population. The extent of variability in such summaries is measured by their respective standard errors. Actually, this is the standard deviation of mean or median or any other summary measure as the case may be.

Standardization (of groups)— The procedure that makes two different groups comparable by bringing them on to a common base or a common standard, such as age-standardization.

Standardization. (of variables)— Subtracting mean from the variable and dividing by the standard deviation (SD): thus standardization makes mean = 0 and SD - 1 Standardized death rate

(directly standardized)— Recalculated death rate when one or more factors affecting deaths (such as age structure) are brought at par with the comparison group, or both brought to a common base. This substantially increases comparability that crude death rate lacks when one groups is young and the other is old. Common base structure (called, standard) of population is chosen by the researcher.

Standardized mortality ratio— Ratio of actually observed deaths to expected deaths based on standard death rates. If this ratio is more than one, the force of mortality is higher in the study group compared to the standard group.

Standard treatment— An approved or widely accepted treatment modality for an ailment.

Statistic— A summary measure for any characteristic in the sample or the group actually studied, such as mean, median or standard deviation of a sample, or proportion of subjects found affected in a sample.

Statistical analysis— Subjecting data to the rigors of statistical methods so that the uncertainty levels are either quantified or minimized, or both.

Statistical fallacies— Many fallacies can occur in the results because of improper use of statistical methods. Some of these are due to (i) use of improper denominator for computing rate or percentage, (ii) not accounting for variable periods of exposure that could affect the rate of outcome, (iii) considering mixture of two groups as one, (iv) misuse of percentages such as 2 out 4 being stated as 50%, (v) using means for emphasizing a point without considering the standard deviation, (vi) inappropriate scales in the graphs, (vii) looking at linearity when in fact the relationship is nonlinear, (viii) ignoring important prerequisites such as randomness, independence, equality of variances and Gaussian form of distribution, (ix) using means where proportions are adequate, or vice-versa, (x) ignoring baseline values, (xi) using too many statistical tests on the same set of data without adjusting P-values (xii) quantitative analysis of codes, (xiii) jumping to cause-effect relationship without sufficient examination of data, and (xiv) multivariate conclusions on the basis of several univariate analyses.

Statistical power— Same as power.

Statistical significance— A result is statistically significant if the chance of wrongly rejecting null hypothesis is less than the prefixed level such as 5%. The implication is that chance differences in samples would produce that kind of result in less than 5 times out of of 100—thus chance is not an explanation for that result, and it is most likely real.

Statistical test— A procedure to find P-value corresponding to a null hypothesis on the basis of the given data. Depending upon the type of data and the type of hypothesis, a large number of statistical tests are available. Most popular of these are Student's t-test and chi-square test.

Statistical threshold (of normal range)— Mean " 2SD where mean and standard deviation (SD) are obtained from measurements in a large number of healthy individuals. There is a chance of classifying nearly 5% healthy individuals with extreme values as sick when this range is used as normal.

Statistics— A science that helps to manage uncertainties in the data. Also, plural of statistic.

Strata— The divisions obtained after stratification (the singular is stratum).

Stratification— Division of subjects into relevant groups.

Stratified random sampling— Separate simple random sampling from each group after stratification.

Strength of relationship— The consistency of change in one factor when the other changers. If one unit change in one factor results in nearly the same change in the other in all the subjects, the strength is high. Note that the strength is not related to the magnitude of change. Small change, if consistent, would mean high degree of relationship.

STROBE— Acronym for STrengthening the Reporting of OBservational studies in Epidemiology: A checklist of items for reporting results of and observational study.

Student's t-test— Same as t-test.

Study design— Same as design.

Study setting— The environment in which the study is conducted. The setting could be a general hospital, a referral centre, private practice, ambulatory care, community, etc.

Sufficient cause— A cause that by itself is sufficient to change the outcome. Exposure to measles virus in a susceptible is sufficient to produce the disease. In fact this cause is both necessary and sufficient. Hanging by rope is sufficient to cause death but is not necessary as a cause for death.

Superiority trial— A clinical trial that has objective to examine if the regimen under test is better by at least a predefined clinically important margin.

Surrogate outcome— Outcomes that are not of direct interest but reflect the outcome of direct interest, such as pallor for nutritional level. Surrogates are generally easy to assess and do not require long follow-up.

Surrogate variable— A makeshift substitute variable that is used when the actually required variable cannot be measured. If the respondents are shy of revealing income, surrogates such as size of house, car, telephone and television can be used to assess the level of income. Since they are surrogate, they may or may not reveal the true status.

Survey— A descriptive study done generally on scientifically selected subjects. Another descriptive study methodology is case series.

Survival analysis: Analysis of survival durations. Survival duration is generic—it can be duration between any specified events such as between end of operation and beginning of consciousness, between beginning of treatment and time at complete recovery, etc. Two popular methods of survival analysis are life table method and Kaplan-Meir method.

Survival curve— A graph that depicts survival pattern of the subjects, over the observed period of time. It begins at 100% (all alive) and shows gradual or rapid decline as the time passes depending on the disease under study.

Survival function— A mathematical expression for survival curve.

Susceptibility — Proneness to catch an infection or a disease. A person who is effectively immunised against tetanus is susceptible to tetanus, and a child is not susceptible to the usual sexually transmitted diseases.

Synergism— A situation where two factors when present together accentuate the outcome more than their individual capacities. Iron and folic acid are synergistic for increasing haemoglobin level.

Synthesis (of research)— The process of combining diverse evidence from different researches to come to a holistic conclusion

Systematic error— Same as bias.

Target population— Same as population. Also called reference population.

Test group— The group of subjects that is receiving or has received the regimen under test.

Test of hypothesis— The procedure used to test whether or not sufficient evidence exists against a null hypothesis: mostly a statistical procedure.

Test of significance— A statistical procedure to test whether or not the observations fall into a specified pattern, such as equal means of two or more groups, or following a linear trend. If they do not, the result is called statistically significant. This requires prior fixing of the level of significance that specifies the maximum tolerable probability of Type I error.

Test-retest reliability— agreement between responses when the same instrument such as a questionnaire is administered to the same set of people again; stability of the responses in repeated we of the instrument.

Therapeutic equivalence— Comparable safety and efficacy of two or more treatment modalities when administered under the conditions specified for each modality.

These conditions could be different for different modalities. Also see equivalence.

Therapeutic trial — A clinical trial on a therapeutic agent or regimen to evaluate its efficacy and safety.

Thesis— A proposal or hypothesis forwarded after a careful investigation accompanied by full details: generally the written work submitted by a candidate in fulfillment of partial requirement for the award of master's degree.

Time-line— A chart or a table that states the durations and dates of beginning and ending various phases of a project, some of which can overlap.

Training sample— The sample of subjects which is used to develop a model. This model is subsequently tested on validation sample.

Translational research— The research that tries to bridge the gap between discoveries and their application to actual life situations.

Transmissibility — used in two senses:

1. The ability to transmit (infection or disease) from one to the other. HIV is transmissible through blood transfusion. Injury is not transmissible.

2. The force of transmission: when exposed what percentage of susceptible get the infection or disease. HIV is more transmissible from male to female than from female to male.

Trial— An experiment on human subjects. See clinical trial, field trial, prophylactic trial, therapeutic trial and vaccine trial.

t -test — A statistical procedure to test hypothesis of equality of two means, and for certain other hypotheses relating to parameters such as regression coefficient.

Two-sided alternative— An alternative hypothesis that stipulates that the parameter value can be higher or lower than the null value. Both directions are admissible. This type of alternative is setup when it is not known that the value is going to be higher or lower than the specified value.

Two-tailed test— See One-tailed test.

Two-way classification— Division of subjects by two characteristics simultaneously, such as dividing cases of diabetes mellitus by their obesity category and smoking category.

Two-way design— A study that is planned to investigate the effect of levels of two antecedent factors, such as effect of obesity (BMI<20.0, 20.0-24.9, 25.0-29.9 or 30.0+) and smoking (none, mild, moderate or heavy) on blood glucose level. Their interaction can also be investigated in this kind of design.

Type I error— The error of rejecting a true null hypothesis, i.e., concluding that there is a difference when actually there is none. The sample or data might be such that this lead to such a wrong conclusion. This error leads to false positive result.

Type II error— The error of wrongly concluding that there is no difference when actually some difference is present. This error leads to false negative result.

Unbalanced design — A design with unequal number of subjects in different groups.

Uncertainty analysis— The analysis that delineates the effect of change in the value of the parameter under assessment on the conclusion. One component of this is the sampling fluctuation in the estimate of the parameters, and the other is the plausible change in the values themselves that can affect the outcome.

Uncertainty principle (in a clinical trial)— The principle that says that the outcome of various arms of trial should be a-priori uncertain. One specific uncertainty situation is that the a-priori chances of each regimen being successful are nearly equal–called clinical equipoise.

Unit of study— The unit (individual, patient, blood sample, biopsy, etc.) that is used to obtain the required information.

Universe — The broad group of subjects for which the findings could be generalized or implicated. Statistically this is broader than the target population and can include future subjects.

Up-and-down trial — A trial where a start is made with an assumed average dose and it is increased or decreased by predetermined step in subsequent subjects depending upon the dose is not effective or effective, respectively.

Vaccine trial — An experiment on human population to evaluate potency, efficacy and safety of a vaccine.

Validation sample — A sample used to validate the results of the study. It could be a Subsample of the original sample that is kept aside for this purpose, or could be a new sample of subjects.

Validity (of a measurement) — Ability to hit the target (or around it): ability to assess what is really intended to be assessed. Weight by itself is not a valid indicator of obesity in adults but body mass index that uses height also is. For a medical test, validity is measured by sensitivity, specificity and predictivities (positive and negative).

Validity (of a study) — The ability of a study to provide correct conclusion, considering the representativeness and size of sample, validity of measurements, and the soundness of methods. See also internal validity and external validity.

Validity (of a survey instrument or a test)— Ability of an instrument (such as a questionnaire or a schedule) or of a test to provide the information that matches with the objectives of the study. For its varieties, see concurrent validity, content validity, construct validity, criterion validity, face validity, and predictive validity.

Vancouver style (or format)— A style of writing research papers agreed by editors of more than 500 medical journals published around the world. It includes instructions on who could and should be authors, what help must be acknowledged, how to structure the text, and how to cite references. The system of citing references matches closely with the system followed by MedLine.

Variable— A characteristic that varies from person to person , or form situation to situation. Platelet count in different persons is variable but number of eyes or number of fingers is not at variable. See quantitative variable, qualitative variable, discrete variable, continuous variable, dependent variable, and independent variable.

Variance— A measure of dispersion or scatteredness of quantitative data obtained as average of the squared deviations from mean.

Virulence— The ability to produce severe form of disease that can threaten life. Rabies is highly virulent disease and cholera is not—measured as percentage of cases who go into severe form. See infectivity, pathogenicity.

Volunteer studies— A study done on volunteers, opposed to randomly selected subjects. Results from such studies can be used to estimate tolerated dose and some side-effects of a test regimen but cannot be used to estimate efficacy.

Waist-height ratio— The ratio of waist circumference to height. Ratio realizes that people with more height can have more waist circumference without being obese.

Waist-hip ratio— The ratio of waist circumference to hip measurement: sometimes considered a more valid measures of obesity than body mass index. Waist-hip ratio measures only central obesity, whereas body mass index is for overall obesity including central obesity.

Washout period— In a cross-over trial, the period elapsed between withdrawal of first treatment, and start of the second treatment. This period allows time for any effect of the first treatment to vanish before the second is started.

Wilcoxon test— Another method to do Mann-Whitney test for comparing central tendency of two groups. Both give exactly same result, and they are algebraically equivalent.

Z-score— Same as normal deviate but some times measured from median median instead of mean, particularly in assessing growth: difference of a value from group mean in terms of how times of SD.

Z-test— A statistical test of hypothesis based on Gaussian distribution, generally used to compare two means or two proportions.

REFERENCES

1. Tao NSN and Murthy NS. Planning of research studies, applied statistical in health. Sciences, Jaypee Brothers Medical Publishers (P) Ltd. New-Delhi, 2008.

2. Ethical guide lines for biomedical research on human subjects, ICMR Guidelines, 2000:30:107-116.

3. Research -Methods and Technique, by-C.R. Kothari (New age International Publisher-Daryaganj, New Delhi-2, Year-2014.

4. A hand book for Clinical Medicine In Traditional Medicine by Farah Ahmad/ Ghazala Javed, Published by Fine Ofset Work-Delhi, year-2005.

5. Introduction to Biostatstics and Research Methodology by P.S.S. Sundar Rao/ J.Richard, 4th Edition., Prentice Hall of India Private ltd, New Delhi, year-2005.

6. Research Methodology by Munir Ahmad R Bublished by Centre for Homeopathy Studies-Bangalore, year2005.3

7. Methods of Biostatistics by T. Bhaskar Rao, 2nd Edition, Published by Paras Medical Publisher-Hydrabad, year 2004.

8. The Journal of Clinical Investigation http://www.jci.org Volume 117 Number 12 Dcember 2007.

9. Park's Textbook of Preventive And Social Medicine by K. PARK, 20th edition, published by Banarsidas Bhannot 1167, Prem Nagar, Nagpur Road JABALPUR, 482001 (INDIA), year 2009.

10. Taber's Cyclopedia Medical Dictionary, 19th edition, edited by Donald Vens, M.D, M.S.J.

11. Quick Reference Dictionary, by Ed Denning, Med, LMT, Published by: SLACK Incorporated, 6900 Grove Road, Thorofare, NJ 08086 USA, ISBN-13: 978-1-55642-646-9 (alk. paper)

Printed in Great Britain
by Amazon